Dangerous Sanctuaries

A volume in the series

CORNELL STUDIES IN SECURITY AFFAIRS

edited by Robert J. Art, Robert Jervis, *and* Stephen M. Walt

A full list of titles in the series appears at the end of the book.

Dangerous Sanctuaries

Refugee Camps, Civil War, and the Dilemmas of Humanitarian Aid

SARAH KENYON LISCHER

Cornell University Press

ITHACA AND LONDON

First published 2005 by Cornell University Press

Printed in the United States of America

Library of Congress Cataloging-in-Publication Data

Lischer, Sarah Kenyon, 1970–
    Dangerous sanctuaries : refugee camps, civil war, and the dilemmas of
humanitarian aid / Sarah Kenyon Lischer.
        p.   cm. -- (Cornell studies in security affairs)
    Includes bibliographical references and index.
    ISBN 0-8014-4285-0 (cloth : alk. paper)
1. Refugees--Services for.   2. Humanitarian assistance.
I. Title.   II. Series.
    HV640L48 2005
    362.87'.8—dc22   2004018219

Cloth printing   10 9 8 7 6 5 4 3 2 1

For Paul

Contents

Tables and Maps

Acknowledgments

Numerous friends and colleagues improved the quality of my work and supported me throughout the writing process. I received expert guidance from Steve Van Evera, Barry Posen, Melissa Nobles, Kenneth Oye, and the late Myron Weiner during my years at MIT. I am also grateful for the detailed comments from Jeremy Pressman and Gerard McHugh on the topics of Palestinian refugees and humanitarian organizations, respectively. Of course, they are responsible neither for my arguments nor my mistakes. David Art, Kelly Greenhill, Sara Jane McCaffrey, Daniel Metz, Jessica Piombo, Monica Toft, Carola Weil, Cory Welt, Beth Whitaker, and Amos Zehavi offered thoughtful comments on earlier drafts. Later drafts benefited from helpful critiques from the participants in the BCSIA International Security Program brown bag seminar, the World Peace Foundation Program on Intrastate Conflict seminars (especially Robert Rotberg), and the Third Annual New Faces Conference at Duke University. I extend many thanks to Roger Haydon at Cornell University Press, Robert Jervis, and the anonymous reviewer. They all read the manuscript carefully and offered many invaluable suggestions.

Everywhere I traveled for my fieldwork, I met warm and wise people willing to help me. UNHCR's Evaluation and Policy Analysis Unit was incredibly helpful and forthcoming during this project. Without the assistance of its director, Jeff Crisp, I could never have completed my research. Many other UNHCR employees, including Joel Boutroue and Quang Bui in Geneva and Arjun Jain in Tanzania, extended their help and hospitality. Anne-Christine Eriksson generously shared her home and her OSCE office with me in Croatia. Bonaventure Rutinwa and Khoti

Kamanga of the Centre for the Study of Forced Migration at the University of Dar es Salaam graciously facilitated my research in Tanzania.

I thank many organizations for their generous sponsorship of this research. Fellowships from Harvard University's Belfer Center for Science and International Affairs, the Harry Frank Guggenheim Foundation, and the Academic Council on the United Nations System gave me the time I needed to write. I am also grateful for funding from the Institute for the Study of World Politics, the John D. and Catherine T. MacArthur Foundation through a grant to the Center for International Studies at MIT, the Mellon-MIT Program on NGOs and Forced Migration—especially its director Sharon Stanton Russell—and the National Science Foundation.

Finally, and most important, I am grateful for the support of my family. I dedicate this book with love to my husband Paul Sherman.

SARAH KENYON LISCHER

Charlottesville, VA

[xii]

Dangerous Sanctuaries

[1]

Refugee Crises as Catalysts of Conflict

"*Increasingly refugees are equated with threats to national and regional secu-rity. . . . Many refugee hosting countries have legitimate security concerns, including cross-border incursions, militarization of refugee camps, and the fear of conflicts spilling over from neighboring refugee-producing countries.*"

—Human Rights Watch, "UNHCR at 50: What Future for Refugee Protection?" December 12, 2000

After organizing the mass killing of hundreds of thousands of Rwandan Tutsi in 1994, the Rwandan Hutu leadership forced over a million Hutu civilians into eastern Congo (then Zaire). During the refugee crisis from 1994 to 1996, perpetrators of the Rwandan genocide established military training bases adjacent to the refugee camps. The militants stockpiled weapons, recruited and trained refugee fighters, and launched cross-border attacks against Rwanda. The militant leaders openly gloated about their manipulation of the Hutu refugees and their plan to complete the genocide of the Tutsi. From the camps, the genocidal leader Jean Bosco Barayagwiza boasted that "even if [the Tutsi-led Rwandan Patriotic Front] has won a military victory it will not have the power. We have the population."[1] In late 1996, the growing strength of the militant groups provoked a Rwandan invasion and attacks against refugees. Until the fighting disrupted their operations, international humanitarian organizations regularly delivered food and supplies to military bases and refugee camps.

Eastern Congo became the epicenter of a regional war in which over a dozen states and rebel groups fought one another and plundered the region's resources. An estimated three million Congolese died as a result of this war, mostly from preventable diseases and malnutrition.[2] A major cause of war was the internationally supported refugee population, which included tens of thousands of unrepentant perpetrators of genocide. Between 1994 and 1996, international donors spent billions of dollars to sustain that population. These same donors refused to fund efforts to disarm the militants or to send peacekeeping troops to do so.

Every year, millions of people flee their homes to escape violent conflict. Often the resulting refugee crisis leads to an expansion of violence rather than an escape.[3] In some cases, refugee crises function as a strategy of war. For exiled rebel groups, a refugee population provides international legitimacy, a shield against attack, a pool of recruits, and valuable sources for food and medicine. In essence, refugee camps function as rear bases for rebels who attack across the border. Refugee-sending states view refugees as an indictment of the government's legitimacy and as a potential military threat. The sending state may pursue refugees across the border, subjecting them to military attack.[4] As cross-border attacks escalate, the risk of international war grows. Eventually, the entire region may be destabilized as more states are drawn in to the conflict.

The recurring pattern of violent refugee crises prompts the following questions: Under what conditions do refugee crises lead to the spread of civil war across borders? How can refugee relief organizations respond when militants use humanitarian assistance as a tool of war? What government actions can prevent or reduce the spread of conflict? This book examines these widely ignored questions, which have profound implications for understanding how refugee flows affect the dynamics of conflicts in various parts of the world.

The spread of civil war due to refugee crises has occurred, or threatened to occur, numerous times throughout history and around the globe. One early attempt to militarize refugees occurred after World War II, when President Eisenhower pursued a plan to enlist stateless Europeans into the U.S. army as a covert anti-communist force. General Robert L. Cutler, special assistant to the president for national security, described Eisenhower's vision as an army of 250,000 "stateless, single, anti-Communist young men, coming from countries behind the iron curtain." Eventually the plan faltered because of European concerns about the divisive political implications of such a force.[5]

In the decades after World War II, the great powers viewed refugees as political actors and often abetted their militarization. Looking back on the Cold War period, Myron Weiner commented: "Since refugees were often regarded as part of an armed struggle in the cold war the question of demilitarizing camps did not arise. . . . It would not be too great an exaggeration to say that in many circumstances UNHCR and NGOs were instruments of the United States and its allies for coping with the humanitarian consequences of cold war conflicts."[6] During the Cold War, refugee crises contributed to the spread of civil war in South and Southeast Asia, Central America, Southern Africa, and the Middle East.

The refugee crisis sparked by the Vietnamese invasion of Cambodia in 1979 created an internationally supported battleground on the Thai-Cambodian border. Hundreds of thousands of refugees straddled the border in a series of camps that were controlled by the various Cambodian rebel groups, including the genocidal but anti-communist Khmer Rouge. The United States supported the anti-communist rebel groups despite the blatant military activity among the refugees and the misuse of humanitarian assistance. The United Nations provided assistance to the refugees but refused to offer legal or physical protection. One expert, Courtland Robinson, convincingly argues that the international response needlessly prolonged the refugee crisis and revitalized the Khmer Rouge.[7]

Cold War politics also affected Nicaraguan and Salvadoran refugees in Central America. During the 1980s at least 300,000 people from war-torn Nicaragua and El Salvador fled to Honduras. The United States supported the militant activities of the anti-communist *contra* rebels based among the Nicaraguan refugees, encouraging cross-border attacks against the sending state. In the UNHCR-assisted camps, "contras were also apparently free to come and go and used the camps for rest, political and logistical support, and recruitment."[8] In contrast, Salvadoran refugees, perceived as enemies of the right-wing government in El Salvador, suffered oppression and attacks at the hands of Honduran and Salvadoran government forces.[9]

In Africa, international agencies supported refugees who sought to topple white dominated governments in South Africa, Zimbabwe, and Namibia. The regional conflict spread as the South African government retaliated with bombing raids against refugee settlements in Angola, Botswana, and other border states, killing hundreds of civilians (as well as some rebels). Donors generally viewed those refugees as victims—rather than perpetrators—of violence and regarded their struggles against apartheid as legitimate.

One of the most enduring and violent situations involves the millions of Palestinian refugees scattered throughout the Middle East. These refugees have been involved in the spread of conflict in Jordan, Lebanon, and the West Bank and the Gaza Strip. In the 1970s the refugees precipitated civil war in Jordan. In the 1980s Israeli-backed forces in Lebanon massacred thousands of refugees as part of a crackdown on militant Palestinian groups. Battles between Palestinian militants and Israeli security forces have raged in the refugee camps of the West Bank and the Gaza Strip. Such a highly politicized and militarized environment has eroded the neutrality of humanitarian organizations. For example, Israel has accused the United Nations Relief and Works Agency (UNRWA), formed specifically to assist the Palestinians, of politicizing its aid work and supporting militant elements.

Since the early 1990s, refugee crises in Central Africa, the Balkans, West Africa, and the Middle East have led to the international spread of internal conflict. In 2001, a United States government analysis reckoned, "the recent military interventions in Fiji and Cote d'Ivoire; ethnic conflicts in the former Yugoslavia, the former Soviet Union, eastern Indonesia, and Democratic Republic of the Congo; and the Arab-Israeli dispute have resulted in part from large-scale migration and refugee flows." That analysis also predicted that migration to less-developed countries would continue to "upset ethnic balances and contribute to conflict or violent regime change."[10]

The humanitarian fiasco in eastern Congo kindled an awareness of the military and political implications of refugee crises. Freed from Cold War politics, policymakers are now more receptive to the idea of reducing military activity affecting refugees. At the same time, however, the great powers have generally lost strategic interest in developing countries and are unwilling to commit resources to demilitarize refugee areas. As the United States, Russia, and the former colonial powers disengage from many conflicts in the developing world, humanitarian agencies often remain the only international presence during a refugee crisis.

HUMANITARIAN ASSISTANCE AS A TOOL OF WAR

Status Quo Policy: Ignoring Militarization

> "Why should UNHCR be worried about weapons?"
> —UNHCR protection officer, Geneva, July 1998.

Despite the political and military implications of refugee crises, the international response to a crisis usually consists of humanitarian assistance. Both governments and humanitarian organizations pay little attention to the politics of the refugee crisis or the conflict that created the displacement. Instead, private charities, UN organizations, and the Red Cross expertly provide food, shelter, health care, and sanitation facilities for the refugees. Western governments often fund international humanitarian organizations as a substitute for political or military involvement. Such donor states generally do not view militarized refugee crises as a threat to national security.

When conflict escalates, governments and humanitarian organizations tend to blame each other. After the Rwandan refugee crisis in Zaire, politicians condemned aid workers for succoring genocidal killers. Aid agencies accused governments of abandoning humanitarians in a military and political quagmire. Yet during the crisis, both states and humanitarian organizations willfully ignored its political and military aspects.

Humanitarian organizations generally assess the political context of the crisis only insofar as it affects the delivery of aid. In many cases, aid agencies regard military activity that does not directly impinge on their activities among the refugees as irrelevant. Aid workers often ignore militarization as long as the weapons and military training remain out of sight—quite literally. During the late 1990s, for example, humanitarian officials conceded that Burundian rebels had mingled with the refugees in Tanzanian camps. Yet aid workers did not consider the camps militarized because the rebels conducted their military activities in the bush and on the Burundi border, evading direct observation. Because of that humanitarian myopia, militants can reap the benefits of international aid—as long as they maintain a low profile.

Practical reasons also encourage humanitarian organizations to ignore militarization.[11] Legally, it is not aid agencies but the receiving state that must provide security in refugee crises. Without support from the receiving state, the unarmed humanitarians have little capacity to oppose military activity. Militarization condoned by the receiving state or a powerful donor state sharply limits the options humanitarian organizations can pursue.

Ethical issues cloud the issue of militarization as well. Humanitarian organizations express ambivalence about encouraging—or forcing—refugees to return home, even when it seems the only solution to militarization.[12] The norm against *refoulement* (forced return) is deeply ingrained, both in the culture of humanitarian organizations and in international law. A second ethical qualm concerns the uneasy relationship between aid organizations and security organizations. Philosophically, many non-governmental organizations (NGOs) oppose the presence of armed guards or security details for humanitarian missions.

Some NGOs view reliance on any form of coercion as antithetical to the humanitarian enterprise.

In situations where refugee crises are exploited as a strategy of war, the purely humanitarian response is not only inadequate, it can be counterproductive. Well-intentioned humanitarian assistance that ignores the existing political risk factors for militarization will end up exacerbating the conflict. Both states and aid organizations often operate under the mistaken assumption that humanitarian activity in the absence of military or political attention to the crisis is better than no action at all. In some instances, as in the Rwandan refugee crisis in Zaire, ignoring militarization while distributing aid did intensify the conflict. Neutral humanitarian action was not possible. In fact, the most helpful response to a potentially violent refugee crisis is a robust peace-enforcement mission with the aim of disarming militants and securing the refugee camps.[13]

Following the debacle in the Rwandan refugee camps, a number of critics exposed the perverse effects of humanitarian aid.[14] These scholars and NGO practitioners uncovered many of the negative effects of assistance during conflict and, in many cases, offered scathing critiques of the existing policies. It remains to be seen how these critiques will influence actual practice during refugee crises.

How Refugee Relief Exacerbates Conflict

"We are going to be feeding people who have been perpetrating genocide."
—Charles Tapp, chief executive of the charity CARE,
quoted in *Rwanda: Death, Despair, and Defiance* (1995)

There are four main ways that humanitarian aid in refugee crises can exacerbate conflict: feeding militants, sustaining and protecting militants' dependents, supporting a war economy, and providing legitimacy to combatants. The optimal conditions for these mechanisms to thrive include a high level of political cohesion among the refugees and low state capability or willingness to provide security.

Feeding militants. At the most basic level, direct assistance to militants, both intentional and otherwise, relieves them of having to find food themselves. Inadvertent distribution occurs when militants hide among the refugees. For example, at the beginning of the Rwanda crisis in 1994, many aid workers were unaware of the genocide that had preceded it. Hutu militants implemented a successful propaganda effort painting the Hutu as victims and ignoring the genocide. David Rieff quotes an

[6]

American engineer who arrived in Goma, in Zaire, technically prepared but politically ignorant: "I went to Goma and worked there for three solid months. But it was only later, when I finally went to Rwanda on a break, that I found out about the genocide, and realized, 'Hey, I've been busting my butt for a bunch of ax murderers!' "[15]

In some cases, NGOs have intentionally provided food directly to militants. In the Zaire camps, some NGOs rationalized that if the Hutu militants did not receive aid, they would steal it from the refugees. Another rationale was strict adherence to the humanitarian imperative of impartiality—that is, providing assistance based on need—without determining if the recipients included hungry warriors. Fabrizio Hochschild, an official under the United Nations High Commissioner for Refugees, summed up this logic when he defended UNHCR action during the Rwanda crisis: "Even the guilty need to be fed."[16]

Sustaining and protecting militants' dependents. Even if assistance does not directly sustain the militants, it can support their war aims by succoring their civilian families and supporters. Humanitarian assistance relieves militants from providing goods and services for their supporters. Rebels can live outside of the camps, while sending their families to the camps to live in relative safety. As a Sudanese refugee in the violence-plagued Ugandan camps confirmed, "the [Sudanese rebel] commanders keep their wives and families in the camps."[17]

Ironically, militants often present themselves as a "state in exile," even though it is the humanitarian organizations that provide many of the functions of the state. As Mary Anderson explains, "When external aid agencies assume responsibility for civilian survival, warlords tend to define their responsibility and accountability only in terms of military control."[18] By sustaining and protecting civilian dependents, aid organizations allow the militant leaders to focus on fighting rather than on providing for their supporters.

Supporting a war economy. Militants can use relief resources to finance conflict. It is not uncommon for refugee leaders to levy a war tax on the refugee population, commandeering a portion of all rations and salaries. Refugee leaders can also divert aid when they control the distribution process. During the Rwandan refugee crisis, militant leaders diverted large amounts of aid by inflating population numbers and pocketing the excess. Alain Destexhe, secretary general of Médecins Sans Frontières (Doctors Without Borders), in discussing Goma, in Zaire, noted that "food represents power, and camp leaders who control its distribution divert considerable quantities towards war preparations."[19] A Liberian refugee in Guinea observed in 2002 that "The same food the UN is bringing here is being used for the war in Liberia."[20]

Armed groups often raid warehouses and international compounds to steal food, medicine, and equipment. Thousands, if not millions, of dollars of relief resources, including vehicles and communication equipment, are stolen every year. In the mid-1990s, aid organizations curtailed their operations in Liberia after the theft of $20 million in equipment during the civil war there.[21] The International Committee of the Red Cross reported that "the level of diversion by the factions had reached a systematic and planned level, that it was integrated into the war strategy. . . . It had become obvious that the factions were opening the doors to humanitarian aid, up to the point where all the sophisticated logistics had entered the zones: cars, radios, computers, telephones. When all the stuff was there, then the looting would start in a quite systematic way."[22]

Defenders of aid organizations are quick to point out that, in many cases, humanitarian assistance forms a negligible part of the resources available to combatants.[23] There are two responses to this argument. First, even a relatively small role does not absolve humanitarian organizations of responsibility. Absolute amounts matter as much as relative measures: The $20 million of equipment stolen in Liberia during the mid-1990s was $20 million that aid agencies could not use for other crises, regardless of the relative importance of aid resources in Liberia's conflict. Second, the nonmonetary benefits of humanitarian aid as a resource of war are also important. The legitimacy conferred by humanitarian activity can bolster the strength of a rebel group, regardless of the cash value of the aid.

Providing legitimacy to combatants. Humanitarian assistance shapes international opinion about the actors in a crisis. To raise money from Western publics and governments, aid agencies tend to present oversimplified stories that emphasize the helplessness and victimization of the refugees.[24] Aid to the Rwandan refugees established a perception of the Hutu refugees as needy victims, obscuring their role as perpetrators of genocide against the Tutsi.

Aid also provides international legitimation of a group's political goals. The ruling party in Angola, the Movimento Popular da Libertação de Angola (MPLA), repeatedly used humanitarian assistance to bolster its political standing during its civil war throughout the 1990s. One member of the opposition, the União Nacional para a Independência Total de Angola (UNITA), explained: "The greatest problem is that people confuse humanitarian assistance as assistance from the MPLA party. The MPLA have taken advantage of this situation and many people think that what [aid] arrives has been given by the MPLA, not by the international aid organizations nor [sic] the government. . . . We don't have access to distribution of humanitarian aid, this is going to affect with certainty the electoral constituency of the future."[25] Rebel groups also manipulate aid agencies to increase their legitimacy and profile in the international media. To gain access to a needy population, humanitarian agencies are often forced to negotiate with unsavory rebel or government groups. The very act of negotiation solidifies the reputation of such groups as powerful and legitimate.

Despite the proven political uses of humanitarian aid, many impassioned arguments suggest that impartiality and neutrality are both possible and desirable. Rieff makes a principled argument that humanitarianism "is neutral or it is nothing."[26] More practically, aid workers fear becoming targets in the conflict and losing access to the needy population if combatants view their work as political. Advocates of strict neutrality rarely admit that by giving aid in a supposedly impartial and neutral manner, their actions may benefit one or more combatants and lead to further war.[27] In reality, any humanitarian action in a conflict zone will have political, and possibly military, consequences no matter how apolitical the intent. Thus, in a militarized refugee crisis, humanitarian organizations may have to decide between aiding both killers and refugees and aiding no one at all.

REFUGEES AND POLITICAL VIOLENCE: THE CENTRAL ARGUMENT

The humanitarian assistance literature and the policy community routinely offer socioeconomic explanations for refugee-related violence. According to one view, large refugee camps become a breeding ground for militant and criminal organizations because they are harder to control. Camps located near the border of the sending state facilitate attacks by refugee militias or the sending state. Another explanation posits that larger numbers of young men among the refugees will lead to greater violence. Finally, poor living conditions are thought to encourage discontent, which leads to militancy.[28]

In fact, none of these four socioeconomic propositions satisfactorily explains the spread of civil war. In militarized refugee crises, reliance on socioeconomic explanations often ends up supporting militants rather than weakening them. When socioeconomic remedies ignore the political motivations behind militarization, the aid can fuel a war. Rather than appeasing militarization, increased assistance feeds the militants' ambitions.

This book offers an alternative explanation more consistent with the realities of refugee-related violence. It suggests that the political context of the crisis better explains the spread of civil war arising from refugee crises. Three attributes of the political context influence whether a refugee crisis will cause the spread of war. These attributes are the origin of the refugee crisis, the policy of the receiving state, and the influence of external state and non-state actors.

The socioeconomic explanations mistakenly disregard the *origins* of the refugee crisis, focusing instead on the *characteristics* of the refugee situation. Yet the cause of the refugee crisis directly influences the refugees' level of military organization. Ignoring the cause of the crisis implicitly assumes that all refugee crises arise from similar political, economic, and military dynamics. This lack of differentiation leads to the mistaken assumption that socioeconomic policies—such as reducing camp size or improving recreational opportunities—will have universally beneficial effects on all refugee groups. In fact, refugee populations must be differentiated according to their political organization and motivation to understand the likelihood of militarization.

This book categorizes refugees by the cause of their flight: situational refugees, persecuted refugees, and state-in-exile refugees. These groups are discussed at length in chapter 2. Situational refugees flee their homes to escape the intolerable conditions and general destruction wrought by civil war, not due to any specific persecution or premeditated strategy. These refugees express a willingness to return home as soon as peace and stability is established. Such refugees are not likely to organize for political or military purposes.

A second type of refugee population flees because of direct persecution or oppression, rather than general chaos. These persecuted refugees escape ethnic cleansing, genocide, or other oppressive policies that target them on the basis of ethnic, religious, linguistic, or political identity. The coalescing event of group persecution can facilitate political or military organization among the refugees and cross-border violence. These refugees generally refuse to return home unless they are assured protection from their persecutors.

The third refugee group is actually a state in exile. This group contains political and military leaders who, in some cases, organize the refugee crisis as a strategy to avoid defeat in a civil war. These groups refuse to return home unless they can do so in victory. State-in-exile groups have the highest propensity for political violence.

Among violence-prone persecuted refugees or a state in exile, the role of the receiving state determines whether or not war will spread. The policy of the receiving state can be analyzed according to two factors—capability and will. A capable receiving state can secure its borders and demilitarize the refugees. The will of the receiving state refers to the state's desire to prevent violence. The spread of civil war is likely in situations where a capable receiving state allies with militant refugees or where an incapable receiving state cannot control militarism. Conversely, a highly capable receiving state with no sympathy for the refugees' militant aims can forestall the spread of civil war.

The interference of external actors often tips the balance of capability in the direction of the refugees or the sending state, thus prompting one or the other to instigate violence. For example, a powerful donor state might pressure the receiving state to allow refugee militarization. Nonstate actors, such as UN agencies and NGOs, also increase the capability of militant refugees by indiscriminately distributing humanitarian assistance. Militants then use the aid to feed combatants and procure weapons. External parties can discourage the spread of war by strengthening the receiving state's capability to police its borders and demilitarize the refugee camps.

Types of Refugee-Related Violence

Recent studies of refugee-related violence rarely specify the type of violence that occurs.[29] Generalization assumes similar causes for all violent outcomes and assigns the same importance to all refugee-related violence. Clearly, however, qualitative and quantitative differences exist among incidents of theft, banditry, rioting, and international war. Disaggregating the types of violence that occur is a first step toward understanding their causes. Each type of violence is likely to have different causes and cures.

Political violence involving refugees manifests itself in five possible types (see table 1.1). The first, and most common, version is a violent cross-border attack between the sending state and the refugees. Usually, such attacks entail the most intense violence of the five types, including the bombing or shelling of camps. Attacks involving the sending state threaten the sovereignty of the receiving state and may lead to international war.[30]

There are numerous instances of cross-border attacks initiated by either the refugees or the sending state. In the 1980s, South Africa conducted repeated bombing raids against suspected African National Congress (ANC) refugees in Angola and Botswana. Those raids killed

[11]

Table 1.1   Types of refugee-related violence

- Attacks between the sending state and the refugees
- Attacks between the receiving state and the refugees
- Ethnic or factional violence among the refugees
- Internal violence within the receiving state
- Inter-state war or unilateral intervention

both refugees and local civilians and heightened regional tensions in southern Africa. As mentioned earlier, Rwandan Hutu militias raided Rwanda from their bases in the refugee camps of eastern Zaire following the 1994 Rwandan genocide. The cross-border attacks targeted genocide survivors and other civilians as well as government infrastructure. Another major instance of violence between refugees and a sending state involved Palestinians and Israeli forces in the West Bank and the Gaza Strip during the first Intifada, from 1987 to 1993, and the second Intifada, which began in 2000. The violence, which ranged from stone throwing to rocket attacks, led to thousands of deaths. During this ongoing conflict, Israel has attacked refugee camps in the occupied territories and Palestinian militants based in the camps have launched cross-border attacks against Israel.

During the Cold War, the United States supported Afghan militants in Pakistan as they fought the communist regime in Kabul. The Soviet-backed forces responded with hundreds of cross-border bombings in Pakistan. Another Cold War crisis involved more than 300,000 Cambodian refugees on the Thai border, subject to attacks from Cambodia, harassment by Thai forces, and abuse by the Cambodian rebel groups that controlled the camps.[31]

Sometimes cross-border attacks against refugees are carried out by sub-state groups rather than national armies. Such attacks also raise the risk of international conflict. In West Africa, both rebels and government forces attacked Sierra Leonean refugees in Guinea during the 1990s. Similarly, in 2001 and 2002 members of the rebel group Liberians United for Reconciliation and Democracy (LURD) attacked Liberian refugees in Guinea, with the connivance of the Guinean army.[32] Since the late 1980s, Sudanese refugees in Uganda have suffered numerous attacks by both Sudanese and Ugandan rebel groups in which hundreds of refugees have died. Those attacks created great tension between the Sudanese and Ugandan governments.[33]

The second type of violence arises out of conflict between the refugees and the receiving state. One of the most extreme instances of this was the fighting between Palestinian refugees and the Jordanian government that led to civil war in 1970. Thousands of refugees died when Jordan cracked down on Palestinian political and military activity, which Jordan's King Hussein viewed as a threat to his regime's survival.[34]

More common are riots between locals and refugees or police actions targeting refugees. Examples include the continuing violence involving Burmese refugees in Bangladesh. The Bangladeshi police and military often use violence to encourage repatriation. Local villagers sometimes join in police attacks against refugees, leading to riots and even more severe police action. Violence between refugees and the receiving state can erupt when refugees protest their conditions. For example, Vietnamese refugees in Hong Kong rioted many times, resulting in scores of deaths, to protest forced return to Vietnam.[35] Similar spirals of violence have occurred in Guinea, where cross-border attacks against refugees and locals led Guinean government forces to retaliate against refugees.

Ethnic conflict within the receiving state may lead to violence against refugees. Burundian Hutu citizens attacked Rwandan Tutsi refugees staying in Burundi in the early 1990s. The ethnic dynamic switched after the triumph of a Tutsi government in Burundi and the Rwandan genocide. In 1994 and 1995, Burundian Tutsi militants allied with the Rwandan Tutsi-led government and attacked Rwandan Hutu refugees in Burundi.

Third, ethnic or factional violence that erupts among refugees can spread conflict to the receiving state. This often occurs when refugee groups include members of different ethnic groups or competing political parties. The ramifications of factional or ethnic violence include lawlessness in the refugee camps and endangerment of the staff of humanitarian aid groups.

Numerous incidents of ethnic and factional conflict have led to refugee deaths and the further spread of conflict. Recent factional fighting among Sudanese refugees in remote Ethiopian camps led to the deaths of dozens of refugees.[36] Conflict between rival Burundian Hutu political parties in the camps in western Tanzania has repeatedly threatened Tanzania's security since the early 1990s. Earlier situations of factional violence include conflict between the Palestinian Liberation Organization (PLO) and its rivals in camps in Lebanon during the 1980s and early 1990s.

Factional violence is less likely to engulf the sending and receiving states than the other types of refugee-related violence. One exception would be cases in which a faction or ethnic group has supporters within the receiving state. When that happens, violence can lead to a broader civil conflict in the receiving state. In many situations, factional or ethnic violence does not occur in isolation but accompanies one of the other manifestations of violence. For the Afghan refugees in Pakistan, for example, conflicts existed with the sending state, with the receiving state, and among refugee factions.

A related type of violence occurs when the refugees create an unstable ethnic balance in the receiving state that encourages a previously oppressed minority to confront the state. During the 1999 NATO war in Kosovo, many observers predicted that the presence of thousands of ethnic Albanian refugees in Macedonia might lead to civil war by upsetting the delicate balance between Slavs and Albanians. Fortunately, the refugees rapid return to Kosovo blunted their long-term impact on Macedonian domestic politics. The arrival of over a million Hutu refugees in eastern Zaire in 1994 led to an upsurge of ethnic conflict among various Zairian groups. The Rwandan Hutu polarized relations between the previously amicable Zairian Tutsi and Hutu, encouraging persecution of Zairian Tutsi by other indigenous ethnic groups.

The fifth type of violence occurs when refugees operate as catalysts for inter-state war or unilateral intervention. In some instances international war occurs when refugees use exile to launch an invasion of their home country. Inter-state war becomes more likely if the receiving state supports the military activity. In 1990 longtime Rwandan Tutsi refugees in Uganda launched an invasion of Rwanda, throwing the latter country into civil war and precipitating the genocide. After the genocide, attacks between Hutu refugees and the sending state escalated into international war in Central Africa, when Rwanda attacked Zaire (now Congo) and the Hutu refugees on the pretext of eliminating the security threat posed by the camps. Another example is the 1979 Tanzanian invasion of Uganda. Allied with dissident Ugandan refugees, Tanzania invaded Uganda in 1979 and toppled Idi Amin's brutal regime. The invasion followed a series of cross-border attacks by Uganda, which accused Tanzania of harboring antigovernment rebels.[37]

Another type of international war occurs when the receiving state perceives the refugees as a threat, regardless of their political or military activity. In 1971, ten million refugees from Bangladesh (then East Pakistan) overran India's West Bengal state over a period of several months. The refugee influx prompted India's invasion of East Pakistan. Ambassador Samar Sen, the Indian representative to the United Nations, explained to the Security Council why India had to intervene militarily. He coined the term "refugee aggression" to describe Pakistan's crime against India: "If aggression against another foreign country means that

[14]

it strains its social structure, that it ruins its finances, that it has to give up its territory for sheltering the refugees . . . what is the difference between that kind of aggression and the other type . . . when someone declares war?"[38] The United States has also been involved in refugee-related interventions. President Clinton affirmed that the 1994 United States intervention in Haiti occurred in part to prevent the arrival of thousands of refugees on Florida's shores.[39]

Although this book offers analysis of all five types of political violence involving refugees, the case studies focus specifically on refugee-related violence that leads to the spread of civil war. Attacks between the sending state and the refugees have the highest risk of escalating into international war between the sending and receiving state, sometimes with the involvement of external powers. Additionally, sending state/refugee violence occurs with more frequency and intensity than any of the other types of violence.

COMPARING VIOLENT AND NONVIOLENT CRISES

Most studies of refugees and conflict confine themselves to crises such as the Rwandans in Zaire—that is to say, the violent cases. This approach closes off the possibility of explaining why some crises lead to the spread of conflict while others do not. For example, most assessments of the Rwandan refugee crisis ignore the Rwandan refugees—both Hutu and Tutsi—living in Tanzania. These refugees experienced much lower levels of violence than the Rwandan refugees in Zaire. The exclusive focus on the Zaire crisis suggests that Rwandan refugees have a high propensity for involvement in violence. Yet one can only understand the causes of that violence, and the possible solutions, by studying the relatively nonviolent situation in Tanzania. Additionally, most research does not differentiate among the types of refugee-related violence, lumping together, for example, theft, banditry, and international war. By studying situations that avoided refugee-related violence and by differentiating between the types of violent outcomes, this book presents a generalizable explanation for the spread of civil war due to refugee crises.

Unlike past studies of refugees and violence that focus exclusively on cases of extreme violence, this study examines in equal measure violent and nonviolent situations (see table 1.2). By allowing a variation in levels of violence over time and space, one can consider a wider range of factors that might contribute to the spread of civil war. Later chapters offer in-depth examination of the following case studies:

- *Rwandan Hutu refugees in Tanzania and Zaire, 1994–1996; Burundian Hutu refugees in Tanzania, 1990s.* Immediately following the 1994 genocide of up to 800,000 Tutsi, the perpetrators of the genocide urged nearly two million Rwandan Hutu to flee the country. Roughly 1.2 million refugees ended up in eastern Zaire and another 500,000 established camps in western Tanzania. From the camps in Zaire, militant leaders established a state in exile and trained soldiers and militia members for the overthrow of the new Rwandan regime. The threat posed by the militarized camps led to the Rwandan invasion of Zaire and the forceful dismantling of the camps in late 1996. By contrast, the Tanzanian camps presented a much lower threat to regional stability. Refugee leaders were unable to militarize the camps to anywhere near the same degree as in Zaire. An essential question for this book is why the two groups of refugees from the same conflict behaved so differently.

  The Great Lakes case studies also allow for a comparison of refugees from different conflicts within the same receiving state. In contrast to the relatively nonviolent Rwandan refugees in Tanzania, the presence of over 300,000 Burundian refugees has repeatedly led to cross-border violence between Burundi and Tanzania in which the two armies mobilized along the border. The Burundian government accused Tanzania of allowing militants to operate in the refugee camps; factions within Burundi threatened to cross the border to eradicate the threat from the camps. The comparison between Rwandan and Burundian refugees illuminates how differences in the sending state (and in the conflicts there) and the policy of the receiving state can influence outcomes.

- *Afghan refugees in Pakistan and Iran, 1980s.* During the Cold War, the United States actively supported military activity involving anti-communist refugee movements, such as the Afghan refugees in Pakistan. As in the African cases, the situations of Afghan refugees in Pakistan and Iran show variation in the levels of violence. With Pakistan's cooperation, the United States spent billions of dollars funding militant anti-communist forces among the three million Afghan refugees in that country. The remarkably low level of military activity among the two million Afghan refugees in Iran provides a stark contrast to the violence in Pakistan. The Afghan comparisons demonstrate variation over time (the Cold War past versus the current crises) and space (Pakistan versus Iran).

- *Velika Kladusa Muslims in Bosnia, 1994 and 1995.* During the war in Bosnia, a renegade group of Bosnian Muslims, led by Fikret Abdic,

Table 1.2 Comparing violent and nonviolent crises (Violent outcomes in italics)

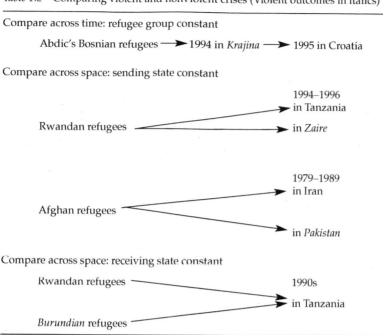

Compare across time: refugee group constant

    Abdic's Bosnian refugees ──► 1994 in *Krajina* ──► 1995 in Croatia

Compare across space: sending state constant

    Rwandan refugees

        1994–1996 in Tanzania

        in *Zaire*

    Afghan refugees

        1979–1989 in Iran

        in *Pakistan*

Compare across space: receiving state constant

    Rwandan refugees

        1990s in Tanzania

    Burundian refugees

challenged the Sarajevo government. During the course of the war, a group of 25,000 of Abdic's followers twice became refugees. On the first occasion, they organized an army of 10,000 fighters and retook their hometown, with military help from the Serbs. The second time the Bosnians were expelled, the Croatian Special Police disarmed them. The refugees peacefully returned home or resettled in other countries after the signing of the Dayton Accords. This case study offers an examination of the same refugee group over time and controls for variables related to history, leadership, and culture.

By comparing violent and nonviolent situations, the case studies pinpoint the attributes of refugee crises that affect the propensity for civil war to spread across borders. The case studies confirm the importance of the political context in causing the spread of conflict and discredit socioeconomic explanations. Currently, policymakers formulate reactions to refugee-related violence on an ad hoc basis, constrained by lack of resources and information. With more systematic information on the causes and characteristics of political violence involving refugees, humanitarian agencies and governments can better target their efforts at prevention.

[2]

Political Incentives for the Spread Of Civil War

Although scholars and policymakers have expressed increasing concern about refugee militarization, there is no existing systematic explanation for the phenomenon of refugee-related violence. The ad hoc explanations offered by the humanitarian assistance literature and the policy community generally focus on socioeconomic factors as both cause and cure. These socioeconomic propositions do not explicitly address the spread of civil war, but rather lump all types of refugee-related violence together. According to these explanations, proximity to the border, large camp populations, the presence of bored young men, and poor living conditions cause cross-border violence. Reliance on these explanations leads to policy prescriptions that focus solely on ameliorating socioeconomic conditions as a cure for refugee-related violence. Closer examination of violent and nonviolent refugee crises confirms the weakness of socioeconomic explanations. In some cases, reliance on socioeconomic policy recommendations actually strengthens militant organizations. The influx of resources does not deter militants from their political goals and inadvertently finances conflict.

A more convincing explanation focuses on the political context of each refugee crisis. This chapter advances a political explanation for the spread of civil war in refugee crises and compares it to the prevailing socioeconomic explanations. Three aspects of the political context determine whether war will spread. The first is the origin of the refugee crisis; refugees who flee targeted persecution or defeat in a civil war will have a higher level of political and military organization than refugees who escape general chaos or destruction. A high level of organization indicates a propensity for later cross-border violence, whether instigated by the refugees or the sending state. Second, given a high propensity for violence among the refugees, the response of the receiving state determines whether violence will occur. A refugee-receiving state that is unwilling or unable to secure its borders and demilitarize the refugees creates a political environment conducive to the spread of war. Lastly, third-party states, international aid agencies, and non-governmental organizations (NGOs) facilitate conflict when they intentionally or inadvertently provide resources to combatants. This political explanation sharply contrasts with the prevailing discussion about militarized refugee crises.

The Origin of the Crisis and Propensity for Violence

Most analyses of refugee-related violence do not differentiate among the dozens of refugee crises active at any one time. Yet not all refugee crises share the same propensity for cross-border violence. The best way to determine the initial propensity for violence is to examine the reason for the refugee flow. The origin determines the political cohesion of the refugees and their initial level of military organization. As mentioned in chapter 1, I create three categories of refugee groups according to the origin of the crisis. These categories are: situational refugees, persecuted refugees, and state-in-exile refugees (See table 2.1). The impetus for their exile, their initial levels of political organization, and their requirements for return to the sending state differentiate these groups and indicate their initial propensity for militarization. Before moving to analysis of these groups, I echo the caveat offered by Myron Wiener in his classification of causes of refugee flows: "Though it is usually possible to

Table 2.1   Types of refugees and propensity for violence

	Origin of Flight	Requirements for voluntary return	Initial political organization	Propensity for violence
Situational refugees	War, chaos, deprivation	Peace and Stability	None or very loose	Unlikely
Persecuted refugees	Group-based persecution	Credible guarantees of protection	Weak, may grow in exile	Somewhat likely
State-in-exile refugees	Defeat in civil war	New government or military victory	Strong, often grows in exile	Very likely

determine the predominant reason for a refugee flow, it is often a judgment call as to whether to classify a particular conflict as [for example] ethnic or non-ethnic. The nature of the conflict also sometimes changes. . . . Some of the conflicts are mixed."[1]

Situational Refugees

Situational refugees have the lowest propensity for involvement in political violence. They have little political cohesion and thus little motivation to divert refugee relief for militarization purposes. Typically, situational refugees report that they left their homes in a panic when the actions of combatants threatened to kill them or destroy their livelihoods. For example, a report on the ongoing war in eastern Congo noted that massive displacement occurred because "the pressure in the villages is so great that people can't live their lives."[2] Similarly, an observer of the 1996 war in Congo (then Zaire) reported that "fear and instability in [eastern Zaire] are so great that many inhabitants have fled their villages even without being directly attacked."[3] Basically, situational refugees like the ones from Congo find themselves in the wrong place at the wrong time. Their villages become the front lines in a war in which the local residents have little stake. If these refugees become involved in violence, it is usually as victims of attacks or as pawns of militant leaders.

The willingness of situational refugees to return home depends on a cessation of hostilities rather than any specific political or military outcome. The goals of these refugees are to earn a livelihood and, as much as possible, to return to their previous way of life. An essential difference between situational refugees and other groups is that situational refugees express a willingness to return to their country as soon as they can live in peace, regardless of the outcome of the conflict.

The less-politicized nature of the situational refugees stems in part from the type of conflict that they have escaped. In many instances, these conflicts garner very low levels of popular support. One often finds that the combatants have engaged in such high levels of brutality toward their own people that they have alienated any potential supporters. In the Liberian civil war, for example, both the government forces and the LURD rebels have preyed on civilians. Refugees from Liberia described the seemingly wanton brutality that caused their flight, explaining that LURD rebels "burned the whole town. Everyone fled into the bushes. . . . Government troops were behind us. They came into the bush and took our clothes and materials."[4] For situational refugees like the Liberians,

[20]

the origin of the crisis reduces the likelihood of their voluntary involvement in military activity.

An example where the origin of the crisis explains an unexpected nonviolent outcome is the flight of more than one million Mozambican refugees to neighboring Malawi during the Mozambican civil war in the 1980s. Despite the large size of the refugee population, its location on the border, and the poor living conditions, humanitarian aid to the refugees in Malawi did not become a tool in the war. The refugee camps did not become militarized, and few cross-border attacks occurred.

During the civil war, the Marxist-Socialist Mozambican government battled the South African–supported Resistência National Moçambicana (RENAMO) rebels in a brutal contest over control of the state. RENAMO attempted to make the country ungovernable, and to that end terrorized the population and demolished much of the infrastructure, including schools, clinics, and roads. Unlike many African civil wars, the conflict lacked a strong ethnic or communal component. The main effect of the conflict was to destroy the peace and threaten the lives of civilians caught in the crossfire. Refugees streamed out of the country to escape the horror and devastation. At the peak of the crisis, Mozambican refugees constituted 10 percent of the population in Malawi and lived mostly in villages and camps less than ten miles from the Mozambique border.

For the most part, the refugees engaged in little political or military activity in support of either side. One observer noted that "RENAMO made no attempt to win over the support of the Mozambican people."[5] RENAMO seemingly had no political goals and focused only on destroying the government, at whatever cost to Mozambicans. In a U.S. State Department study, refugees expressed overwhelmingly negative attitudes toward RENAMO and neutral attitudes toward the Mozambican government.[6] These situational refugees desired a return to peace and stability.[7] One refugee asserted that "we can't possibly go until we are absolutely certain that the hostilities have subsided."[8] Once the combatants reached a peace agreement in 1992, hundreds of thousands of refugees voluntarily returned to Mozambique without demanding any additional political preconditions or guarantees.

Persecuted Refugees

A second type of refugee population flees because of direct persecution or oppression. These refugees have a greater propensity for involvement in political violence than do situational refugees. Persecuted refugees escape ethnic cleansing, genocide, or other violent policies that target them for ethnic, religious, linguistic, or political reasons. The experience of persecution helps create politically cohesive refugee groups that lend themselves to military activity. Humanitarian assistance to persecuted refugees is more likely to exacerbate conflict than aid to situational refugees.

During the war in Bosnia, for example, combatants tried to expel all members of the opposing ethnic group in order to create ethnically homogeneous areas. In repeated instances, Muslim residents fled in terror when Serb militias entered a town. Often an attack on a Muslim neighbor convinced other Muslims to flee before they too experienced a direct attack. One Bosnian Muslim refugee described the impetus to flight: "First [the Serbs] sent written notices saying that Muslims and Croats had to leave the area immediately. Our neighbors came and warned us to go, because they said that if they tried to help us they would also be killed."[9] The war created groups of refugees united by the experience of ethnically based persecution, so they were determined not to return home until the risk of such persecution had vanished.

For persecuted refugees, the political outcome of the conflict bears directly on their willingness to return home. The goals of persecuted refugees often include political change, for example power sharing or other credible guarantees that their group will not be persecuted if it returns home. One displaced Bosnian Muslim reported that her family would return home "only if as Bosniacs they would be free and equal citizens in Republika Srpska."[10] Situational refugees, on the other hand, will likely return home as soon as conditions are peaceful, regardless of the political outcome of the conflict. These refugees have no reason to expect targeted persecution and merely require a cessation of war in order to go home.

The coalescing event of group persecution increases the receptivity of refugees to political or military activity. In many instances, refugee or rebel leaders draw on the experience of persecution—and often exaggerate it—in order to rally support for military activity. Due to the causes of their flight, persecuted refugees are more vulnerable to propaganda and manipulation than situational refugees. Refugees who have experienced persecution also fear repeated attacks by the sending state. Therefore, they will be more willing to take measures perceived as defensive or preventive. These refugees may find that ambitious leaders manipulate a defensive interest in survival for offensive purposes.

Persecuted refugees also face a higher probability of cross-border attacks by the sending state than situational refugees. Depending on

[22]

the cause of their flight, the sending state may view the refugees as a threat for reasons of ethnicity, religion, or political affiliation. Thus, even if the refugees do not organize politically or militarily while in exile, they remain vulnerable to continued attacks. The sending state will likely view the internationally supported refugee camps as a threat to its security.

In some cases, a group of persecuted refugees becomes more prone to violence over time, creating a state in exile. This is especially likely for long-term refugees who see no hope of return until radical change occurs in their homeland. As time passes, a leadership may emerge that unites the refugees behind a program of political and military action.[11] For example, the Palestinian refugees who were expelled to neighboring states following the 1948 war constituted a persecuted refugee group. Over time, organized militant groups, such as the Palestinian National Liberation Movement (Fatah) and the PLO, emerged among the refugees. Under the leadership of these organizations, militarized refugee populations engaged in cross-border warfare against Israel. For aid agencies, this suggests that protracted refugee relief may help to build and sustain a militarized population.

The Burundian Hutu population in Tanzania offers another example of persecuted refugees who became involved in political violence. The brutal ethnic civil war that started in 1993 in Burundi led to the death of hundreds of thousands of civilians and the displacement of many more. The conflict pitted the Tutsi-dominated government and army against an array of Hutu rebel forces. Both sides targeted civilians based on their ethnicity. The government rounded up Hutu villagers into "regroupment" camps in order to prevent the rebels from gaining their support. The Hutu rebels, conversely, sought to create a vast population of Hutu refugees in order to undermine the legitimacy of the Tutsi government and provide cover for rebel activity. As of December 2002, 370,000 Hutu refugees from Burundi were living in camps near the Tanzanian-Burundi border.

The ethnic polarization that led to the refugee flows allowed Hutu leaders to mobilize support in the camps, as did the tacit support of the Tanzanian government for the Hutu rebel activity. Tanzania hotly denied the Burundian government accusations that rebels freely operated in the refugee camps, but observers confirmed that Burundian Hutu refugees were engaging in both political and military activity. Many extremist political parties developed in the camps, most with military wings. Rebel groups recruited young men from the camps for military training and subsequent cross-border raids.[12] As one analyst explained, "this should come as no surprise, considering the traumatic experiences which caused the flight."[13] The Burundian army threatened to retaliate by attacking the camps, leading to a Tanzanian military buildup on the border.[14]

Humanitarian assistance exacerbated this conflict even though military activity occurred clandestinely. The militant parties increased their resources by enforcing a war tax on refugees, in both food and cash. The camps sustained the militants' dependents and followers, freeing the rebel parties from the responsibility of providing material support. The refugee camps themselves did not function as military bases but were still highly politicized. When a UNHCR team assessed the security situation, it found a high level of political activity, including political meetings.[15] This allowed the rebel parties to enhance their legitimacy and support among the refugees.

Although the Burundian refugees displayed a high level of political and military organization, they did not flee as a state in exile. Refugees fled persecution and the threat of injury based on their ethnicity. The rebel leaders did not organize the exile in the face of defeat, but they took advantage of the refugee situation in order to pursue their ongoing conflict against the Burundian government. Unlike Afghan refugees in Pakistan and Rwandan refugees in Zaire, the Burundian refugees did not regard themselves as a state in exile and were never recognized as such by any external party.

State-in-Exile Refugees

The third and most violence-prone group occurs when the refugee group includes a highly organized political and military leadership. This type of population is a state-in-exile refugee group.[16] In some instances, the leadership has organized the refugees as a strategy of war. Such leaders hold aggressive goals, which likely include a radical change in the government of the sending state. Because such outflows include many civilians, states and international agencies often designate them as refugee populations. The Rwandan Hutu refugees in eastern Zaire provide a recent example of the state-in-exile phenomenon. These refugees fled Rwanda in 1994 under pressure from the leaders of the genocide, who used the refugees as a valuable resource for their militant purposes.

Of the three categories of refugee groups, state-in-exile refugees are the most likely to use humanitarian relief as a resource of war. Indeed, the leaders, facing military defeat, often encourage a refugee crisis to facilitate their war aims. The strong political organization exercised by the leaders enables them to divert large amounts of assistance to support their conflict. In the Zaire crisis, humanitarian aid to the refugees essentially functioned as the infrastructure for the state in exile.

State-in-exile refugees usually return home either in victory or as a result of forced repatriation after rejecting power-sharing or amnesty offers from the sending state. For example, the Rwandan Hutu refugees in Zaire refused all attempts by the Rwandan government to orchestrate their return, leading to the conclusion that "the extremists were not opposed to return as such, merely to a return that they did not control."[17]

State-in-exile refugees present a greater threat to the sending state than other types of groups, thus increasing the chance of preventive cross-border attacks against the refugees. Large and politically active refugee populations serve as an indictment of the sending state regime and a constant threat to its security. State-in-exile refugees challenge the legitimacy of the sending state government, providing fodder for domestic and international critics.

Although state-in-exile refugees exist within a strong and politicized leadership structure, many of the refugees may have little desire to become involved in violence. The nature of the exile group makes it more likely, however, that these refugees will serve as a political and military resource for their leaders. By maintaining an iron grip on the information that reaches the refugees and controlling the distribution of humanitarian aid, leaders can convince many refugees of possible threats to their safety and of the need to mobilize. Leaders emphasize real and imagined injustices to foster fear of return among the refugees. In the Rwandan Hutu camps, leaders successfully nurtured a belief in Hutu victimhood, distorting or erasing the genocide that preceded the refugee flight. Hutu leaders also played on fears created by real injustices in Rwanda, such as the 1995 massacre of unarmed displaced Hutu by the Rwandan Patriotic Army at Kibeho camp.

Most state-in-exile groups gain strength over time. The longer it takes to separate the militants, disarm the refugees, and develop alternate solutions to the crisis, the more time the group has to organize and grow. In exile, the militants improve their security situation vis-à-vis the sending state. They also have greater freedom to raise funds and develop alliances. Time in exile gives leaders the opportunity to expand their popular support. As a crisis drags on, discouraged refugees may begin to believe that the only escape from an intractable situation is through violence.

[25]

The Palestinian refugee crisis provides a clear example of an unresolved and highly politicized refugee crisis that over time developed into a state in exile. The refugee crisis began with an estimated 600,000 to 840,000 refugees resulting from the 1948 war with Israel.[18] The Palestinian refugees went primarily to the West Bank, the Gaza Strip, and neighboring states.[19] Following the 1967 war between Israel and Egypt, Syria, and Jordan, hundreds of thousands of Palestinian refugees fled to Jordan. As of 2002, the United Nations had registered 3.9 million Palestinian refugees, including the descendants of the 1948 refugees. This seemingly intractable refugee crisis—arguably more intractable than any other in the world—has become intertwined with broader political issues and regional conflicts. Although many scholars and policymakers view it as an exceptional case, many aspects of the Palestinian crisis fit into the framework described in this book.

The refugees did not flee as a state in exile, but over time their shared experience of persecution coalesced into a highly organized and militant state in exile. In the period from 1956 to 1964, political parties emerged among the refugee population, including the Palestine National Liberation Movement (Fatah) and the Palestinian branch of the Arab Nationalist Movement. The PLO formed in 1964 and created the Palestinian Liberation Army (PLA). As in the Afghan state in exile, the competing Palestinian factions experienced fragmentation and bitter conflict. Eventually Yasir Arafat's PLO became the dominant, although not the only, resistance movement.

By September 1970 the Palestinians had over 5,000 full-time and 20–25,000 part-time fighters, based mostly in Jordan. A decade later the PLO had moved its fighters to Lebanon and amassed equipment including artillery, rocket launchers, tanks and armored personnel carriers, and anti-aircraft and anti-tank weapons.[20] The Palestinian state in exile also consolidated itself by developing social and economic organizations among the refugees, including the Palestinian Red Crescent Society.

In the Palestinian situation, the issue of return to the sending state is more highly contested and politicized than in many refugee crises. Usually refugee demands center on the right *not* to return to a crisis area, especially while hostilities are ongoing. In this conflict, Palestinian demands for return and Israeli refusals to allow it constitute the heart of the dispute.[21]

All five types of refugee-related violence listed in table 1.1 have affected Palestinian refugees during their decades of displacement. Repeated cross-border attacks occurred between Israel and the refugee militants, which escalated to Israeli attacks on the receiving states and the 1982 invasion of Lebanon. During the early years of the crisis, the Palestinian militant organizations based in Jordan and Lebanon conducted small-scale guerrilla raids across the border into Israel until a mass armed movement emerged in 1968. Following the battle at Karameh, in which 300 Palestinian fighters (with Jordanian army assistance) inflicted relatively heavy losses on a much stronger Israeli force, thousands of new recruits came from the Palestinian refugee camps to train with the PLO and other resistance forces.[22] Conflict between Israeli forces and Palestinian militants has continued through the decades, leading to pitched battles in the crowded, politicized refugee camps in the West Bank and the Gaza Strip.

Despite cultural and religious affinities and sympathy for the Palestinian cause, the major receiving states (Jordan, Syria, and Lebanon) did not encourage the development of a strong, unified Palestinian state in exile. Yezid Sayigh reported that "the threat to internal stability, and the risk of inviting Israeli retaliation, has been sufficient to bring the host governments into direct confrontation with the Palestinian movement."[23] Dramatic confirmation of the risks of a militarized refugee presence occurred in Jordan in 1970. Despite Jordan's generous treatment of the refugees, including granting citizenship, the Palestinian refugees sparked a civil war and nearly toppled the government of King Hussein. Thousands of Palestinian civilians and militants died during Hussein's subsequent harsh crackdown on Palestinian activity.[24]

Following the civil war, the Jordanian government evicted the PLO and the Palestinian militants moved their bases to Lebanon. The Palestinians developed a thriving state in exile that generated about 15 percent of Lebanon's GDP in 1981.[25] Conflict with the receiving state continued as the Lebanese government sought to control and restrict Palestinian political activity. Tensions culminated in 1982 when Lebanese forces backed by Israeli tanks, massacred some several thousand Palestinian civilians in the Sabra and Shatila refugee camps.[26] The Lebanese then expelled the PLO, which established a new headquarters in Tunis.

Like the Cambodian refugees on the Thai border, Palestinian refugees were neither assisted nor protected by UNHCR. In 1949 the United Nations formed a special agency, the United Nations Relief and Works Agency for Palestinian refugees (UNRWA), with a mandate to provide humanitarian assistance. Over time, UNRWA became the main lightning rod for the fierce debate over the politicization of aid to Palestinians. One expert admitted that "although the agency did not create Palestinian nationalism, nevertheless, over the years refugees, both as beneficiaries and employees, mapped out a Palestinian identity onto its various sites and spaces."[27] Critics condemn American support for UNRWA and call for the institution's dismemberment.[28]

THE RECEIVING STATE RESPONSE TO MILITARIZED CRISES

Capability and Willingness

According to international law, the refugee-receiving state bears the primary responsibility for ensuring the safety of the refugees and maintaining the civilian nature of the refugee populated area.[29] The duties of the receiving state include disarming and demobilizing any noncivilian exiles who wish to integrate into the refugee camp, preventing the flow of arms to refugee areas, protecting the refugees from attack and intimidation, and separating those who do not qualify for international protection—for example, war criminals—from the refugees. In the optimal case, the receiving state provides physical and legal protection to the refugees while humanitarian organizations provide material assistance.

The receiving state response is critical to preventing the spread of civil war among violence-prone refugee groups, whether classified as persecuted or state in exile. As noted in chapter 1, two factors determine how the policy of the receiving state will affect the spread of civil war. The first factor is the *capability* of the receiving state to secure its borders and demilitarize the refugees. The second factor is the receiving state's *willingness* to prevent violence. Capability refers to the ability of the state to protect its borders and maintain peace and stability on its own territory.[30] Willingness describes the state's attitude toward providing protection and enforcing security in refugee-populated areas. Numerous domestic and international factors affect a state's willingness and capability.

As the independent measures of capability and willingness can both be high or low in any given instance, there are four possible policy responses to a violence-prone refugee situation, as shown in table 2.2. A common scenario features a capable receiving state that supports one of the parties to the conflict and is unwilling to maintain the civilian nature of the refugee camps. Most cases of cross-border attacks and international war fall into this category.[31] When a state has high capability, its political preferences will largely determine whether war spreads. A sympathetic receiving state may allow or abet military activity by the refugees. The state may pressure or coerce humanitarian organizations to divert assistance to combatants and loyalists. In the 1980s, a

Table 2.2 Possible receiving state policies

		Capability to prevent violence	
		High	*Low*
Willingness to prevent violence	*High*	Cross-border violence unlikely	Cross-border violence not controllable but not supported
	Low	Active support of cross-border violence more likely	Active or tacit support of cross-border violence more likely

sympathetic and powerful Thai government allowed Khmer Rouge militants to use the refugee camps as rear bases in their struggle against the Vietnam-sponsored regime in Cambodia. If a capable receiving state is allied with the sending state, it may allow cross-border "hot pursuit" raids by the sending state or forcibly eject the refugees.

A highly dangerous but less frequent situation occurs when the receiving state has little capability and little willingness to prevent violence.[32] Both the sending state and the refugees can more easily engage in cross-border violence when the receiving state cannot impose political order. Most commonly, the receiving state is allied with one of the combatants. In such a situation, the receiving state usually refuses international help that would improve security in the refugee areas. In the Rwandan refugee crisis of 1994 to 1996, the Zairian government combined unwillingness with incapability. The government was allied with the Hutu extremists in the camps and was unable to secure its border with Rwanda. The result was international war.

The third scenario is a receiving state with high willingness to prevent violence but low capability. When this happens, the outcome depends on external assistance to demilitarize the refugee-populated area. Without external assistance, the civil war may spread to the weak receiving state. Guinea from 2000 to 2002 is an example of a weak receiving state that sought external assistance to improve the security of its refugee population. The government of Guinea, host to over 400,000 refugees, was unable to prevent repeated cross-border attacks from both Liberia and Sierra Leone against refugees and local Guineans. After suffering numerous attacks, the government consented to a relocation effort funded by external donors that moved thousands of refugees away from the insecure border with Liberia and Sierra Leone.[33]

Most conducive to stopping the spread of war is a highly capable receiving state with a high willingness to protect its borders and maintain the civilian character of refugee populated areas.[34] In this scenario, attacks by both refugees and the sending state become less likely. Militant refugees will find it difficult to obtain arms, conduct training, and launch attacks when the receiving state adequately polices the refugee area and the border with the sending state. Unlike Zaire, the willing and capable Tanzanian government managed to prevent the spread of war during the Rwandan refugee crisis. In addition to preventing refugee-instigated attacks, adequate security measures reduce the sending state's perception of the refugees as an aggressive threat. A capable receiving state is more able to provide a deterrent to opportunistic attacks by the sending state, especially if the sending state hopes to avoid international war with its neighbor.

All too often, receiving states lack the capability to protect refugees and secure the border. The majority of receiving states are developing countries with extremely limited resources for their own citizens, much less for thousands of refugees. In such states, institutions like the police and the judiciary have grossly inadequate funding and competence to deal with a large influx of refugees. A poor state's capability also depends on the existence of generous allies willing to fund improved border security and law enforcement measures. In addition, the presence of a large and militant refugee state in exile may decrease the state's capability, as happened when the Palestinians took up residence in Jordan.

International and domestic politics affect the receiving state's willingness to provide security. Ethnic ties between the refugees and groups in the receiving state can increase domestic pressure to overlook refugee-instigated violence. Ethnic alliances between the refugees and the receiving state can also pressure the government to prevent cross-border attacks instigated by the sending state. The type of government in the receiving state also influences policy. For example, in Tanzania, the Rwandan refugee crisis occurred during an election year, so leaders sought to placate their constituents with harsh measures against the refugees. A nondemocratic leader faces less domestic public pressure but must still respond to international demands and avoid sparking a rebellion or coup attempt. The receiving state's past experience with asylum seekers also influences its response to a refugee crisis.

Interaction with the Sending State

A sending state that perceives a refugee group as a threat will likely oppose the establishment of internationally funded refugee camps. The sending state will interpret the camps as an international condemnation of its legitimacy and ability to control its borders. It may also fear that the refugee camps will supply militants with resources (recruits or supplies) and lend their cause international legitimacy.

The sending state response to the crisis will depend in part on its relationship with the receiving state. The sending state will be less likely to attack the refugees if the receiving state is willing and able to prevent militarization. In addition, a relatively powerful receiving state is more able to deter opportunistic attacks by the sending state.

If the receiving state cannot control military activity, it may become an attractive target for the sending state. Rwanda invaded Zaire in 1996 to establish a zone of security on the border and to fulfill larger political and economic objectives, such as overthrowing President Mobutu and installing a friendlier regime. In this context, Rwanda viewed the international support of the refugees as contributing to its insecurity.

Another possible scenario is an alliance between the sending and receiving state, in which the receiving state allows cross-border attacks against the refugees. Such an alliance would encourage opportunistic attacks against the refugees regardless of their level of militarization. A prime example of this was the 1994 wave of Rwandan government attacks against Rwandan Hutu refugees in Burundi. Unlike the refugees in Zaire, these Rwandan Hutu were not militarized and lived in fear of the Burundian Tutsi military. The Burundian military allowed cross-border attacks by Rwandan Tutsi forces that killed over 250 defenseless Hutu refugees.

The receiving and sending states may also collude to reduce refugee flows, resulting in violence against prospective refugees. For example, both China and North Korea view massive Korean outflows as a security threat and strive to prevent would-be refugees from settling in China. This has led to violent protests and roundups of North Koreans in China.

The receiving state may also ally with rebel forces in the sending state. For example, a Ugandan human rights organization asserted that the Ugandan government's alliance with the Sudanese rebel army (SPLA) "compromises [the government's] ability to provide protection for those seeking asylum from the war in southern Sudan."[35] Similarly, in 2002 the Guinean military allowed Liberian LURD rebels unimpeded access to defenseless Liberian refugees in Guinea. Human Rights Watch reported that rebels entered the camps to recruit fighters by force and steal supplies in full view of the Guinean camp guards.[36]

The receiving and sending states are not the only influence on whether violence occurs; international actors also provide an impetus for either war or peace (see table 2.3). These actors include third-party states, multilateral organizations (e.g., regional or international peacekeeping forces), international agencies (e.g., UNHCR), and NGOs. External actors exacerbate conflict when they provide military, political, or economic resources to the refugees or the sending state, or they can discourage the spread of conflict by helping the receiving state secure its border and demilitarize the refugee areas.

A third-party state allied with the refugees may encourage or coerce the receiving state and humanitarian organizations to support militant exiles. By providing resources to the refugees and their leaders, the external supporter increases the feasibility of cross-border attacks. During the Cold War, the United States persuaded UNHCR to aid militant refugees, for example the liberation movements in southern Africa and the anti-communist Afghan rebels based in Pakistan. The United States, China, and Saudi Arabia also provided direct military aid to the Afghan rebels.

An external power allied with the sending state may pressure the receiving state to expel the refugees or limit their opportunities for military activity. The third-party state may condone, or even assist in, hot-pursuit raids against the refugees. For example, in 1996 the United States quietly supported the Tutsi-led Rwandan regime as it prepared for attacks on the Hutu refugee camps in Zaire.

Inaction by external states also exacerbates conflict by passively allowing refugee militarization. During the Rwandan refugee crisis, no external actor was willing to pay the political and military price of

Table 2.3   International influences on the spread of civil war

	State actors	Non-state actors
Encourage spread	• Military/political aid to combatants • Pressure receiving state to allow militarization • Pressure humanitarians to assist militants	• Feed rebels • Succor dependents of militants • Support war economy • Legitimize militants
Prevent spread	• Help secure borders • Help demilitarize camps • Restrain sending state	• Withhold assistance from militants • Help secure borders • Help demilitarize

separating the Rwandan militants from the refugees. In vain, UN Secretary General Boutros-Ghali appealed to member states for assistance in Zaire. Initial UN plans to separate the militants from the refugees fell through when aid agencies realized that they would have to move 60,000 to 100,000 militia and army members (and their families) at an estimated cost of $90 to $125 million. Such a move would have required high levels of coercion, since the militants would have refused to separate willingly from their power base—the refugee population. State inaction facilitated the spread of civil war in eastern Zaire.

Third-party states can encourage peace in two ways. Wealthy donor states can help the receiving state secure the border and demilitarize refugee areas. External states can also restrain the sending state from attacking the refugees. Tools for restraining the sending state include diplomatic and/or economic pressure and military force. Multilateral external actors, such as a UN peacekeeping force, can also help secure borders and demilitarize the refugees.

Non-state actors, such as international agencies and NGOs, also influence whether civil war spreads. In militarized situations, aid can fuel the conflict by feeding all exiles, regardless of their civilian status, and ignoring militarization in the refugee area. High levels of aid also allow militants to sell donated food and buy weapons. An implicit "don't ask, don't tell" policy of aid provision allows militarization to continue as long as it does not occur right under the noses of the aid workers. Chapter 1 discusses in detail the ways in which aid becomes a tool of war.

There are two ways that humanitarian organizations can reduce violence: by providing their own security or by making assistance contingent on security. For example, starting in the late 1990s UNHCR provided funds to the Tanzanian government for improving the police presence in the refugee area. In Zaire, UNHCR paid members of the army to guard the Rwandan camps. A potentially powerful, but rarely used, form of leverage is the humanitarian assistance itself. UN agencies and NGOs can coerce the receiving state and militant groups to enforce security and demilitarize by threatening to withdraw assistance. Based on past experience, militant exiles assume that humanitarian groups will automatically feed and house the refugees, whether militants are there or not. The state-in-exile phenomenon might occur less often if the promise of generous international aid was less certain. This would necessitate a credible threat to withdraw humanitarian aid in highly militarized crises. Chapter 6 discusses these controversial options in greater detail.

CONVENTIONAL WISDOM: SOCIOECONOMIC EXPLANATIONS

The discussion thus far has emphasized the political reasons that refugee crises occur and the sources of political and military support available to potentially militant refugees. Despite the importance of politics, current discussions of refugee militarization focus on socioeconomic explanations of the phenomenon and generally ignore the political context of the crisis (see table 2.4). The socioeconomic explanations, taken together, do not constitute a systematic theory but rather a collection of common factors cited by humanitarian aid workers and policymakers as causes of conflict. Socioeconomic factors include the size and location of camps, the number of men in the population, and the living conditions in the camps. In practice, none of these socioeconomic characteristics satisfactorily explain cross-border violence involving refugees. Adherence to those explanations leads to ineffective policy and can even exacerbate violence.

Numerous policy pronouncements urgently cite large refugee camps as security threats. As one UNHCR policy paper recommends, "refugee camps should be located at a reasonable distance from the border . . . and should ideally not exceed 20,000 refugees."[37] One analyst's recommendation to "scatter refugees to reduce militia control" implies that concentrated populations contribute to conflict.[38] The camp size explanation argues that many small refugee camps, instead of one or two large ones, would reduce violence between the refugees and the sending state. Advocates reason that large camps are harder to manage and more prone to social problems than small camps.[39] A second, related question is whether large refugee populations in absolute terms are more involved in violence, regardless of the size of the camps.

Surprisingly, case study research reveals refugees in both large and small camps engaged in conflict with the sending state.[40] Apparently refugee militants share the view of policymakers that small camps are easier to control and organize. In eastern Zaire, refugees in small camps (fewer than 20,000 people) fell under even tighter control by the militants than refugees in the larger camps. Small groups of Nicaraguan and Salvadoran refugees in Honduras led to the spread of civil war from

Table 2.4 Socioeconomic explanations

- Large camps
- Border camps
- Bored young men
- Poor living conditions

their sending states. In the Honduras crisis, the overall size of the refugee population and the size of the camps were both well below UNHCR specifications. In 1983, there were only 19,000 Nicaraguan refugees in Honduras and 7–10,000 Salvadoran refugees. Both groups were perceived as threats by their sending states. The example of the Bosnian Muslim renegade refugees, presented in a later chapter, also illustrates the point. In that crisis, a group of 25,000 refugees formed a rebel army and launched an attack on the Bosnian army. In these situations, the political context of the crisis, not the size of the refugee camp, caused the spread of civil war.

The overall number of refugees seems logically more relevant to the spread of war than the size of the camp. Parties to a conflict generally view larger populations as a greater potential threat (and as a greater strategic resource) than smaller populations. Both the sending state and the refugee leaders realize that a large population, in absolute terms, provides a greater resource for military mobilization and offensive activity.[41] A large population of refugees relative to the size of the sending state also offers a greater indictment of the sending state government and its ability to govern its own population.

Systematic data analysis confirms that larger refugee populations are more often involved in political violence (of all types) than small populations.[42] For example, in 1998, 9 percent of refugee populations with fewer than 100,000 refugees were involved in political violence.[43] Conversely, 29 percent of large populations (over 100,000 refugees) were involved in political violence. Thus one can conclude that larger populations are more often involved in political violence than smaller populations.

Moving from all types of political violence to the subset of attacks between the refugees and the sending state—that is to say, attacks that may lead to the spread of civil war—reveals different findings. The analysis of cross-border attacks between the refugees and the sending state during 1998 shows a rough parity between large and small groups. Of the eleven populations involved in cross-border attacks, six were small groups and five were large groups, with the dividing line again at 100,000. The popular focus on large groups stems from the fact that their activities will more likely involve higher levels of violence, which in turn will mean more casualties, more recruits, and so on. The salient point is that small refugee groups are no less likely to engage in cross-border attacks than large ones.

Observers frequently claim that refugee populations encamped near the border of the sending state are more likely to become involved in violence because the short distance makes it easier for both parties to launch attacks.[44] The Organization of African Unity (OAU) Convention states that "for reasons of security, countries of asylum shall, as far as possible, settle refugees at a reasonable distance from the frontier of the country of origin."[45] Ideally, UNHCR would like to locate refugee camps more than 20 miles from the border of the sending state, for the security of both the refugees and the states involved. UNHCR directs its staff that "when in doubt always locate or move the site away from the frontier."[46]

There are two ways to evaluate the "border camps" explanation for violence. First, one can compare different border camps with similar characteristics to see if there is variance in the level of cross-border violence. For example, the Rwandan Hutu refugees in both Zaire and Tanzania lived within walking distance of Rwanda, yet cross-border violence affected the Zairian camps much more than in Tanzania. That comparison suggests that an additional factor may be responsible for levels of violence within border camps, although a single example does not prove that camp location is irrelevant to violence.

A second way to evaluate the explanation involves comparing border camps to camps located far from the border, holding other characteristics constant, as much as possible. One then asks whether the border camps experience higher levels of violence. A systematic test of this proposition is difficult because the vast majority of camps are located near the sending state border. Despite the OAU condemnation of border camps, most refugee camps exist near the sending state border. The predominance of border camps generally stems from the preference of the receiving state and the simple fact that refugees on foot cannot move easily toward the interior of the receiving state. For their part, refugees often prefer border camps because they can return home more easily.[47] State-in-exile refugee groups may intentionally settle on the border in order to conduct cross-border attacks more easily.

Some evidence emerges from individual case studies, but it does not lead to generalizable findings. For example, variations in the cross-border violence affecting the Afghan refugees did not correlate with the distance of the camp from the border.[48] Without more comparisons, however, a conclusive finding is not possible.

The problem with the border camps explanation as enunciated by humanitarian organizations is that it ignores the political nature of camp location, treating it merely as a logistical difficulty. A recent optimistic statement by an official at the United Nations Office for the Coordination of Humanitarian Affairs (OCHA) offers an example of this viewpoint: "It is still possible to apply standards and principles when dealing with problems of protection. Some of these things are actually very straightforward and practical issue [*sic*] to adopt, for example on refugees—to ensure that refugee camps are 50 km away from an international border is a practical measure that doesn't necessarily cost, it isn't an issue of capacity, it's primarily an issue of political will."[49] The OCHA analysis suggests that since *only* political will is involved, and not money, relocation of refugee camps should not be difficult. UNHCR also discusses camp location in technocratic terms, even while conceding "the tendency of host governments to see site selection only as a political issue."[50] In reality, the receiving state and the refugees may strenuously—even violently—oppose camp relocation for political, economic, and military reasons. Thus, what aid organizations and governments treat as a purely socioeconomic issue—camp location and size—is actually deeply intertwined with political factors.

In addition to the location and size of camps, humanitarian aid workers and scholars often suggest that the gender and age balances in the refugee population contribute to violence. This explanation argues that the mere presence of young men in camps—especially those without legitimate activities to occupy their time—encourages refugee-related violence. According to this argument, leaders easily recruit these bored young men for violent purposes or organize them into criminal bands.[51]

The "bored young men" explanation has two strands. One is that refugee populations with an abnormally large number of young men are more likely to engage in war. This sociological explanation rests on the (generally valid) assumption that young men are the most likely perpetrators of aggression in a society. Tony Vaux, an experienced Oxfam worker and author, quotes Steven Pinker to make the point: "Maleness is by far the biggest risk factor for violence."[52] Valerie Hudson and Andrea den Boer's application of the gender balance theory to international security can be applied to refugee populations. They argue that an unnaturally high proportion of young men "may provide an aggravating catalyst to the mix of insecurity factors leading to conflict."[53]

A second strand of the gender theory focuses more on the activities available to men, rather than the number of men per se. This explanation holds that refugee assistance must provide more activities, such as sports, vocational training, and farming to occupy young men. Paul Collier, a World Bank official, has developed this theory for civil war in general. He argues that "other things being equal, we might expect that the *proportion of young men* in a society . . . would be a factor influencing the feasibility of rebellion. . . . Relatedly, the willingness of young men to join a rebellion might be influenced by their other income-earning opportunities."[54] This basically fits with the living conditions explanation discussed below and suggests that men can be distracted from political violence through recreational or income-generating activity.

The demographics of refugee populations make gender imbalance an unlikely explanation for the spread of civil war.[55] The chief UNHCR statistician reports that in the initial stages of a refugee crisis, the demographics of the refugee population resemble the structure of the population of the country of origin.[56] UNHCR finds that "generally speaking, the gender selectivity of mass refugee outflows is limited." The age distribution also tends to mirror the general population.[57] Relying on demographic data, one would not expect more violence in refugee populations than among non-uprooted populations.[58]

A glaring problem in the gender imbalance theory is its disregard of any political motivation for militarization.[59] The explanation suggests that all bored young men, whether in situational or state-in-exile groups, are equally susceptible to military recruitment. In fact, state-in-exile and persecuted refugees have a much greater propensity for military organization than situational refugees. Surprisingly, state-in-exile groups may have even less than the usual amount of men because they remain outside of the camps to fight.[60]

A disproportionate number of men could signify aggressive intentions or simply reflect the type of population that was expelled. For example, when the Rwandans fled to Zaire with their army and militia, the group likely included large numbers of men. However, the cause of the ensuing violence was that the army had been able to escape intact, not the number of men in the camps. The gender imbalance theory treats all men as similarly dangerous, even though there is clearly a difference between an "extra" 20,000 male militia members and 20,000 male farmers. During the civil war in Sudan, thousands of boys became separated from their families and moved to the refugee camps in Ethiopia and Kenya. The movement of these teenagers did not result from any militant ambition among the refugees, but rather from their banding together to survive the harsh conditions of exile.

The fourth socioeconomic proposition suggests that poor living conditions increase the willingness of refugees to support military activity. The humanitarian assistance literature often argues that increased material incentives—humanitarian assistance, farming land, freedom of movement, opportunity to engage in commerce, educational opportunity, and recreational activity—will forestall the spread of civil war. As UNHCR explains, "Refugee camps (like other large, poor and densely-populated human settlements) have an inherent propensity to insecurity, especially when their inhabitants are deprived of educational, agricultural or income-generating opportunities and have little prospect of finding an early solution to their plight."[61]

The basic idea is that refugees, especially young men, require distraction from the pull of aggressive leaders and the temptation to improve their standard of living through violence. For example, an OAU-sponsored conference stressed that aid agencies could reduce militarism and improve security in the Rwandan refugee camps by encouraging "educational, cultural and sporting activities . . . targeted particularly at those adolescent males who are most likely to become involved in destabilizing criminal, political or military activities."[62] UNHCR recommends "providing structured activities and primary schools for children" in order to "reduce recruitment into the armed forces."[63] A UNICEF-sponsored evaluation of humanitarian assistance quotes an Afghan relief worker: "When people are self-reliant they won't need to go join the warlords . . . [but] if you are starving, you have to go and fight."[64] The living conditions explanation implies that refugee camps with low levels of humanitarian aid and very restrictive conditions are likely to become hotbeds of violence.

The flaws in this explanation stem, in part, from its overgeneralization to all refugee groups and its complete avoidance of the political contexts of crises. As currently enunciated by the humanitarian aid community, this explanation assumes little or no political motivation behind the tendency of refugees to support cross-border attacks. The living conditions explanation also fails to distinguish between types of refugee populations, implying that even situational refugees might become violent if their living conditions become too unsatisfactory. The theory could be improved by recognizing the possibility that living conditions might affect some types of violence (crime) more than others (international war).[65] As a corollary to this theory, it seems likely that the very lowest living conditions would not produce violence, as some basic level of food, water, and shelter is required for political mobilization.

The living conditions explanation, looking at the same refugee group over time and also comparing different groups, fails to explain the actions of deprived refugees. For example, among Rwandan refugees the variation in levels of assistance over time does not correlate with the variation in violent activity. In addition, refugees who enjoyed relatively good conditions (compared to the average for developing countries and to other refugee groups) exhibited variation in levels of violence. These findings suggest that the level of military activity depends on the political motivation of the refugees rather than just material incentives.

In practice, the converse of the living conditions explanation often holds true. Higher levels of aid can actually fuel the conflict and enable the spread of civil war. In cases where aggressive leaders control the refugee population, the militants extract resources from the refugees in order to prosecute the war. The Rwandan refugee crisis prompted an unprecedented outpouring of humanitarian aid, which the militants easily diverted to their cause.

Humanitarian organizations usually focus on short-term solutions to poor living conditions in their attempts to forestall violence. The case studies show that this does not curtail the spread of civil war, and may even encourage it. Another socioeconomic approach that seems more promising—and also more difficult—is the establishment of long-term improvements in the refugees' living conditions. This includes finding durable solutions to the crisis, for example resettlement abroad or local integration into the receiving state. In the few instances where such options have been available, it has limited refugees' militancy. During their second flight in 1995, many militant Bosnian Muslim refugees accepted resettlement abroad, breaking their ties with the militant leaders. The availability of that option made it much easier to weaken the hard-core militant elements and allow the peaceful return of the rest of the refugees.

In their focus on peripheral or irrelevant factors, the socioeconomic explanations obscure the political context of the violence and hinder policy measures to prevent the spread of war. Humanitarian organizations probably rely on socioeconomic explanations because these agencies have little control over the political context. For policymakers, hiding behind socioeconomic explanations allows them to foist the problem onto the humanitarian agencies. However, viewing refugee crises purely as humanitarian emergencies often facilitates the spread of civil war.

REFUGEE CRISES AND THE "GREED OR GRIEVANCE" DEBATE

> *"Conflicts are far more likely to be caused by economic opportunities than by grievance."*
> —Paul Collier, in *Greed and Grievance, Economic Agendas in Civil Wars* (2000)

Current theories of civil war focus on economic motivations for violence and disregard historical or political grievances as a cause of conflict.[66]

Although these theories do not directly address the role of refugees or the international spread of conflict, the findings from militarized refugee crises call into question the emphasis on economics as an exclusive cause of civil war. In many instances of refugee-related violence, the refugee militants have been unresponsive to economic enticements to reduce violence. While there are clear economic incentives to perpetuate refugee crises, such as stealing humanitarian aid, most refugee militants did not gain economically by instigating conflict. For the subset of civil wars studied in this book, grievance played a greater role than the economic literature would predict.

One variant of the "greed" theory, advanced by Paul Collier and Anke Hoeffler, argues that the ability to finance rebellion is the major cause of civil war. Their econometric analysis discounts ethnic and religious divisions, political repression, and inequality (what they term "grievance") as causes of civil war. They find that dependence on primary commodity exports is the most "powerful risk factor" for civil war. Such commodities—diamonds, oil, timber—are easily exploitable and highly profitable. One aspect of the greed argument assumes that "all countries might have groups with a sufficiently strong sense of grievance to wish to launch a rebellion, so that rebellions will occur where they are viable." That implies that grievance is a universal and static variable across all states.[67]

The findings on militarized refugee crises clearly demonstrate that a universal grievance theory does not explain why some refugee crises lead to the spread of civil war. Refugee groups harbor varying levels of grievance. Situational refugees have no intention of becoming militarized or starting a war. These refugees have a low level of grievance around which to organize and rarely become involved in violence. Persecuted and state-in-exile groups have higher levels of grievance, but those levels still vary considerably. Only among state-in-exile groups is a rebellion almost sure to occur, given sufficient resources. Among persecuted groups, it is not a foregone conclusion that an infusion of resources will lead to war.

The most straightforward form of the greed theory argues that groups engage in civil war for material gain, not to achieve political goals. David Keen persuasively argues that not all groups engaged in war desire a political victory.[68] Rather, for some groups, the economic gains from war itself outweigh the benefits of political and military victory. This argument makes sense for some civil wars, such as the one in Sierra Leone, where the primary prize was not the state but rather the abundant natural resources. However, the theory does not fit well in many situations where refugees instigate the spread of civil war. Refugee armies have not generally fought for plunder or material gain but rather for political influence. Refugee situations are so politically tenuous—refugees have neither sovereign territory nor the legal right to govern themselves—that the continued limbo of their situation does not allow militant refugees to consolidate much economic gain.

One aspect of Keen's argument worth exploring in later research is the role of economic incentives in prolonging refugee crises. Militant refugees and many other groups (including NGOs) profit from refugee crises and have been accused of preventing the resolution of many protracted crises, such as the Palestinian and Afghan cases. Incentives to prolong refugee crises, not war, seem more analogous to Keen's theory in the case of militarized refugee crises. During a conflict or the preparations for one, a refugee crisis provides substantial economic and political benefits to the militants.

The militant refugees studied in this book fought to redress political grievances and gain political power. The Rwandan Hutu refugee militants were motivated primarily by political goals and the desire to eliminate the Tutsi government. The militants used the exile to gather resources for the war, but this was not the motivation for the war. During their conflict, the Hutu took advantage of Zaire's natural resources and funneled gold out of the country. Rather than staying in Zaire and enriching themselves, they imported weapons and continued to attack Rwanda. Their attacks did not consolidate their economic power—instead they precipitated the Rwandan invasion and the dismemberment of the camps. For the Hutu refugees, varying levels of aid did not produce corresponding variation in the level of violence. More aid did not sate the political aspirations of the Hutu militants, it just enabled them to extract more resources from the refugees, for example in food taxes.[69]

The Mujahideen in Afghanistan also fought for political, not economic, goals. In fact, the life of a Mujahideen was singularly unpleasant. Staying peacefully in the refugee camp would have represented a material improvement in terms of food, health care, and employment opportunities. The Mujahideen had few rewards in terms of plunder or other economic opportunities. They risked their lives to defeat communism, defend Islam, and garner power for their tribe.

Another variation of the economic explanation is the idea that wars occur due to declining standards of living.[70] The case studies directly address the theory of deprivation as a cause of conflict. As shown in all the cases, poor living conditions (both absolute and relative) did not cause refugees to support military activity. The most militant cases are those in which refugees have better than average conditions. Further research could examine if the findings from the refugee crises are applicable to other aspects of civil war.

The economic theories of war are most persuasive when they acknowledge the importance of political goals and grievances. The refugee crises studied here suggest that the initial existence of political goals is a prerequisite to the spread of civil war. Capability, in the form of state support and international influence, leads to war once a high level of political organization among the refugees has been achieved. It is possible that a high level of capability encourages better political organization, but this is more likely to occur in persecuted and state-in-exile groups and not in situational groups. No doubt war profiteers existed and flourished in all of the conflicts studied here. Nevertheless, economic gain was not the primary impetus for the spread of civil war in the Rwandan, Afghan, or Bosnian refugee crises.

[3]

Afghan Refugees

THREE DECADES OF
POLITICAL VIOLENCE

After the Soviet invasion of Afghanistan in 1979, nearly six million Afghans fled their homes—around three million went east to Pakistan and two million moved west into Iran. In Pakistan, Afghan resistance parties created a powerful state in exile that waged a relentless guerrilla war against the Soviet-backed regime in Kabul. In contrast, the potentially militant refugees in Iran lacked the capability to mobilize against the Afghan government. The two receiving states had fundamentally different foreign policy goals, domestic politics, and attitudes toward the refugees. The refugee crises occurred in the political context of the Cold War, with Afghanistan serving as a proxy battleground for the larger struggle between East and West. Massive donations from anticommunist governments and humanitarian organizations sustained the refugees' war effort in Pakistan during the 1980s. The political context of the crisis explains why refugees in Pakistan were able to internationalize the civil war, whereas those in Iran could not.

Without the refugees, the Afghan resistance could not have mounted such a successful campaign against the Soviet invaders. In Pakistan, the refugees lived in camps controlled by the Afghan resistance parties. The Pakistan government and American donors accepted the primacy of the resistance parties and channeled humanitarian and military assistance through them. President Zia ul-Haq of Pakistan relished the opportunity the refugee crisis provided to increase his standing with the West. International aid organizations provided the infrastructure for the Afghan state in exile, relieving the resistance parties from the burden of sustaining their followers. The resistance parties launched cross-border attacks against Afghanistan and organized raids into the interior of the country. In response, the Soviet-backed Afghan regime shelled and bombed the border areas of Pakistan. The refugee population provided legitimacy for the resistance and a mechanism for funneling weapons to the anti-communist forces.

The refugees in Iran had a very different experience. Like the Pakistan groups, these refugees fled persecution by the Soviet-backed government. However, the Iranian government prevented the emergence of a state in exile. The refugees in Iran did not translate their political goals into military action. Most refugees in Iran lived in urban areas, not camps, and became economically self-sufficient. The government blocked interference by external states and aid organizations. Resistance parties engaged in limited political activity and chafed at the Iranian restrictions against military activity. Iran deeply distrusted Western states and saw the United Nations as a tool of the West. Whereas Pakistan viewed a friendly, malleable Afghanistan as a vital national interest, Iran was preoccupied by its war with Iraq.

Fundamental misunderstandings about the role of refugees in conflict have long hindered analysis of the Afghan refugee crises. Scholars and policymakers have rarely examined the role of the refugees in the war and have completely neglected any systematic comparison between the crises in Pakistan and Iran. Scholars of Afghanistan or of military history have ignored the refugee issue, viewing it as purely humanitarian. Olivier Roy wrote in his seminal study of the Afghan resistance that "refugees who have fled to Pakistan or Iran fall outside the scope of this study; a refugee ceases to be a member of a resistance movement."[1] Clearly, in practice, this was simply not true in the case of the Afghan refugees. The humanitarian literature also treats the military aspects of the refugee crisis as irrelevant. Thus, studies of the war and of the refugees exclude analysis of the vital role of the refugees in internationalizing the conflict.

BACKGROUND OF THE CRISES—CIVIL AND INTERNATIONAL WAR

The Cold War conflict in Afghanistan began with the 1973 coup that ousted King Zahir Shah, who had ruled for forty years. Muhammad Daoud, a secular nationalist from the dominant Pushtun ethnic group, replaced the king. The coup initiated a period of political instability in which communist, nationalist, and Islamist forces battled for supremacy. Perceiving a threat from Daoud's regime, Islamist resistance groups began to establish themselves in Peshawar, Pakistan, during the

1970s. Although Afghan communists helped Daoud to power, he drew away from the USSR over the five years of his rule.

As Daoud's regime weakened, the Afghan communist factions saw an opportunity to grab power. The communists, led by Nur Muhammad Taraki, in April 1978 staged a coup, later called the Saur Revolution. The coup leaders deposed and killed Daoud and renamed the country the Democratic Republic of Afghanistan. At the time of the coup, neither of the two communist factions (Khalq and Parcham) had more than about five thousand supporters.[2] The unpopular new government planned a complete social, economic, and political transformation, which failed utterly and nearly brought down the new regime. The new measures aimed to change the land tenure system, provide literacy training to women, and reform the bride price system. These reforms outraged most Afghans, who preferred to cling to their traditions. Even among the supposed beneficiaries of the reforms, the communists never established a base of popular support. Violent opposition to the communist government quickly became widespread. Uprisings began in the northeast, where the Islamic fundamentalist parties were strongest, and moved to the west. By the end of 1979, three-fourths of the country was in rebellion.[3]

In late 1979 the government again changed hands when Prime Minister Hafizullah Amin ousted President Taraki and had him killed. Amin's government was no more stable or successful than its predecessor. Amin's weakness alarmed the Soviets, who feared that the collapse of his government would allow American and Chinese influences to succeed in the region. The Soviet Union also worried that the fall of a communist government on its border would erode the USSR's credibility. As the communists teetered on the edge of collapse in December 1979, Soviet troops entered the country, killed President Amin, and installed Babrak Karmal as the new leader.

The conflict in Afghanistan pitted the Soviet Union and the new Afghan government against an array of resistance parties, grouped together as the "Mujahideen."[4] At the apex of their involvement in 1986 and 1987, the Soviets had around 150,000 troops in Afghanistan. The Afghan government troops were little help to the Soviets, as a majority of them deserted or defected to the rebels. The Mujahideen were able to field between 150,000 and 200,000 fighters throughout the conflict.[5] However, neither side was able to achieve a decisive victory. Until 1986, the Soviets controlled the air and about 20 percent of the land, most of it urban areas. The Mujahideen controlled 80 percent of the land, most of it rural. For the Afghan people, the war led to 1.25 million deaths and nearly 6 million refugees out of a prewar population of 16 million.

The Soviets employed brutal, and ultimately unsuccessful, measures to eradicate the Mujahideen resistance. These methods included destroying entire Afghan villages with extensive bombing campaigns and imprisoning or executing anyone suspected of supporting the Mujahideen. The Afghan army also forcibly conscripted men to fight against the resistance. These conscripts obviously lacked loyalty to the government and would trade their weapons to the rebels in exchange for food or drugs. The Soviet invasion united its opponents in the causes of national liberation and protection of Islam.

In 1986, the conflict began to favor the Mujahideen. The United States increased its military aid, including surface-to-surface 120mm rockets, radio equipment, and, most importantly, Stinger anti-aircraft missiles. The Stingers enabled the Mujahideen to defend themselves against the Soviet helicopter gunships and bombers.[6] President Karmal resigned in May 1986 and was replaced by Najibullah, a Soviet loyalist and former head of the secret police. Without a prospect for victory and facing domestic discontent, the Soviets began to contemplate withdrawal from Afghanistan. The Geneva agreements negotiated in March 1988 led to a complete Soviet withdrawal in February 1989.

The Soviet withdrawal did not bring peace or massive refugee repatriation, however. The Najibullah government remained in power until 1992, when it was overthrown by a coalition of Mujahideen and army generals. Without the Soviet enemy, the Mujahideen parties were unable to maintain even a minimal level of cooperation. Civil war among the factions raged until 1996, when the fundamentalist Taliban gained control of most of the country and established a strict Islamist state—according to its own interpretation of Islam. The Taliban regime provided safe haven for the Al Qaeda terrorist organization, which also recruited veterans of the anti-Soviet war. In 2001 the U.S. war on terrorism in Afghanistan dislodged the Taliban and installed a transitional government. The new regime, headed by Hamid Karzai, encouraged many refugees to return. Despite the changes, however, as of January 2003 some four million Afghan refugees remained in neighboring states.[7]

ORIGIN OF THE REFUGEE CRISES—COMMUNIST PERSECUTION

> *"In general, all the Afghan refugees regard communism*
> *as inherently incompatible with Islam."*
>
> —Kerry M. Connor, in *Afghan Resistance* (1987)

Unlike other militarized refugee groups such as the Rwandan Hutu and renegade Bosnian Muslims, the Afghan refugees began as a persecuted group, not a state in exile. Over a period of months, the refugee population in Pakistan strengthened its political and military organization to the extent that it transformed into a state in exile. The two million refugees in Iran, however, never coalesced into a state in exile, despite the hopes of resistance party leaders. The changes that occurred among the refugees in Pakistan demonstrate how time and external support contribute to the formation of a state in exile.

The refugees fled Afghanistan due to their anti-communism, their resentment of foreign rule, the widespread cruelty practiced by the regime, and their adherence to Islam.[8] The Soviets and their Afghan allies committed numerous massacres in villages as a warning against supporting the rebels.[9] The demonstration effect of these massacres caused thousands to flee. The Soviet forces also conducted massive aerial bombing campaigns.[10] One refugee explained that his family left Afghanistan after Russian bombs killed five hundred villagers.[11] Analyst Lawrence Ziring concurred: "Given the severity of the fighting, the reluctance to take prisoners, the destruction of innocents through indiscriminate bombing and shelling, the families of the Afghan rebels, the Mujahiddin, were put to flight."[12] Islam provided an additional reason to flee the country. The Qur'an praises those "who leave their homes in the cause of Allah, after suffering oppression." Based on Mohammed's flight from Mecca to Medina in 622 A.D., the Islamic concept of *hijrah* encourages Muslims to leave territory that has been occupied by infidels.[13]

The refugees had strong political leanings against the communist regime. The war that followed the Soviet invasion "became a war in which the absolute majority of the Afghan people began to participate in one way or another."[14] The communist-oriented People's Democratic Party of Afghanistan (PDPA) had a few hundred adherents in 1978 and was otherwise unrepresentative of the population—for example, members were atheists. Roy found widespread willingness among the population to help the resistance: "Throughout the country there is no shortage of willing guides, people who will lend out their horses, provide shelter, education and finance, without any coercion."[15] This indicates that ordinary Afghans were not simply caught in the crossfire, like situational refugees, but had political goals that included the withdrawal of the Soviets. Once in Pakistan, shared anti-communism and adherence to Islam helped the resistance parties consolidate their power among the refugees. In Iran, however, the resistance leaders were unable to capitalize on these shared experiences.

A survey of refugees in Peshawar, Pakistan, suggests a persecuted refugee group with strong political opinions about the conflict. Nearly a quarter of the 771 family heads interviewed left to avoid military conscription into the communist army. Another 12 percent cited anti-communism as the impetus for flight, and 18 percent left to avoid prison, harassment, or arrest. Nearly 25 percent cited Soviet bombing that threatened their lives or livelihood as a cause of flight, and 15 percent of the respondents admitted being active in the resistance at the time they left Afghanistan.[16]

Despite their strong political opinions and goals, the arriving refugees did not constitute a state-in-exile group. The resistance parties were weakly organized at the outset and lacked military capability. As the refugee numbers grew and international assistance increased, resistance parties amassed supporters and resources.

The two million refugees in Iran did not form a state in exile and received much less attention than the refugees in Pakistan. Iran shunned overtures from the international community, refusing offers of international aid. Therefore, aid agencies and external governments knew very little about the situation of the refugees in the early years of the crisis (1979 to 1983). There were no cross-border raids or covert weapons shipments to catch the attention of the international media. Both refugee groups fled Afghanistan for similar reasons—to escape persecution—but once in exile the groups developed very differently.

THE SUPERPOWER EFFECT: AFGHAN REFUGEES IN PAKISTAN, 1979 TO 1989

Building a State in Exile

"The atheist forces invaded our country, destroyed our mosques, killed our children and started teaching communism in the schools. . . . For the sake of our religion we migrated. We now swear that we will fight until we eliminate the very germ of communism from our country."

—Resistance leader to refugees, quoted in "Whose Side Is Time on This Time?" *The New York Times* (October 3, 1982)

At the time of the Soviet invasion in December 1979, around 300,000 Afghan refugees lived in Pakistan. A year later, Pakistan reported 1.5 million Afghan refugees; by 1981, the figure had reached nearly two million. The refugees fled to the Northwest Frontier Province (NWFP) and Baluchistan, poor regions bordering Afghanistan. The mostly Pushtun refugees shared ethnic ties with local Pakistanis.[17] The early arrivals to Pakistan lived in tent cities on the border, called "refugee tented villages" (RTVs). Over time, these developed into sturdier mud brick structures. As of 1987, there were 312 refugee tented villages (although most refugees no longer lived in tents) in Pakistan, the vast majority in the Northwest Frontier Province (see map 3.1). At its peak in the mid- to late 1980s, the refugee population in Pakistan numbered about three million.[18]

The development of a state in exile out of the weak, disorganized resistance parties emerged over time and with significant external support. Roy confirms that when the Soviets invaded, "the Mujaheddin commanders, who were to gain such prominence in the future, were still

Map 3.1   Afghan refugee flows to Pakistan and Iran, 1979 to 1990. UNHCR, *State of the World's Refugees* (Oxford: Oxford University Press, 2001), 117. Modified by the author.

confined to remote mountain regions."[19] The refugee crisis provided a fertile ground for the Mujahideen parties to expand their influence in the relative security of Pakistan. When the refugees entered from 1979 to 1982, many had no previous contact with the political parties. As the refugees registered for assistance, party activists enlisted them as members. The parties stressed the idea of *jihad* (holy war), which "brought to the forefront feelings of identity of purpose and unity amongst members of the resistance."[20]

The refugee crisis offered the necessary opportunity to create a viable resistance movement in a relatively secure environment. As scholar Anthony Hyman reported, "One of the main advantages for Afghan opposition parties of a center in exile—not Peshawar alone but in Quetta, in Delhi, and in Iranian towns like Tehran, Meshed, Qum— is freedom to organize, instead of persecution (or worse) in Afghanistan."[21] In 1978 and 1979 political parties started establishing headquarters in Peshawar. By 1980, over twenty parties were active in Peshawar and Quetta.[22] Pakistan recognized only six of these (seven by 1981). Throughout 1979 the parties had a low level of external support and thus few resources to provide to the guerrillas. This quickly changed after the Soviet invasion in December 1979. The infusion of external support—political, military, and humanitarian—enabled the transformation of a persecuted refugee group into a state in exile.

The coalescing event of communist persecution made recruitment much easier for the Mujahideen parties. The resistance leaders openly enlisted members and sought popular support in the camps based on the unifying factors of Islam and anti-communism. Support for the Mujahideen struggle was reflected in many aspects of camp life. Refugee education included chants of anti-Russian slogans and weapons training for children as young as nine.[23] Over the first months of the crisis, the rebels developed more polished methods of raising political awareness among the refugees. Their control over millions of refugees provided a legitimacy to the Mujahideen parties, which might otherwise have been viewed as peripheral to the conflict inside Afghanistan.

The formation of the state in exile—that is, the consolidation of the resistance parties and their control of resources—discouraged return to Afghanistan. That attitude separated the Afghan refugees from persecuted or situational refugee groups, which have a much lower threshold for return. The Afghan refugee delegation to a 1987 conference on their plight "was adamant that the vast majority of refugees would return willingly to their homeland—but on their own terms, not on conditions imposed by others."[24] At the same conference, a member of the Cultural Council of Afghanistan Resistance outlined the conditions for refugee return. The conditions included a complete Soviet withdrawal and the formation of a non-communist government in Kabul. The resistance representative insisted that virtually all the refugees would refuse to return before the Soviets withdrew.[25] Confirming the political motivation of the refugees, one commentator explained: "By and large market mechanism and monetary incentives are not the dominant factors determining the Afghan code of behavior. . . . The decision to return or to continue to live in the refugee villages are collectively deliberated and factors such as security, the availability of food and the prevalent political situation are important determinants in decision making."[26] For the Afghan refugees, a cessation of hostilities or amnesty program would not be enough to induce return. The refugees demanded a complete victory over the communist government.

Pakistan recognized seven of the resistance parties and funneled resources to those deemed most useful to Pakistan's aims. The Islamic fundamentalist parties won more support than the traditionalist or westernized groups. The fundamentalist *Hizb-i-Islami* party, led by Gulbuddin Hekmatyar, received the most military assistance from Pakistan. Hekmatyar had a strong following among the refugees and was infamous for his attacks against competing resistance groups. Another powerful fundamentalist party was *Jamiat-i-Islami,* led by Burhanuddin Rabbani. According to scholar M. Nazif Shahrani, the resistance parties "played important roles in the RTV councils and administration of community affairs."[27]

Like everything else in Afghan politics, the resistance movement had deep cleavages along ethnic, religious, and clan lines.[28] The primary split was between traditionalists and Islamic fundamentalists. There were also rifts between the parties in exile and the guerrillas based within Afghanistan. The Peshawar parties tried to form an alliance but it immediately crumbled and was formally dissolved in 1981. One analysis of the conflict noted, "many of the political parties seem to be expending most of their energy bickering and fighting each other and are riven with corruption and nepotism."[29] In May 1985, the seven main rebel groups in Peshawar formed an alliance, the Islamic Unity of Afghan Mujahideen, at the urging of Pakistan and other donors, especially the Saudis. This unity was extremely tenuous and did not merge the groups financially or militarily. The state in exile never achieved the cohesiveness of a strongly centralized state, yet the Soviets were unable to capitalize on the divisions within the resistance.

Waging War from the Refugee Camps

"[The refugee villages] are part supply bases and clearing stations for the Mujahedeen guerrilla fighters, part forward registration point for the U.N. High Commissioner."

—George Reid, *Red Cross, Red Crescent* (Jan 1987)

"As a safe haven and source of at least minimal food, housing, and medical care for fighters' families and survivors, camps . . . are a key—if indirect— underpinning for the Afghan resistance."

—Carol Honsa, "Inside a Pakistani Camp for Afghan Refugees," *The Christian Science Monitor* (December 9, 1981)

The refugee influx into Pakistan led to the spread of civil war across the Afghan border. The cross-border attacks perpetrated by the refugees led to Afghan government reprisals, which violated Pakistan's sovereignty and killed its citizens. Despite the intense violence, the conflict did not escalate to international war between Pakistan and the Soviet Union. Pakistan limited the spread of conflict to protect its own security interests and maintain a firm grip on the Afghan rebel parties.

The refugee crisis enabled the development of a state in exile and expanded the conflict across the border as refugees and fighters mixed freely. In 1982, journalist Edward Girardet reported, "Similar to dozens of other camps and villages along Pakistan's 1,400–mile border with Afghanistan, Terimangal [camp] serves as both temporary haven for refugees fleeing the war—and launching point for Afghan resistance supply convoys."[30] Compared to the dangerous situation in Afghanistan, the refugee camps provided a safe haven for fighters and civilians. An experienced NGO official noted, "By-and-large, the vast majority of Afghans in Pakistan face a security environment roughly on par with that of the indigenous population and in many ways vastly improved over the situation in Afghanistan."[31]

The resistance parties presented a serious security threat to the Afghan regime. By 1987, seven military training camps were operating in Pakistan, training up to 20,000 Mujahideen per year.[32] Mujahideen activities included commando raids into Afghanistan to strike government targets and re-supply the local resistance fighters. Nearly all refugee men spent time with one or another of the resistance parties fighting in Afghanistan. Mujahideen activities prevented the Soviets from controlling the countryside. The Mujahideen brought dozens of Soviet prisoners of war into Pakistan, which increased the risk of Soviet reprisals.[33]

The border between Afghanistan and Pakistan was ideal for guerrilla warfare. The border is 1400 miles long and includes over 300 mountain passes. Called the Durand Line, it was drawn by the British in 1893. The British and succeeding rulers found it virtually impossible to police. In addition, the Pushtun ethnic group straddles the border and has traditionally ignored its existence.

Over the course of the war, the Soviet-backed Afghan regime conducted hundreds of cross-border attacks and violations of Pakistani airspace. Numerous sources report helicopter gunship attacks on UNHCR-recognized refugee camps.[34] For example, in November 1980, the U.S. mission to the United Nations complained about "the serious escalation of provocative actions from the Afghanistan side along the Pakistan-Afghanistan border." The U.S. report detailed three helicopter gunship attacks in two months, one of which occurred "well inside the Pakistan territory."[35] In 1984, air attacks against frontier towns and refugee camps in Pakistan killed more than one hundred people. There were 62 reported violations of Pakistan territory by Afghan/Soviet soldiers and 459 airspace violations.[36] In 1986, a U.S. National Security Council secret memo noted, "The Soviets are increasing the frequency of their cross-border strikes into Pakistan, and occasionally Iran, while inciting a terror campaign in Pakistan."[37] Despite the frequent cross-border attacks, the conflict did not escalate to international war between Pakistan and the Soviet Union, mainly due to Pakistan's restraints on the rebels' activities.

Pakistan: A Complicit Receiving State

A complex web of humanitarian, political, and military goals influenced Pakistan's response to the Afghan refugees.[38] Pakistan generously allowed millions of refugees into the country and, with international assistance, provided adequate care for them. In addition to humanitarian aid, the government of Pakistan offered a safe haven and military assistance to the anti-communist resistance groups. Ties of religion, ethnicity, and culture encouraged Pakistan's sympathetic response toward the refugees. One Pakistani administrator explained, "We are all Pathans. . . . Our customs, religion, and traditions are the same."[39] The geopolitical realities of the situation tempered those sympathetic ties, however. Throughout the crisis, Pakistan walked a fine line between aiding the Islamic rebels and preventing a large-scale Soviet counterattack. The refugees threatened Pakistan's domestic stability, even as they strengthened its influence abroad.

Pakistan allowed the Mujahideen parties control over the refugees as long as the resistance activities did not threaten Pakistani interests. As refugees entered the country, they registered in a UNHCR-run refugee tented village to receive assistance. In reality, this meant registering as a supporter of one of the seven dominant resistance parties, since they controlled the refugee villages. Pakistan did not interfere in internal Afghan refugee affairs and ignored the resistance parties' heavy-handed tactics. As one Pakistani official warned, however, "if [refugees] start introducing bloodshed into the bazaar, then let me assure you, we will crack down hard."[40]

Even had it wanted to, Pakistan did not have the capability to control the Afghan border, with its more than three hundred mountain passes. As President Zia explained to the Soviets, sealing the border was "physically impossible" for the Pakistan government. Pakistan also would not have been able to fend off a full-scale Soviet assault, which is why Zia made sure that rebel activity did not provoke the Soviets to invade Pakistan.[41]

Regional politics greatly influenced Pakistan's actions. Zia's ultimate goal was to establish a "Muslim belt south of the Soviet Union under Pakistani influence."[42] By bolstering the Mujahideen, Pakistan wanted to increase its influence vis-à-vis India, more so than against Moscow. Pakistan focused support on the Sunni resistance parties rather the Shi'a parties because a Shi'a-dominated Afghanistan would lean toward Shi'a Iran. Helping a Muslim nation in distress also bolstered Zia's prestige in the Muslim world.

Despite its goals for creating a friendly (and pliable) Afghanistan, Pakistan limited the military activities of the Mujahideen resistance parties. Pakistan maintained an uneasy balance between supporting the resistance and avoiding significant Soviet retaliation. Pakistan feared direct confrontation with the Soviets and also the Soviets' ability to support dissidents and provoke ethnic quarrels within Pakistan. A Rand Corporation study explained that the Soviet strategy was to "intimidate Pakistan into curtailing support for the resistance and eventually denying it the sanctuaries on Pakistani territory that are vital for its operations."[43]

Soviet threats succeeded to the extent that Pakistan limited Mujahideen activity. Zia required arms flows to be covert and restricted the type and amount of weapons so as not to provoke the USSR. Pakistan's Inter-Services Intelligence Directorate (ISI) completely controlled the distribution of the arms. Pakistan also controlled the political activity of the resistance parties (e.g. press conferences and public meetings). Soviet pressure, in the form of terrorist bombings in urban centers, caused Pakistan to order the resistance parties to move their headquarters out of Peshawar in 1984.[44]

Domestically, the influx of millions of Afghan Pushtun refugees threatened to destabilize ethnic politics in Pakistan. Even before the refugee crisis, tension existed between the Pushtun (often called "Pathans" in Pakistan) in the western provinces and the central government, including talk of a separate Pushtunistan. The government needed to prevent the formation of a pan-Pushtun alliance that would threaten its sovereignty. Roy explained, "The Pakistanis were obsessed with the fear that the resistance might develop in the same way as the Palestinian groups had done, enjoying the support of millions of refugees."[45] Pushtun refugees also exacerbated ethnic tensions between local Pushtun and Baluchis. Despite this, the government dared not alienate its Pushtun citizens by disregarding the plight of the Afghan Pushtun refugees. To prevent the emergence of a strong nationalistic Pushtun resistance movement, the Pakistan government found it useful to keep the resistance parties squabbling and divided.

In addition to the Pushtun issue, the refugee crisis threatened Zia's regime by stoking discontent among Pakistanis. Local residents in the refugee-populated areas expressed resentment toward the services provided to the refugees. Locals viewed the refugees as an economic burden and as competition in commerce and employment. Because Afghans received UNHCR assistance, they could work for lower wages than local Pakistanis. Refugees were active in the transportation industry and the arms trade, and also smuggled goods, including drugs. Further, the refugees brought three million livestock with them into Pakistan. Locals observed not only the refugees' material benefits but also their ability to express themselves through political parties. The example set by the Mujahideen parties led to Pakistani protests against Zia's dictatorship and demands for the right to form political parties. After that, Zia pressured the refugee parties to keep a lower profile. Despite these tensions, however, there were remarkably few violent incidents between refugees and locals.[46]

Superpower Politics

"Assistance to the refugees serves important U.S. interests in the region—including stability in Pakistan, assurance of continuity for [Pakistan's] role in giving haven to the refugees, and the viability of the resistance in Afghanistan."

—U.S. Department of State, "Afghan Refugee Situation—An Overview" (1982)

For the United States, the Soviet offensive in Afghanistan threatened both the policy of containment of communism and the free flow of oil to the West. American leaders feared that the invasion signaled the global expansionist aims of the USSR.[47] President Jimmy Carter's initial response included an Olympic boycott, suspension of SALT II arms control talks and trade embargoes. The Carter administration cancelled seventeen million tons' worth of grain sales and reduced Soviet fishing quotas. The Reagan administration took a more activist stance regarding Afghanistan. Unlike his predecessor, President Ronald Reagan wanted to "roll back" Soviet influence, not merely contain it. Visiting India, Jeanne Kirkpatrick, American ambassador to the United Nations, explained the United States position: "What India calls rearming of Pakistan in a way that raised tensions, we call helping Pakistan as it confronts the problem of refugees and the Soviet presence on its border."[48] The United States wanted to ensure that Pakistan was strong enough, economically and militarily, to withstand Soviet pressure.

American support for the Mujahideen increased dramatically in 1984. Up until 1984 the United States had given over $350 million for Afghan refugee relief, much of it via UNHCR and the World Food Programme (WFP).[49] In the late 1980s, the United States provided around $150 million per year in humanitarian aid.[50] In 1985, the Reagan administration added $470 million in military aid for the fiscal year 1986 and $630 million for 1987.[51] The United States channeled its military assistance through Pakistan's Inter-Services Intelligence Directorate (ISI), which distributed it to the resistance parties as it saw fit. In practice, this meant that the fundamentalist parties received the bulk of the aid, not pro-Western parties. The United States did not view the refugee militarization as a problem. One State Department official cabled back in an overview of refugee relief that "the refugee situation in Pakistan is being relatively well handled."[52]

Until 1985, the United States took great pains to hide its direct involvement in Afghanistan; this was the policy of "plausible deniability." Pakistan and the United States wanted to avoid triggering a massive Soviet retaliation against Pakistan. Pakistan also did not want to lend credence to Soviet propaganda that the Afghan resistance parties were American stooges. As part of plausible deniability, the weapons provided to the Mujahideen were Soviet-made or Soviet-designed (produced in Egypt, China and other countries). Despite the concealment, American involvement was something of an open secret. In Washington, observers labeled the program as "covert overt" by the mid to late 1980s.[53] After the provision of American-made Stinger missiles in 1986, plausible deniability was not an option.

Splits emerged among U.S. policymakers about the goals and methods of American policy toward Afghanistan. One analyst noted in 1987 that "the institutional ideological differences among various departments of the government and the Congress are creating policy problems that will be difficult to undo in the long run."[54] One faction, anti-communist and anti–arms control, pushed for more aid to the resistance. This was characterized as the "Bleeder" view, because the premise was that it would bleed the Soviets dry. The "Bleeders" were motivated in part by American failure in Vietnam and the desire to inflict such an experience on the Soviets.[55] Other factions wanted to limit the assistance to further plausible deniability and insulate Pakistan from attack. In the end, the "Bleeder" view dominated U.S. policy decisions.

Humanitarian Infrastructure of the State in Exile

"WFP takes the lead from donor governments, and if the donors and the [government of Pakistan] aren't worried about the workings of the food distribution mechanism, including possible diversion, the WPF will not modify its own program."

—WFP official to Pakistani official, quoted in
"Visit of WFP Emergency Unit Director to Pakistan,"
United States Embassy, Pakistan, (September 2, 1983)

"Perhaps more clearly than in other refugee situations, the humanitarian and political dimensions of the Afghan refugee situation were mutually reinforcing."

—Aristide Zolberg et al., *Escape from Violence* (1992)

The humanitarian organizations in Pakistan provided the infrastructure of the Mujahideen state in exile. This suited the purposes of the Pakistan government, the Mujahideen parties, and the anti-communist external donors. International assistance allowed the resistance parties to focus their resources on waging war in Afghanistan, rather than on providing goods and services for the refugee population. The assistance clearly benefited the anti-communist rebels and their supporters by sustaining fighters and their dependents, contributing to the war economy, and boosting the legitimacy of the militant leaders.

From the beginning of the crisis, international humanitarian organizations eagerly provided assistance to the refugees. In 1983, seventeen registered private voluntary organizations worked with the refugees, spending millions of dollars on food, health care, shelter, and other necessities. The largest and most active organizations included the Salvation

Army, Catholic Relief Services, Church World Services, Cooperation for American Relief Everywhere (CARE), and Save the Children. By the late 1980s, the number of international NGOs had jumped to over sixty. During those later years of the crisis, the total cost of humanitarian assistance had reached $400 million per year. The United States paid one third of this, with Pakistan and UN agencies sharing responsibility for the rest. In 1982, for example, UNHCR spent $77 million in Pakistan, supplying tents, health care, clothes, water, fuel, and supplementary food such as tea and sugar.[56]

Humanitarian aid supported the resistance movement by providing food, shelter, and medical care directly to fighters. Neither the aid agencies nor the Pakistani authorities balked at registering Mujahideen fighters as refugees. Mujahideen recruits did not lose their right to food rations upon their return to the camps from a stint in battle. One Western advocate for the refugees asserted that it was impossible to distinguish between a man's roles as refugee in Pakistan and as rebel in Afghanistan because nearly all refugee men periodically crossed the border to fight in the *jihad*. Thus, she argued, "to strike such persons off the registration lists [for humanitarian aid] would, in my opinion, be unjust."[57]

The camps provided a safe haven for the families of the fighters. As one man explained, "After I settle my family in Pakistan, I will go back to Afghanistan for jihad (holy war) against the Russian Army."[58] A common pattern was for male family members to rotate every few months between fighting and camp life.[59]

It was common knowledge that widespread corruption in humanitarian aid distribution benefited the war economy. Resistance parties and local Pakistani officials diverted millions of dollars of relief aid before it even reached the refugees.[60] A 1983 UNHCR evaluation admitted, "Large profit margins for refugee leaders and those involved in distribution at the village level have become well established and widely recognized. . . . Although much is known about the extent of diversion, no one has yet been successful in doing much about it."[61] Five years later, in 1987, UNHCR was still lamenting the "pervasive corruption" and had made no headway in reducing it.[62]

The resistance parties strengthened their legitimacy and power by controlling the flow of donated goods. Pakistan allowed the Mujahideen parties to distribute aid in many camps. This contributed to the misappropriation of aid and the exaggeration of population numbers. When the party leaders distributed aid to new arrivals, they also registered them with the party and recruited them as fighters for the resistance.

At the time, observers generally considered the Afghan refugee program a model operation and made no mention of the extensive militarization of the population. Aid organizations expressed little concern about the politicization and militarization of the crisis, which clearly contravened international law regarding the civilian and neutral character of refugee camps. Journalist Edward Girardet rhapsodized, "As one of the largest relief operations since the end of World War II, the Afghan refugee situation in Pakistan appears to be among the best managed. . . . Considering its size, there have been surprisingly few major problems."[63] A World Food Programme official noted that "there have been only minimal law and order problems among the refugees."[64] These observers did not classify the spread of the Afghan conflict as a problem for the relief operation.

NGOs assisting the refugees depended on Pakistan, the United States, and UNHCR for funding contracts and access to the refugee population, thus, as an NGO official admitted, "many of the aid agencies operated with little or no pretense of neutrality."[65] The U.S. government funded many NGOs with the explicit aim of influencing the Afghan conflict. The financial relationship brought with it a closer alignment between U.S. policy and NGO activities. That Pakistan was not a signatory to the 1950 Refugee Convention further reduced UNHCR's leverage.[66]

The humanitarian assistance that poured into Pakistan and basically bypassed the Afghans in Afghanistan is in some measure responsible for the size and duration of the refugee crisis. Logistically and politically it was more difficult to serve the needy within Afghanistan. One critic, Gowher Rizvi, scathingly suggested: "It would perhaps not be unfair to suggest that some of these organizations [NGOs] have developed an institutional stake in the continuing presence of the Afghans in Pakistan and may not relish the prospect of Afghans leaving Pakistan. . . . The continuation of NGO 'services' and 'facilities' inside Pakistan, albeit quite unintentionally, has the effect of rewarding those who opt to stay in Pakistan and, by implication, deprive such opportunities to those who return home."[67] The incentives of the refugee assistance program encouraged large, long-term refugee flows that sustained the NGOs as well as the refugees.

Socioeconomic Explanations

"The most essential needs of most of the refugees have been satisfied, and starvation, epidemics, and large-scale public disorder have been avoided."

—U.S. Department of State, "Afghan Refugee Situation— An Overview" (1982)

"The money is not so important. . . . What we need is antiaircraft guns."

—Refugee, Jamrud camp, quoted in "Refugees in Pakistan Clamor for
Arms," *New York Times* (July 20, 1980)

Socioeconomic explanations do not account for the strong popular support for the Mujahideen among the refugees. The socioeconomic explanations for the militarization of refugee populations hold that large camps and camps near the border will lead to political violence. Another explanation is that poor living conditions will predispose the refugees toward military activity. Refugees (especially young men) will be easily recruited by promises of food and other material incentives. Considering the high level of military activity in the Pakistan camps, the socioeconomic explanations would predict large border camps with an excess of young men and poor living conditions. However, the evidence from Pakistan contradicts most of the socioeconomic explanations. The camps were not large by UNHCR standards; there were relatively few young men, and the living conditions compared favorably with other refugee situations and the conditions in Afghanistan. Political incentives better explain the activities of the resistance.

Most of the refugee camps were near the Pakistan/Afghanistan border, but not necessarily within walking distance. The locations varied from a few miles to well over 60 miles from the Afghan border. One expert stated that the levels of military activity did not correlate with the distance of the camp from the border since virtually all the camps were within striking distance of Soviet planes.[68] A counterargument is that the camp location favored the Mujahideen, which relied on ground transport to cross the border. Considering the pattern of fighting, in which rebels alternated between living in refugee camps and infiltrating Afghanistan, "the effect therefore of the position of the camps   and the activities which this facilitated was to effectively extend the zone of the war."[69]

There was clearly a strategic element to the camp location in the border provinces. Pakistan did not want to move the camps because there was not enough public land available. The refugees also did not want to move further away from the border. One elderly refugee, wounded in battle and waiting for new weapons, explained, "We want to live here, as close as possible to our country."[70] In addition, refugees and rebels often crossed the border to tend their farms back in Afghanistan. For Pakistan to move the camps would have signaled an unwillingness to aid the Mujahideen in their struggle. Thus, the location of the camps may have had a significant impact on the spread of violence, but the location was also intertwined in the political context of the crisis.

[61]

The size of the refugee tented villages varied widely, despite Pakistan's directive that they should not exceed 5,000 persons. The RTVs ranged in size from 5,000 to over 120,000 people.[71] Most of the settlements held between 30,000 and 50,000 refugees.[72] Relative to the massive camps deplored by UNHCR (such as those in Goma, Zaire, that housed hundreds of thousands), the size of the RTVs should not have presented a problem. The camps did not approximate overcrowded urban areas, although they were more cramped than traditional Afghan living conditions. In general, the size of the refugee settlements seems to have played no role in the militarization and cross-border attacks.

Contrary to the expectations of the "gender balance" explanation, the number of men in the camps bore no relation to the level of militarization. Compared to a non-uprooted population, the camps had fewer young men than expected. The refugee population consisted of 48 percent children, 28 percent women, and 24 percent men.[73] Most of the able-bodied men did not stay in the refugee camps but returned to Afghanistan to fight or protect their property. Often men rotated their presence in the camps—for example, one brother stayed in Pakistan with the family while the other brother was fighting in Afghanistan. In the mid-1980s, refugees reported that nearly every family had at least one man fighting the Soviets.[74] Despite the dearth of men in the camps, the refugee population in Pakistan was highly militarized and provided extensive support to the Mujahideen state in exile. The "men in camps" explanation fails to account for situations in which men rely on the camps, but do not necessarily live in them.

Poor living conditions in camps also cannot explain why so many men joined the resistance. In fact, the living conditions for refugees were better than their past situation in Afghanistan and were comparable to the local residents in Pakistan. Pakistani analyst Hasan-Askari Razvi noted, "A large number amongst the poorest refugees are better-off in Pakistan as compared with their position in Afghanistan."[75] A UNHCR evaluation concurred: "Most of the refugees have obtained a relatively high standard of living compared to their former standard and to that of similar local groups."[76] Refugees usually built mud/brick huts for their families after their initial stay in UNHCR-provided tents.[77] The settlement pattern in the villages was open and similar to Pakistani villages.[78] Thus it does not seem likely that refugees supported the rebels out of desperation to improve their living conditions.

Rates of infant mortality and malnutrition among the refugees were better than in Afghanistan both before and during the war: "The physical health of women and children in the refugee camps in Pakistan is not only better than it was in Afghanistan, but also better than the surrounding Pakistani villages."[79] A 1987 UNHCR evaluation reported that "malnutrition is rare and it is believed most [Afghan refugees] are well-nourished."[80] The prescribed official food basket for the refugees included wheat, oil, sugar, tea, and dried milk. These often arrived erratically, and sugar, milk, and tea were especially hard to obtain. Nevertheless, donated food appeared for sale in local markets, apparently sold to generate revenue for the resistance movement.[81] One observer found that "the active Mujahideen, who, like most soldiers, spend only a fraction of their time actually fighting, have taken to planting crops themselves in abandoned areas."[82]

Unlike many refugee populations, Afghans enjoyed freedom of movement and employment in the receiving state.[83] Refugee entrepreneurs competed successfully with the locals in running transport businesses, especially in Peshawar. One survey in 1988 reported that two-thirds of male refugees had employment.[84] An American diplomat reported that the government of Pakistan "has put no legal restrictions on work by Afghans and has encouraged their employment on approved UNHCR projects as a way of keeping the refugees busy and out of trouble."[85]

Contrary to the material incentives explanation for violence, poor living conditions did not induce refugees to support political violence. Compared to life in Afghanistan, local Pakistani villages and to other refugee situations, conditions in the refugee villages were adequate (if not superior). An additional refutation of the material incentives explanation is that life as a Mujahideen fighter was difficult and offered little opportunity for material gain. Fighters did not join to enrich themselves from plunder or because the resistance could offer better conditions than the refugee camps.

One incentive that can blunt violence is a durable solution to the refugee crisis, such as resettlement abroad. Most Afghan refugees in Pakistan did not have the option of exchanging their refugee status for a more durable solution such as resettlement, peaceful return, or local integration. Neither Pakistan nor the resistance movement favored such durable solutions. The rebels clearly understood that long-term solutions would dissipate the influence of the Mujahideen. A representative from the Cultural Council of the Afghanistan Resistance maintained: "As far as the Afghan refugees in Pakistan and Iran is [sic] concerned, it is important for them to remain as refugees: They are fighting for their independence and national survival. . . . They are there to fight to return home and resume their lives in their country in dignity and peace."[86]

Thus the maintenance of the population as refugees gave an advantage to the Mujahideen.

A Surprising Calm: Afghan Refugees in Iran, 1979 to 1989

A Nonviolent Persecuted Refugee Group

"The Afghan freedom fighters [in Iran] were not free to move and did not seem to be supported at all."

—Journalist Christina Demeyer, 1984, quoted in "Arms Shipments to the Afghan Resistance," in *Afghan Resistance* (1987)

"Overall, the Iranian factor has remained a side issue in the Afghan equation, with Pakistan's position as a 'frontline' state attracting far greater attention."

—Edward Girardet, *Afghanistan: The Soviet War* (1985)

The Afghan refugees in Iran never formed a state in exile. Like the refugees in Pakistan, they arrived as a persecuted refugee population, sharing the common experience of communist attacks. Would-be rebel leaders attempted to procure support from Iran and mobilize the population—to no avail. Some small-scale political activity—and even smaller-scale military activity—did occur, but the Afghan resistance never established a firm base in Iran. The lack of political violence resulted from Iran's policy of withholding military and political support from the refugees. Because of Iran's reluctance to support the Mujahideen and Iran's own turbulent revolutionary politics, the government excluded international actors from intervening in the refugee crisis. Unlike Pakistan, the rebel movement did not receive generous infusions of foreign military and humanitarian assistance.

Iran has a long history of accepting Afghan migrants, especially those that share ethnic and religious affinities with locals. For decades, cultural ties and better economic conditions acted as a magnet to draw Afghan labor to Iran. Before the Soviet invasion, there were already up to 600,000 Afghan workers in Iran, mostly in urban areas.[87] Following the Soviet invasion in 1979, hundreds of thousands of Afghan refugees poured into Iran. The post-1979 refugees were concentrated in border provinces (Sistan-Baluchestan and Khorasan) and urban centers. Nearly all the refugees spoke Iran's state language, Farsi (also called Dari in

[64]

Afghanistan), and some, mainly the Hazara, shared the Shi'a Islam practiced in Iran.[88]

The precise number of refugees in Iran was difficult to determine. The United States government reported "it [is] difficult if not impossible to get a firm figure on the number of Afghans. . . . The distinction between Afghan refugees and those who came earlier is increasingly blurred."[89] In 1983, the Iranian government estimated that there were 1.5 million refugees. By 1987, Iran increased its estimate to 2.4 million Afghans. A registration carried out by the government in 1990 estimated 2.2 million refugees. These estimates were likely inflated, but not dramatically so.[90]

Like the Afghans in Pakistan, the refugees in Iran fled persecution by the Soviets and their Afghan allies. Many refugees demonstrated their aspirations to fight the communist-backed Afghan regime but were thwarted from achieving these goals. Unlike a situational refugee group, the refugees did not desire only peace and stability to return. They required an end to their persecution and radical changes in the Afghan government. Despite their goals, the refugees lacked the political and military organization to threaten the Afghan regime. The refugees' political organization consisted of a fractured group of Shi'a resistance parties, which were unable to mount a military campaign.

The level of political violence was low, especially compared with the highly militarized camps in Pakistan. An unknown number of Mujahideen came to Iran to work for a few months and then returned to Afghanistan to fight, but they did not engage in military activity while in Iran.[91] Early in the conflict, rebel leader Gulbuddin Hekmatyar claimed that small rebel units based in Iran made "hit-and-run raids" on Afghanistan.[92] Some refugees donated part of their income to the opposition parties.[93] Afghan resistance groups wanted more support and some reportedly offered to fight against Iraq in exchange for Iranian support of the Afghan rebels.[94] Generally, the Iranian authorities rebuffed the refugees' attempts at political action. In one instance, Afghan refugees briefly occupied the Soviet Embassy in Tehran but were ejected by Iranian revolutionary guards.[95]

The Soviet Union did not engage in much cross-border military activity against Iran, but it did clearly express its willingness to counter any perceived threat. In one cross-border incident in March 1980, Soviet MiG planes violated Iranian airspace.[96] Later, in April 1982, the Soviets destroyed two Iranian border posts and killed armed Afghan refugees.[97] The Soviets also based a large number of troops at Shindand as a buffer zone between Afghanistan and Iran. These actions seemed designed to prevent the emergence of rebel activity, rather than to counter existing organizations.[98]

Iran: A Different Political Agenda

"[The Afghan rebel representative] was asking for arms assistance, and the Ayatollah spoke instead of humanitarian assistance."

—United States Embassy, Iran, "Limited Iranian Response to Afghan Rebel Appeal" (May 21, 1979)

"Any help to Afghan rebels is equal to damaging the Iranian Revolution and aiding U.S. imperialism."

—National Voice of Iran radio, quoted in FBIS Daily Report (March 4, 1980)

Unlike Pakistan, Iran did not view a pliable Afghan government as a vital national interest. As the refugee crisis occurred, Iran was at war with Iraq, embroiled in the hostage crisis with the United States, and reeling domestically from the Islamic revolution. As an Islamic nonaligned state, Iran carefully tried to balance its actions to avoid provoking the USSR, while also condemning Soviet interference in an Islamic country. Iran exhorted the Afghan people not to "depend on the solutions imposed by the West and East . . . [which] want to preserve their illegitimate interests in Afghanistan."[99] Iran agitated against superpower influence in the region, but did not commit itself to any further military actions.

Iranian government policy toward the refugees ensured that a state in exile could not coalesce. Iran restricted the political and military activity of the refugees and successfully controlled its border with Afghanistan. Roy explained: "The parties based at Peshawar were not allowed to transport weapons and ammunition into Afghanistan via Iran, a fact which posed insurmountable logistic problems for the Herat Jamiat [rebel party]. The refugees in Iran . . . were subject to much closer surveillance by the police than their brethren in Pakistan. No Iranian contingent went to fight in Afghanistan."[100] The Iranian Revolutionary Guards (*Pasdaran*) monitored the borders, confiscated arms from the guerrillas, and prevented entry of refugees. Geographically, the 388 mile Iran/Afghanistan border was easier to control than the much longer, and more mountainous, Pakistan/Afghanistan border.

In 1983 the Deputy Minister of the Interior, Abbas Akhundi, announced that Iran would support refugees' political activity only "if the refugees do not adhere to any ideology inspired from east or west."[101] Iran allowed resistance parties to open offices but provided no further assistance, with the exception of meager aid to certain pro-Khomeini Shi'a groups. Apparently Iran considered aiding the Sunni groups based in Peshawar between 1980 and early 1982. The U.S. Defense Intelligence Agency reported that "land mines, shoulder-fired antitank rockets, heavy machine guns, uniforms and boots were supplied to at least the Hizb-e-Islami."[102] These "negligible" contributions did not satisfy *Hizb-i-Islami*, especially when Iran refused to express public support for the rebels. The government maintained relations with the Soviet-backed Afghan government, meeting only covertly with rebel leaders.[103] Early in the crisis, Iran distanced itself from the Peshawar parties, considering them too dependent on the West.

After Iran cut its ties with *Hizb-i-Islami* in Peshawar, it restricted its support to Shi'a groups. These groups included *Harakat-Islami, Hazara Nasr,* and *Pasdaran,* a party controlled by the Iranian Revolutionary Guards.[104] Some Iranian Revolutionary Guards also volunteered as advisors to ethnic Hazara resistance groups.[105] Paradoxically, Iranian support of the Shi'a groups increased inter-group fighting among the resistance, rather than strengthening it against the Soviets.[106]

Iran's primary motive in restraining the resistance was to avoid active hostility with the Soviets. Scholar Anthony Hyman confirmed that for both economic and military reasons, "Iranian leaders realized that having good-neighbourly relations with their northern neighbor was a geographical necessity."[107] Iran lacked the capability to repulse any potential Soviet cross-border attacks. Iran's oilfields were vulnerable to Soviet attack across the Afghan border and the long Soviet border. Economically, Soviet transit routes boosted Iran's trade and the government hoped to use Soviet technical experts on industrial projects. The economic incentives were especially important, as Iran was suffering from an American and European trade embargo. The Iranian government also wanted the Soviets to reduce their arms sales to Iraq. A United States government analysis explained:

> Although the Afghans in Iran have experienced harsh treatment, the measures undertaken against them have been aimed more at maintaining a balance in Iran's official relations with Kabul and Moscow and not for the sole purpose of extinguishing the resistance's presence in Iran. While Iran has made strong efforts to sanitize and clear its border with Afghanistan, it has done so to avoid provoking Soviet retaliation for Iran's selective support of the resistance.[108]

Despite its sympathy for the Afghan resistance and its condemnation of the Soviet invasion, Iran could not afford to risk Soviet reprisals by arming the Mujahideen.

Iran also had domestic security reasons for limiting the refugees' military activity. Numerous separatist groups in Iran representing Baluchis, Kurds, Azerbaijanis, Azeris, and others pressed the central government for more autonomy. Considering the high concentration of refugees in Baluchi territory, Iran's central government feared the demonstration effects of a militant refugee group on Baluchi separatism.[109]

Local citizens met the refugees with a mixture of sympathy and resentment. Part of the sympathy stemmed from shared cultural, religious, and ethnic ties, especially for Shi'a refugees.[110] The Shi'a, a minority in Afghanistan, were a majority in Iran. Roy predicted that "the goal that Iran seems to be pursuing is to strengthen its control over the Shi'a minorities and to use them as pawns in its policy of regional expansion."[111] Control of the Shi'a Hazaras would give Iran more leverage in Afghan affairs or a future Afghan regime.

Despite historical and cultural ties, Roy reported that "Iranians felt traditional mistrust for the Afghans, an attitude which existed before Khomeini's time."[112] The refugees hurt the economy and the environment. Refugees brought their livestock with them and the fodder and grazing needs depleted local resources. The Afghans reintroduced diseases that had been eradicated in Iran, among them malaria and cholera, which cost the government over $150 million to combat. Poor Iranians resented the government's support for the Afghan refugees, especially since the war with Iraq had internally displaced two million Iranians. These resentments were behind the attacks and anti-Afghan demonstrations that occurred in Tehran in late 1983.[113] Since the end of the Cold War, Iran has repeatedly threatened to expel the refugees and curtailed their options regarding employment and free movement.[114]

Isolation from International Influences

International humanitarian organizations played a minimal role in the refugee crisis in Iran. The government excluded all organizations until 1983, when it permitted UNHCR to set up a modest program. In 1984, UNHCR spent $7.5 million in Iran, less than a tenth of what it spent in Pakistan. This rose to $14 million by 1987.[115] UNHCR's main responsibility in Iran was to procure relief items from abroad. The mandate evolved over time to include long-term development projects that benefited the refugees (income generation, health care, and schools). In

1987, the World Food Programme (WFP) opened an office in Iran. By the 1990s, an NGO mission reported "the Iranian Government's willingness to meet the basic needs of the Afghan refugee population over this long period, with the result that there is not a need for NGOs to play a major role in providing for the refugees within Iran."[116]

Iran provides an example of how a capable state can prevent external influences during a refugee crisis. Iran distrusted western aid agencies and took full responsibility for assisting the refugees for the first three years of the crisis. Iran's policy also excluded third-party states from supporting the Mujahideen or otherwise becoming involved in the crisis. Unlike many receiving states, including Pakistan, Iran did not use the refugee presence as a way to gain international funding or legitimacy.

Inconclusive Socioeconomic Explanations

"Much about the conditions of these refugees remains murky."
—U.S. Committee for Refugees, *World Refugee Survey: 1988 in Review*

It is unclear how much socioeconomic conditions influenced the low level of political violence among Afghan refugees in Iran. In this case, the political explanations and the socioeconomic explanation make similar predictions, with the exception of the gender balance theory. Socioeconomic conditions for refugees in Iran differed greatly from those in Pakistan. However, the political context also differed significantly between the two states. In the Rwandan crises, socioeconomic factors were nearly constant between Tanzania and Zaire, allowing a focus on the political factors. The high level of variation in the Afghan crises makes it difficult to untangle the interactions between socioeconomic and political factors in the case of refugees in Iran. The one certain finding is that the number of men in the population did not determine the level of violence.

In Iran, refugees did not live in camps, crowded on the border. When refugees arrived, they came through transit camps for registration and medical checks, but then moved to urban areas. In the late 1980s only 75,000 refugees lived in government-run camps. Most of the others were absorbed into the local economy and found employment as manual laborers. Because of the Iraq war, Iran experienced a shortage of workers and some refugees were able to open small businesses. However, once the Iraq war ended in the late 1980s, Iran's labor market tightened, causing the government to restrict the refugees to low-skill trades. By

1986, Iran did not permit refugees free movement but directed them to where there were labor shortages.

Even though the refugees did not live in crowded border camps as in Pakistan, they still remained relatively near the border and tended to cluster together within urban areas. Fifty percent of refugees lived in Khorasan and Sistan-Baluchestan provinces, which bordered Afghanistan. In the city of Mashad, capital of Khorasan province, Afghan refugees made up 31 percent of the population. Recognizing that demographic pattern, the Iranian government established Afghan refugee councils in urban areas with heavy Afghan populations as forums to discuss refugee issues. Despite the concentrated settlement patterns of Afghans, little organized political activity occurred.

In both Iran and Pakistan, refugees had adequate shelter, food, and medical care relative to other refugee populations and to conditions in Afghanistan. The available evidence supports Iran's claims that refugee conditions were satisfactory.[117] Afghans utilized the same health services as Iranians. For refugees in camps or other collectives, the Ministry of Health established a network of primary care centers, most staffed by refugees.[118] Refugee children attended Iranian primary schools. A Western assessment mission found that "the refugees are provided with basic health, education, water and electricity services which are generally of a reasonable standard, together with food coupons." Health care in Khorasan province was "of a reasonably high standard."[119] The adequate conditions in Iran did not seem to blunt the ambitions of the would-be rebels. They continuously expressed frustration at Iran's lack of political support.

Unlike most refugee groups, the gender and age balance of the refugees in Iran did not correlate with the non-displaced population. The majority of the refugees were working-age men. The Iranian government estimated that 11 percent of refugees were between 10 and 19 years of age and that 36 percent were between 20 and 29. Only 1.9 percent were under seven years old. According to Iranian statistics, 87 percent of the refugees were single or came without their families. In addition, surveys report that between 67 and 82 percent of the refugees were men.[120] This differs markedly from most refugee populations, which generally mirror the gender ratios of non-displaced groups—that is to say, roughly equal.[121]

The gender balance explanation suggests that a high level of violence would be associated with this refugee population since the single young men would make willing recruits for rebel forces. The disproportionate number of fighting-age men in Iran did not, however, translate into militant activity. This is due, for the most part, to the Iranian disinclination to support the Mujahideen. Without the support of the receiving state or external donors, the potential rebels could not act. The refugees also enjoyed better long-term employment prospects than they would have if Iran had housed them in camps.

To determine the importance of socioeconomic factors (except for the demographic balance), one would need to resort to a counterfactual. Namely, one would have to imagine that Iran maintained its opposition to militarization, but housed the refugees in large border camps. The refugees would not have been free to become self-sufficient and international assistance would have been required for their upkeep. The question is whether this change in living conditions would have increased militarization. Obviously, it is impossible to prove a counterfactual. But it seems likely that the refugees would have still faced great difficulty in achieving political and military organization—much as the thwarted Rwandan state in exile in Tanzania did.

CONCLUSION: A NEW POLITICAL CONTEXT, NEW TYPES OF VIOLENCE

Virtually all analyses of the Afghan conflict and the refugee crises ignore the two million refugees who fled to Iran.[122] The exclusive focus on the violent situation in Pakistan obscures the true causes of the conflict, however. The refugee crisis in Iran provides an essential comparison to the Pakistan crisis. Both states hosted millions of Afghan refugees, including many who aspired to overthrow the communist regime in Kabul. The refugee populations in each state had different ethnic backgrounds but shared the experience of Soviet persecution, adherence to Islam, and hatred of communism. The surprising lack of violence involving the refugees in Iran allows for a systematic examination of the causes of violence in Pakistan.

The evidence presented here confirms the importance of the political context of the crisis. The role of the receiving state and international influences determined whether or not the persecuted Afghans could coalesce into a militarized state in exile. Pakistan's support for the resistance parties, coupled with billions of dollars in aid from the United States and Saudi Arabia, provided the backbone of the Mujahideen struggle. Pakistan balanced its support for the resistance with its fear of massive Soviet reprisals, thus managing the violence such that full-scale international war did not erupt. The would-be militant leaders in Iran faced a different response to their ambitions. Iran refused to support the resistance and prevented external interference in the crisis. Thus, the two million refugees in Iran did not form a state in exile or cause the spread of civil war.

The end of the Cold War changed the political context of the Afghan conflict, but it did not resolve the war. Although the Soviet forces withdrew in 1989, most refugees did not return and the rebels continued to fight the Soviet-installed Najibullah government, which finally lost power in 1992. Still peace did not come. After the fall of the communist government, the rebel forces fractured even more and the conflict degenerated into chaotic civil war. Thus, many of the refugees remained in exile as the rival Mujahideen groups wreaked destruction on Afghanistan—mercilessly shelling Kabul and carpeting the country with landmines.

A generation of refugees came of age during this second decade of conflict in the 1990s. These teenagers did not remember their homes in Afghanistan and were educated in the Islamic-run *madrassah* education system in Pakistan, which allegedly receives financial backing from Saudi Arabia. Some of these refugee-scholars became radicalized and eventually formed the fundamentalist Taliban movement. The Taliban took power in Afghanistan in 1996, imposing its own strict version of Islamic law on the country. These refugee-scholar-soldiers shunned their former benefactor, the United States, even as they continued to benefit from past military assistance. Without the years in exile under the tutelage of fundamentalists in Pakistan, it is unlikely the Taliban would have emerged.

The third decade of the conflict in Afghanistan demonstrated that other national interests emerged in the West to fill the vacuum left by the end of the Cold War. The war on terrorism that began after September 11, 2001, involved the United States in Afghanistan more directly and to an even greater extent than during the 1980s. The unsolved refugee crisis also remained a security threat for the region. Many Taliban and al-Qaeda supporters escaped into Pakistan and Iran during the American attack on Afghanistan in 2001. Due in large part to the sympathy of the Afghan refugees and the locals in Pakistan's North West Frontier Province, finding those enemy elements proved extremely difficult, in some cases impossible. Once again, the refugee camps became a locus of militant activity, but this time the exiles presented a threat to American national security interests.

[4]

From Refugees to Regional War in Central Africa

Since the early 1990s, internal conflicts have caused millions of deaths in the Democratic Republic of Congo (formerly Zaire), Rwanda, Burundi, and Uganda. In Congo alone, over three million people died from the effects of war between 1998 and 2003.[1] These many internal conflicts did not remain isolated from each other, but rather spread across national borders, escalating the costs of war. The potent mix of millions of refugees, thousands of rebels, and abundant humanitarian assistance acted as a catalyst for the spread of conflict in the Great Lakes region of Africa.[2] A locus of this regional destabilization was the 1994 Rwandan genocide and the resulting refugee crisis.

The conflict in Rwanda traces its roots to the ethnic polarization that occurred at the end of the colonial period. Under Belgian colonial rule, the minority Tutsi group enjoyed favored status at the expense of the majority Hutu group (roughly 85 percent of the population). As independence approached, the relationship between the Belgian colonial government and their Tutsi protégés deteriorated, causing the Belgians to shift their support to the Hutu.[3] Increasing ethnic tensions erupted in the 1959 revolution, culminating in the suspicious death of the king, Mutara Rudahigwa. His death sparked violence between Hutu and Tutsi, spurring thousands of Tutsi to flee the country. After independence, the Hutu-dominated First Republic was established under the rule of Gregoire Kayibanda. Small groups of Tutsi refugees conducted raids across the border to destabilize the new government, but the attacks usually led to crackdowns on local Tutsi civilians. After a Tutsi refugee incursion in December 1963 almost reached Kigali, between 10,000 and

14,000 Tutsi were massacred and even more fled the country. The 1972 Tutsi-led genocide of the Hutu in Burundi also raised ethnic tensions in neighboring Rwanda, leading to a coup d'état in which Juvenal Habyarimana took power in 1973.[4]

Over the following decades, hundreds of thousands of Tutsi established themselves in neighboring Uganda—200,000 of whom were classified as refugees.[5] During this period, the Banyarwanda, as they were known, became highly integrated into Ugandan society, although they did experience periods of persecution. In 1982 President Milton Obote expelled thousands of Rwandans from Uganda, including many who claimed Ugandan citizenship. Those affected by the expulsion languished in camps in Rwanda for three years before returning to Uganda.

The human rights organization African Rights argues that "the harsh reality they encountered in Uganda in the early eighties was the psychological turning point for many Tutsis," one that led to their later militancy.[6] In reaction to Obote's persecution, many Tutsi joined Yoweri Museveni's resistance movement and formed their own political entity, the Rwandan Patriotic Front (RPF).[7] As allies of Museveni, the refugees had access to military training and equipment. Museveni took power from Obote in 1986 with the help of 5,000 well-trained and armed Tutsi soldiers.[8] After his ascension to power, Museveni felt domestic pressure to disassociate from the Rwandan Tutsi, popularly perceived as foreigners. Ugandan attitudes toward the refugees hardened in the late 1980s and the refugees' positions of authority began to erode. As life became more difficult, the refugees considered more seriously a return to Rwanda. However, as Mahmood Mamdani noted, these militant refugees believed that "the return home could only be armed."[9]

The army of the Rwandan Patriotic Front invaded Rwanda on October 1, 1990, while both Museveni and President Habyarimana were abroad (see table 4.1). An estimated 4,000 Tutsi rebels were involved. Immediately after the invasion, the Rwandan Hutu security forces killed hundreds of Tutsi civilians and arrested thousands more. Between 1990 and 1993, around 2,000 Tutsi died in ethnically motivated violence around the country.[10] The invasion actually played into the hands of the Hutu extremists by lending credibility to their ethnic propaganda. The invasion and the ensuing civil war vastly increased the recruitment of young men into extremist Hutu militias.[11]

Negotiations to end the stalemated civil war resulted in the Arusha Accords, a power-sharing agreement between the government and the RPF signed in 1993. The pact did nothing to reassure either party and provided an opportunity for hardliners on each side to regroup. International

Table 4.1   Timeline of the Great Lakes crisis since 1990

1990		Tutsi exiles launch invasion of Rwanda.
1993		Arusha Accords signed by Rwandan government and Tutsi rebels.
	October	Burundian President Ndadaye assassinated.
1994	April	Rwandan President Habyarimana dies when his plane is shot down.
	April–June	Rwandan genocide. Hutus kill up to 800,000 Tutsi.
	April	250,000 Hutu refugees flee east to Tanzania.
	June	France launches humanitarian intervention, Operation Turquoise.
	July	Over a million Hutu refugees flee to Zaire.
	July–Sept.	Cholera epidemic kills 50,000 refugees in Zaire.
1994–1996		Hutu forces based in refugee camps conduct cross-border attacks against Rwanda. Sporadic retaliation by the Rwandan government.
1996	July	Buyoya stages a coup in Burundi, ousting Hutu leader.
	November	Rwandan government attacks Zaire camps, 600,000 Hutu refugees return to Rwanda from Zaire.
	December	Tanzanian army forces 250,000 Hutu refugees back to Rwanda.
1997	May	Fall of Mobutu government in Zaire. President Kabila renames country the Democratic Republic of Congo (DRC).
1998		Hutu militias continue cross-border attacks against Rwanda.
	August	Rwandan-backed forces resume civil war in DRC.
1999		Lusaka peace accords signed. War continues in DRC.
2003	April	International Rescue Committee estimates over 3 million war-related deaths in DRC

observers overestimated the Habyarimana government's willingness to resolve the Tutsi refugee problem and underestimated the strength of the RPF forces amassing across the border in Uganda. Despite the presence of a United Nations peacekeeping contingent (UNAMIR), Hutu hardliners prepared for genocide.

The details of the genocide that occurred from April to July are now well recorded, although at the time most great powers pled ignorance.[12] Experts generally agree that between 500,000 and 800,000 Tutsi and some moderate Hutu perished at the hands of the killers, often referred to as "genocidaires." The genocide ended when the RPF defeated the Rwandan government forces. The RPF captured Kigali airport on May 22, 1994; on July 4 it took complete control of the city.

The genocide and subsequent defeat of the Hutu forces in 1994 spurred massive refugee outflows to neighboring states. Nearly two million Hutu refugees fled at the instigation of an estimated 20,000 Hutu soldiers and 50,000 militia members, who joined the refugees in exile.[13] The first outflow occurred on April 29, 1994, when nearly 250,000 Hutu crossed the Rusumo bridge into Tanzania. The refugees included many *Interahamwe* (Hutu militia) and local government officials implicated in the genocide. An even larger refugee movement occurred as the Tutsi-led Rwandan Patriotic Front (RPF) appeared poised to take over the entire country in July. At the urging of their leaders, over a million people fled to eastern Zaire, bringing with them most of the resources of the Rwandan government. The populations that arrived in Tanzania and Zaire constituted states in exile and exhibited a high propensity for violence.

From the beginning of the crisis, the Rwandan Hutu refugees served a valuable strategic role for the planners and executors of the genocide. The refugees provided international cover for the genocidaires and also served as an indictment of the new Tutsi-led regime in Rwanda. The militants extracted resources from the refugees and used the camps as recruitment pools. The well-funded camps quickly became the launching point for violence directed against the new Rwandan government.

Although limited cross-border attacks against Rwandan targets originated from Tanzania and Burundi, the vast majority of the violence emanated from eastern Zaire. From the camps in Zaire, the refugees organized to destabilize the Rwandan government. Cross-border attacks against Rwanda occurred throughout 1995 and 1996, with Hutu assailants targeting genocide survivors and abducting local men to participate in the militias across the border.[14] The conflict escalated sharply in late 1996, when the Rwandan government and Zairian rebels attacked the refugee camps, dispersing nearly a million people. Since that time, international and civil war have continued nearly unabated in the region. In contrast, the refugee presence in Tanzania did not cause the spread of civil war. Despite their goals of attacking Rwanda, the militants in Tanzania were unable to act.

The internationalization of conflict in the Great Lakes was also intertwined with the hundreds of thousands of Burundian refugees that fled to Tanzania in the 1990s. Ethnic civil war erupted in Burundi in 1993 after Tutsi soldiers assassinated the elected Hutu president. The conflict cost the lives of at least 250,000 Burundians and created nearly 500,000 Hutu refugees. Both sides in the conflict, the Tutsi-led government and the Hutu rebel parties, terrorized civilians as a strategy of war. The Tutsi army rounded up Hutu peasants and forced them into squalid "regroupment" camps to depopulate potential rebel havens. The Hutu

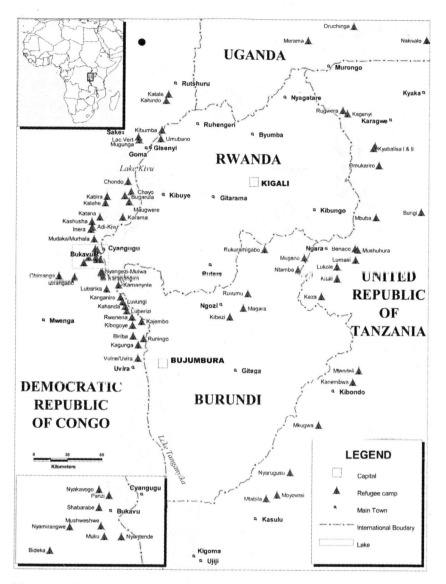

Map 4.1 Refugee camps in the Great Lakes region, 1995. UNHCR mapping unit, Geneva, 1999. Modified by the author.

rebels encouraged the peasants to flee the country, often forcibly. The presence of up to 500,000 refugees in Tanzania served as an indictment of the Burundian government and a valuable resource for the rebels. From the camps in Tanzania, rebel leaders amassed and trained recruits to launch cross-border attacks on Burundi. The government of Burundi responded with "hot pursuit" raids into Tanzania, repeatedly leading the two states to the brink of war.

RWANDAN REFUGEES AND THE SPREAD OF WAR IN ZAIRE

A Violent State in Exile

> "The refugee population, complete with its army, finances, and government, is like a second and smaller unofficial Rwanda outside the official one. . . . The vast majority of the refugees have absolutely no intention of returning to Rwanda as long as the RPF government is in power."
>
> —Gérard Prunier, "Rwanda: Update to End of July 1995," UNHCR (August 1995)

> "We are in a state of virtual war in the camps."
>
> —UNHCR official, August 1994, quoted in Rwanda: Death, Despair, and Defiance (1995)

The Rwandan refugee population in Zaire constituted a state in exile from the early days of the crisis. Numerous sources concur with the Organization for African Unity (OAU) description of the camps as "a rump genocidal state."[15] The post-crisis UNHCR evaluation characterized the refugee flow as "a strategic retreat by the former Government of Rwanda and its armed forces following a genocide."[16] In the fall of 1994, officials in the Bukavu region reported that "a prime minister and defense minister had been elected, the latter's mandate being to 'liberate' Rwanda."[17] In April 1995, the Hutu leaders issued a communiqué from Kinshasa announcing the formation of the Rwandan government in exile located in Zaire.[18]

As the RPF victory appeared imminent in mid-July 1994, the leaders of the genocide created the state in exile by moving over a million people into eastern Zaire. Within less than a week, 850,000 Hutu had walked to Goma in the Kivu district of Zaire, camping just across the Rwandan border on inhospitable volcanic terrain (see map 4.1).[19] A second outflow occurred in August, when the closure of the French-protected zone in southwest Rwanda pushed over 300,000 Hutu in the direction of Bukavu, Zaire. The exiles included much of the political and military leadership.

The UNHCR official in charge of the Goma camps reported that, unlike most refugee movements, "the majority of the refugees were led into Zaire, not really forced out by the winning side."[20] One refugee described the meetings in which the leaders told the people to move toward Zaire: "People were given a deadline, by which time they must be in Zaire. We were told that whoever did not leave by the deadline, which I think was 30 June, would be swept away by the Interahamwe who would come from behind."[21] Indeed, Hutu soldiers shot into the air to stampede people toward the border. One UNHCR official described the refugees as "a defeated, angry population" in which the leaders exercised tight social control through fear.[22]

The fleeing refugees took with them to Zaire nearly everything of value in Rwanda, from the entire state treasury down to door handles and window frames. One UNHCR official recalled seeing ex-FAR (former Rwandan army) tanks and two or three warplanes parked at Bukavu airport.[23] Aid workers observed Rwandan public transport buses and gold Mercedes being driven around the camps.[24] Emissaries of the defeated Hutu regime in Kenya stole the assets of the Rwandan embassy there and sent them to the militants before Kenya had officially recognized the new RPF government in December 1994.[25]

In the first few months of the refugee crisis, chaos and violence ruled the camps in eastern Zaire. From July 1994 until about October, a virulent cholera epidemic killed 50,000 refugees, which—to say the least—greatly added to the confusion.[26] During that time, the militants openly battled for control of the refugee population and made no secret of their ambition to invade Rwanda and topple the RPF. Human rights observers noted men walking around the camps wearing uniforms and "armed with every conceivable type of weapon."[27] A UNHCR official at the Goma camps reported that in August 1994 "gang battles were raging for control of lucrative aspects of camp life."[28] That same month a group of machete-wielding *Interahamwe* dissuaded several hundred refugees from repatriating. Numerous refugees were killed after merely obtaining information about repatriation.[29] Militants set up roadblocks within the camps and instituted neighborhood security patrols to monitor refugee activity.

After the initial period of chaos, militant Hutu leaders established complete control over the camps in eastern Zaire, demonstrating a high level of political and military organization. Once the cholera epidemic subsided, aid workers found: "The old commune and village structures remained intact and senior officials and Interahamwe militias[,] who had directed the original genocide, established control in the camps. Soldiers of the defeated Rwandan army retained both their cohesion and pitched tent just outside civilian camps."[30] The same local authority structures that existed in Rwanda now governed the camps in Zaire, enabling the genocidal leaders to maintain tight control. In December 1994, the refugee-run Commission Sociale restructured the Goma camps into *quartiers* (districts), *sous-quartiers* (sub-districts), *cellules* (neighborhoods), and *nyumba kumi* (groups of ten houses). The Bukavu camps were also organized by *quartier* and *sous-quartier*, but unlike the Goma camps, the people did not live according to their location back in Rwanda. Still, in many Bukavu camps—especially Kishushu and Inera, which had a high proportion of former military and militia—the former authorities held "complete control" over the camps.[31]

In addition to geographically based organization, the refugees organized themselves politically, forming a variety of groups. During 1994, the ex-FAR remained aloof from camp politics, but by 1995 the military elements dominated the political organization of the camps. A World Bank mission reported: "There was an underlying power structure based on a committee of fifteen or seventeen members, made up of former government, military and business leaders, and possibly directed from abroad which still controlled most of what went on in the camps. It appeared that elected leaders would not go against the decisions of this committee."[32] In April 1995, a group of refugees formed a political party in Mugunga camp called Rally for Democracy and the Return to Rwanda (RDR). The RDR claimed no link with the extremist Hutu government in exile, yet it circulated similarly racist propaganda and asserted that the party would resort to "military action as a final option." Thirteen senior officers in the ex-FAR pledged their support for the new party days after its founding.[33]

The refugee crisis provided an excellent opportunity for the genocidaires to improve their military capability. The leaders and their recruits established military camps in close proximity to the refugees. A U.S. Committee for Refugees (USCR) observer noted in 1996 that "it is an open secret in Goma that many of the commanders of FAR are now living and training recruits at Lac Vert Chiefs of Staff camp, several kilometers southwest of Mugunga camp."[34] In addition to the purely military camps, the militants infiltrated the "civilian" camps and used them as bases from which they launched cross border attacks against

Rwanda. The military might of the former Rwandan army (ex-FAR) and militia groups actually grew while in exile. Before the 1990 invasion by the RPF, the FAR had a troop strength of 5,000. This number rose to 30,000 after the invasion. Human Rights Watch reported that by 1995 the group under control of the ex-FAR in the Zairian camps boasted a strength of 50,000 people, due to new recruits and the absorption of former militia members.[35] The OAU estimated that around 10 percent of the refugees—over 100,000 people—were actually militants and war criminals.[36]

The militants used the relative security of exile to stockpile weapons in and around the camps. Aid workers confirmed that weapons shipments destined for the Hutu military leaders regularly arrived at Goma airport. In an assessment mission in March 1995, Human Rights Watch observed military training by ex-FAR and militia in Bilongue camp and an arsenal of weapons in Panzi camp. The weapons were jointly transported by the FAZ (Zairian army) and the ex-FAR and included "assault rifles, mortars, grenades, and landmines." Stewart Wallis of Oxfam reported midnight shipments brought in on twelve Russian-built Ilyushin aircraft. Zaire confiscated heavy weapons (including armored cars, helicopters, 120mm armored mortar carriers, rocket launchers, anti-aircraft guns, and military trucks) but stored them in Zairian warehouses that were maintained by the ex-FAR.[37]

Cementing their status as a state in exile, the refugees refused to return home without a complete victory. Ex-FAR Colonel Theoneste Bagasora warned that the coming war would be "long and full of dead people until the minority Tutsi are finished and completely out of the country."[38] An extremist newspaper circulated in the camps proclaimed that "to be able to return, the refugees must win three wars: a war of arms, of politics, and of information."[39] As one refugee in Goma told reporters, "We came here with our orders and we now wait for our return orders."[40] Interviews with refugees in Mugunga camp, which housed 150,000 refugees and had a high concentration of former military, militia and political elites, revealed that the refugees demanded many changes to return. Interestingly, the refugees seemed to view themselves as holding a strong bargaining position. Their demands included: a new government in Rwanda, an international guarantee of safety, mass (not individual) repatriation, and land tenure rights.[41] At a UN/OAU-sponsored workshop in the region, a refugee from Goma affirmed that the refugees were prepared to establish a government in exile rather than return to Rwanda.[42]

The Spread of Rwanda's Civil War

After the cholera epidemic subsided in October 1994, the focus of militant activity shifted from controlling the camps to destabilizing the new Rwandan regime. Small-scale incursions began in October 1994; over the next year, the attacks increased in intensity and frequency. As the refugee crisis dragged on, the former regime strengthened its military and political power. By mid-1995, Human Rights Watch found that the former Rwandan army (ex-FAR) had rebuilt its military structure and "maintained a direct link with the political establishment through the self-declared government-in-exile's Ministry of Defense."[43] By 1996, the refugee leaders had gained resources and military recruits, leading to an increase in the number and lethality of attacks. The early attacks focused on economic sabotage, but once the RPF began to counter those attacks effectively, the refugee militants began targeting local civilian leaders and genocide survivors.[44]

The Rwandan government responded to the security threat by launching its own cross-border attacks.[45] Tensions rose between Rwanda and Zaire, as Zaire accused Rwanda of attacking its territory three times in the first half of 1995. On April 11, 1995, Rwandan forces crossed the border and killed thirty Hutu refugees at Birava camp. This was followed by a mortar attack in Kibumba camp that wounded two Zairian soldiers. Throughout 1995 and 1996, the RPF attacked suspected *Interahamwe* training bases, both within and outside Rwanda.[46]

The conflict between the Hutu refugees and the Rwandan government quickly escalated, drawing in participants from many neighboring states and rebel groups. The influx of Hutu refugees also led to increased violence against Zairian Tutsi, which was encouraged by the Zairian government. The persecution of Zairian Tutsi provided the perfect pretext for Rwandan intervention in Zaire. Rwanda initially offered covert support for anti-Mobutu exile groups and created the Alliance des Forces Démocratiques pour la Libération du Congo-Zaire (ADFL) under the leadership of Laurent Kabila, a longtime Mobutu opponent. The Banyamulenge, as the Tutsi living in South Kivu are known, began to resist displacement in October 1996 in alliance with Kabila. In late 1996, Rwanda's covert assistance escalated into a cross-border invasion meant to secure eastern Zaire and eliminate the threat of Hutu attacks.

As the invasion neared the refugee camps, the UN Security Council proposed a multilateral force to help the refugees return en masse. As soon as the Rwandan-backed ADFL rebels realized that the proposed force would not disarm the refugees or separate the militants, they targeted the camps for attack. Rwandan Vice President Paul Kagame admitted afterward that the Security Council resolution in favor of the multinational force strongly influenced the timing of the Rwandan action.[47] The RPF wanted the chance to eliminate the threat posed by the Hutu militants.

In the face of the ADFL advance, Hutu extremists, unwilling to relinquish their most important asset, herded the refugees from camp to camp. Although camp conditions were extremely poor, a U.S. Committee for Refugees delegation observed that "among the skeletal figures roamed young Rwandan men in good condition, seemingly oblivious to children lying motionless at their feet."[48] The standoff between the Hutu genocidaires and the invading forces reached a peak at Mugunga camp, housing over 600,000 refugees at the time. The ADFL sealed off the camp from humanitarian access and refugees cowered amid heavy artillery fire.[49]

On November 15, 1996, following the unrelenting attacks on the refugee camps, an unprecedented mass reverse migration occurred. The estimated 600,000 refugees congregated in Mugunga camp poured into Rwanda. This unforeseen mass return prevented the separation of militants from refugees, thwarting the Rwandan government's desire to punish the genocidaires. In the confusion, thousands of refugees also fled westward through the Zairian forest, among them many leaders of the genocide. During this period of confusion, the Rwandan-backed forces allegedly massacred thousands of refugees as they fled. Once in power, the ADFL successfully suppressed investigation of the massacres.[50]

To the satisfaction of most Zairians and the rest of the world—except France—the corrupt and decaying Mobutu regime crumbled under Kabila's onslaught. The ADFL forces successfully took Kinshasa, the capital of Zaire, in April 1997. One of the new government's first acts was to rename the country the Democratic Republic of Congo (DRC). The government of Rwanda expected that Kabila, as a protégé of the RPF, would improve security along the eastern border of the DRC.

Kabila soon disappointed his Rwandan benefactors, however. Much to the RPF's dismay, cross-border violence continued in the aftermath of Mobutu's overthrow and the return of the refugees. The thousands of Hutu militants that had escaped the RPF onslaught regrouped in the Congolese forests. As President Museveni had discovered in Uganda a decade earlier, the new leader of Congo found his reliance on Tutsi forces unpopular with his domestic audience. In July 1998, Kabila ended the military cooperation agreement between Rwanda and Congo. He increasingly scapegoated the Tutsi—domestic and foreign alike—as a strategy to consolidate power. Rather than enacting democratic reforms, the new government encouraged attacks on Tutsi and allowed the *Inter-ahamwe* and ex-FAR to continue their military activities in eastern Congo. The OAU reported that these two groups never lost sight of their goal of invading Rwanda and toppling the government.[51]

In response to continuing cross-border attacks against Rwandans and Congolese Tutsi refugees, Rwanda once again invaded the Congo and supported the local opposition to Kabila's government.[52] The 1998 war resulted in international involvement on an even greater scale than in 1996. The OAU noted with alarm the spread of war and warned that "political rivalries and ethnic distinctions are becoming intertwined, with the result that an ugly new ethnic polarization threatens to engulf a huge swath of Africa."[53] Eventually, many of the warring parties signed the Lusaka peace accords in 1999. The peace agreement called for a Chapter VII peacekeeping force with a mandate to disarm the militias and supervise the withdrawal of the many foreign troops in Congo. In 2003, in response to continuing fighting and human rights abuses, the UN Security Council increased the authorized force from 5,000 to 10,800 UN troops.[54] Following the peace negotiations, a transitional government took power in Kinshasa in July 2003 that included representatives of most rebel parties.

MOBUTU'S ZAIRE: UNWILLING, INCAPABLE

"A cleverly twitching corpse."

—Description of Mobutu's government during the refugee crisis, quoted in "Zaire's Crises of War and Governance," United States Institute of Peace (1997)

The origin of the Rwandan refugees as a defeated state in exile made the spread of civil war likely. To prevent violence, the receiving state would have needed to secure its borders and police the refugee camps. Zairian authorities showed neither the will nor the capability to thwart the clearly militaristic ambitions of the refugee state in exile, however. To the contrary, Human Rights Watch determined that "Zairian forces close to president Mobutu Sese Seko have played a pivotal role in facilitating the re-emergence as a powerful military force of those directly implemented in the Rwandan genocide."[55]

The actions of the central government, embodied by President Mobutu, stemmed from its conflicting policy goals and weak capability. Two international factors pulled Zairian policy in opposite directions:

[84]

Zaire's alliance with the Hutu extremist movement and Mobutu's concern about his international reputation. Domestically, Mobutu's power had begun to crumble in the face of demands for democratization. Mobutu attempted to use the refugee crisis to regain his international standing and distract his domestic opponents. This strategy worked for a while, but in the end, Mobutu underestimated his opponents' resolve and overestimated his own government's ability to withstand attack.

Mobutu's government had long been allied with the Hutu regime in Rwanda. Mobutu and Habyarimana both opposed Museveni's rise to power in Uganda in the 1980s. Following the RPF invasion in 1990, Zaire sent several hundred troops to help Habyarimana quell the rebels.[56] Both Zaire and Rwanda benefited from France's view of the Great Lakes conflicts as an arena for Anglo-French competition.

The history of friendly ties continued after the genocide. During the refugee crisis, Mobutu regularly entertained visits from the former chief of staff of the Rwandan army, Augustin Bizimungu, and other ex-FAR officers.[57] Demonstrating its sympathy for the Hutu militants, the Zairian government made only a halfhearted attempt to disarm the refugees, even in the presence of the international press. At the highly publicized refugee crossing from Gisenyi to Goma in July 1994, Zairian officials confiscated weapons at the border. UNHCR witnessed the piles of weapons that accumulated as the refugees entered, but over time the refugees ended up reclaiming those weapons anyway.[58] The later crossing in August 1994 at Bukavu received much less press attention, so the Zairian troops made no effort whatsoever to disarm the exiles.[59] As the crisis dragged on, the local authorities repeatedly refused to secure the border with Rwanda or move the obviously militarized camps further away. Rwandan Vice President Paul Kagame deplored Mobutu's refusal to separate the militants from the refugees, rightly claiming, "Zaire could do it if it had the will and the support of the international community."[60]

Despite his alliance with the militant Hutu, Mobutu was highly sensitive to international perceptions of the refugee crisis. He hoped to rehabilitate his international standing by manipulating the refugee situation. To this end, Mobutu's government encouraged the perception that Zaire's stability, under Mobutu's leadership, was essential to resolving the crisis. This image temporarily distracted attention from the lack of democratization and increased the willingness of other governments to deal with Mobutu.

Responding to international pressure to end the refugee crisis in August 1995, the Zairian government began a forced repatriation operation that expelled about 12,000 refugees from Kivu over a four-day period. Some relief officials hoped that this expulsion would trigger a mass return and break the power of the leaders. Other observers condemned the brutally executed return forced on the refugees as Mobutu's calculated plot to extort increased international aid from donors. Mobutu suspended the expulsions following a promise from aid organizations to reconsider Zaire's request for increased assistance.[61]

By the end of 1995, Mobutu had milked the maximum political capital out of the refugees. The rest of the world now realized that Mobutu's government could not or would not provide the solution to the crisis. As the political value of the refugees changed, so did Zaire's attitude towards repatriation. Mobutu had hoped to gain international support and recognition from the refugee crisis, as well as to aid the regime of the late President Habyarimana. Instead, as Bonaventure Rutinwa noted, "as the mood in the international community became decidedly pro the new regime in Kigali, [the] refugees increasingly became a potential liability to their hosts."[62]

Although Mobutu encouraged the militants, the Zairian state had limited capability to support military activity. By the mid-1990s the reach of the central government hardly extended to the far-flung provinces in the east. Local authorities had much more power and sided with the Rwandan refugees, encouraging anti-Tutsi militarism. The central government could not have enforced security in the refugee-populated areas even if it had wanted to.[63]

Zaire's lack of capability provided a permissive environment for cross-border attacks, both by the refugees and the Rwandan government. As Mobutu's government and economy collapsed, the threat of civil war in Zaire grew. In 1994 the economy shrank by 7.4 percent and inflation was truly out of control, at over 23,000 percent.[64] Law enforcement in Zaire could not provide security in the camps—indeed, in many cases it contributed to the insecurity.

The desperation of the central government stoked ethnic conflict in the refugee-populated areas and led to a wider war. As his power waned, Mobutu relied on anti-Tutsi sentiment to bolster his position in eastern Zaire. An alliance of indigenous Zairian ethnic groups and the newly arrived Hutu refugees formed to persecute and expel Zairian Tutsi. The attempt to use ethnicity as a divisive factor in Kivu backfired when Rwandan forces entered, an act that eventually led to Mobutu's downfall. The invasion from Rwanda and the emergence of the Zairian ADFL rebel force also strengthened the alliance between the Zairian army and the Hutu militias, creating a multinational anti-Tutsi alliance.[65]

The combination of a militaristic state in exile and a sympathetic, albeit incapable, receiving state enabled the spread of the Rwandan civil war to Zaire. The alliance with Mobutu strengthened the refugees' capabilities and also alarmed the Rwandan government. Zaire's weakness encouraged the Rwandan invasion and the local anti-Mobutu rebellion. The capability and attitude of the receiving state also directly affected the international influences on the crisis.

International Support for Violence

In eastern Zaire, virtually all international actors involved in the crisis contributed to the spread of civil war, whether intentionally or not. External support, especially from France, allowed the militant refugees to continue the war and even strengthen their forces. Sudan, China, and the Angolan UNITA rebel movement also aided Mobutu's government. The Zairian ADFL rebels gained assistance or sympathy from the governments of Rwanda, Burundi, Angola, Uganda, the United States, and also from the Southern Sudanese rebels. No international force attempted to demilitarize the refugee areas or secure Zaire's borders. As a failing state, Zaire lacked the capability to prevent external interference in the crisis. As an ally of the Hutu militants, Zaire willingly abetted international involvement on their behalf.

Many French government officials viewed the Rwanda crisis as part of a larger Anglo-French competition. The French saw the invasion of the English-speaking Tutsi rebels from Uganda as the first move in an Anglo-Saxon plot to diminish French influence in the Great Lakes region. French officials thus perceived support for Zaire and the Rwandan Hutu as vital to French national interests. Loss of French influence in Africa would call into question France's claim to "medium-power status in the international system."[66]

As a long time ally of the Habyarimana regime, France sent military assistance to the government after the RPF invasion in 1990.[67] The French supervised an expansion of the Rwandan army from 5,000 in 1990 to 30,000 in 1994 and continued to provide weapons to the Hutu force during the genocide.[68] Immediately after the imposition of the arms embargo on Rwanda in May 1994, France diverted its arms shipments across the border to Goma airport. Human Rights Watch found evidence of five shipments that arrived during May and June of 1994, which were then taken across the border to Gisenyi, Rwanda.[69]

Under the guise of humanitarianism, France provided aid to the genocidal Hutu regime during and after the genocide. With its Operation

Turquoise, France set up an ostensibly humanitarian zone in the southwest corner of Rwanda that also provided safe haven to the defeated Rwandan army (ex-FAR). Within the zone, the ex-FAR continued to receive weapons and the Hutu leaders reestablished propaganda hate radio. France further antagonized the Tutsi-led RPF forces by declaring that it would defend the zone by force, if necessary. In the most egregious example of the partisan stance of French forces, the French allowed former military and government officials to escape to Zaire after the RPF victory. The French forces disarmed the departing genocidaires, but turned the weapons over to the Zairian army rather than to the UN peacekeepers. Once the extremists had established themselves in the camps, the French reportedly facilitated meetings of key leaders, including Colonel Theoneste Bagasora and Jean-Baptiste Gatete. Analyst William Cyrus Reed found that the French saw to it that the former government of Rwanda "possessed a large, well-equipped military and that it could escape to Zaire, with its command structure and key troops largely in place."[70]

The United States played a smaller role than France, but it did tacitly support the 1996 Rwandan invasion of Zaire. Although Mobutu had been a longtime client of the United States, by the end of the Cold War he had outlived his usefulness. As a corrupt autocrat, he embodied the opposite of the "New African Leaders" promoted by the U.S. government in the 1990s. In her tour of the Great Lakes in 1997, U.S. Secretary of State Madeleine Albright lauded Uganda's President Museveni as a "beacon of hope" and praised Congo's Laurent Kabila and Rwanda's Paul Kagame for their promises of democracy, good governance, and liberal economic policies.[71]

Rwanda's alliance with the United States meant that the RPF could take military action against the refugees without fear of universal international condemnation. After his trip to Washington in June 1996, Rwandan Vice President Paul Kagame reported that he "was not disheartened" by the American response to his plans.[72] In late 1996, the American government helped delay implementation of an international force to assist the refugees because it would have had no mandate to disarm or separate the refugees from the militants.

The Americans were aware that the Rwandan military was training Zairian Tutsi and intending to disperse the camps. In 1996, Richard McCall, chief of staff for the U.S. Agency for International Development (USAID) announced that "it is time to look at other options to maintaining the current status of the refugee camps no matter how difficult it is to reconcile those options with refugee conventions."[73] Although there was evidence that placed Rwandan army officers at the massacres of

Hutu refugees in eastern Zaire, the United States exerted no pressure regarding the killings. The diplomatic and political assistance from the United States clearly hastened Mobutu's downfall.[74]

Regional states also played a major role in the expansion of the conflict. In alliance with Rwanda, Uganda participated in the attacks on the Hutu rebels in eastern Zaire.[75] Rwandan Vice President Kagame and Ugandan President Museveni had close personal ties and complementary security interests in the region. Two anti-Museveni rebel groups, the West Bank Liberation Front and the Holy Spirit Movement, operated from bases in eastern Zaire. The Ugandan rebels were supported by the Sudanese government, which accused Museveni of aiding the Sudanese rebels in Uganda. Like Rwanda, Uganda hoped that the invasion would eliminate the rebel threat on the Zaire border.[76] The Rwanda-Uganda alliance later split and the two states further exacerbated conflict by backing competing Congolese rebel groups.

The Hutu refugees, and their patron Zaire, also received support from neighboring states and rebel groups. Kenya seemed generally sympathetic but offered little material support. Gérard Prunier noted that Kenya sheltered only a few thousand refugees, although many of them were high-ranking officials responsible for the genocide and enjoyed the tacit welcome of the government.[77] Zaire's main source of external support in the region came from a non-state actor, the UNITA rebel movement. Mobutu was a long-standing supporter of UNITA's war against the Angolan government and a close ally of Jonas Savimbi, the UNITA leader. As Angola sided with the Rwandan alliance for the purpose of rooting UNITA out of its Zairian sanctuary, UNITA joined Mobutu in the fight for his regime.

Humanitarian Foundations of the State in Exile

> "I know some of them have killed a lot of people. But I don't care about the past. My job is to feed everyone irrespective of the past."

—Humanitarian aid worker in eastern Zaire, quoted in *Rwanda: Death, Despair, and Defiance* (1995)

> "Uniformed groups with weapons are being fed by the international community."

—Paul Kagame, vice president of Rwanda, quoted in "West Accused of Giving Aid to Defeated Rwandan Army," *Guardian* (December 9, 1994)

[89]

Zaire's weak central government provided little or no oversight of the many UN agencies and hundreds of NGOs that descended on eastern Zaire following the refugee crisis. Major international organizations included UNHCR, the World Food Programme (WFP), and the International Committee of the Red Cross and NGOs such as CARE, Médecins sans Frontières, International Rescue Committee, Oxfam, American Refugee Committee, Caritas, and Médecins du Monde. The humanitarian organizations competed fiercely for the billions of dollars in aid contracts and for public recognition of their charitable activities.[78] International donors spent $1.4 billion on relief contracts for Goma, Zaire, between April and December 1994. UNHCR alone spent $115 million in Goma between July and October 1994. The chaotic situation and abundant aid provided a windfall for the militants, who used it to support their planned invasion of Rwanda.[79]

Humanitarian organizations contributed to the spread of civil war in all of the four ways outlined in chapter 1. Aid agencies provided food directly to militia members and soldiers. The internationally supported camps also sustained the militants' supporters. The billions of dollars of aid contributed to the war economy. And the international images of the refugees as victims legitimated the militants' position in the camps.

Most directly, aid supported war by providing food to the militants. Human Rights Watch reported in 1995 that the militant elements benefited from the resources of the international aid effort through direct assistance from aid agencies. Caritas Internationalis, for example, continued to supply aid to the military camps Panzi and Bilongue, refusing to distinguish between civilian and military recipients. Caritas only required that recipients present themselves for their rations without uniforms or weapons.[80]

The internationally supported camps allowed the militants to focus on their war plans rather than on the survival of their followers (or hostages). As political and military leaders back in Rwanda, the militants had to concern themselves with providing goods and services to their constituents. In the refugee camps, aid organizations functioned as the infrastructure for the state in exile, providing food, health care, sanitation, education, and other services.

The outpouring of relief aid bolstered the war economy in numerous ways. Militants exaggerated refugee numbers and controlled distribution mechanisms to skim off aid. Armed refugees prevented UNHCR workers from conducting a census of the refugees. Initially, humanitarian organizations relied on refugee *commune* leaders to present lists of the population and control the distribution. This allowed for a high level of food misappropriation. Despite the adequate supplies of food, inequitable distribution led to malnutrition among the disadvantaged refugees.[81] Over time, aid organizations transitioned to a distribution system that targeted groups of families and more successfully prevented misappropriation.

The diversion of aid meant that the sale of relief goods profited the militants' agenda. A visitor to the camps reported that "relief blankets were being sold to raise money for, among other things, arms."[82] Humanitarian organizations also swelled the war chests of the genocidaires by paying them as camp administrators. Terry reports that aid agencies rented refugee vehicles that had been looted from Rwanda.[83] Militants also levied a war tax on the refugees, collecting one dollar a month in the name of an orphans fund.[84]

There was also outright theft of donated goods. For example, during the civil war in Zaire in 1996 and 1997, Kabila's rebel forces stole 15,000 gallons of fuel from the UNHCR depot to ferry troops across the country. Many NGOs also reported vehicles stolen by rebel fighters. On the opposing side, Mobutu's forces commandeered UN planes to deliver weapons to Rwandan Hutu refugees in the camps.[85]

The humanitarian organizations bolstered the legitimacy of genocidaires by accepting them as refugee leaders. A UN official in Zaire confirmed this policy: "Mobutu's government was nowhere to be found. It was natural to turn to the Hutus."[86] This allowed the militant leaders a platform to spread misinformation and intimidate refugees. One refugee administrator, Laurent Bucyibaruta, a former prefect of Gikongoro until the genocide, offered his version of recent Rwandan history: "Not just Tutsi died, even more Hutu died. . . . [There were] mutual massacres between Hutu and Tutsi. A confrontation between everyone ensued. The authorities were in great insecurity."[87] The rumors and distortions peddled by the militants gained greater credence among the refugees since these same genocidaires were often employed by international organizations and allowed to represent the refugees.

In November 1994, a coalition of NGOs threatened to withdraw from the camps due to the militarization. The militants' response showed their understanding of the goals and incentives that powered the humanitarian organizations. Violence and intimidation became much less overt. Yet the camps remained as militarized and the populations remained under the complete control of the genocidal leaders. As a result of these "cosmetic" changes, aid workers received fewer threats and rarely observed military activity taking place in the open. The militants managed to give the aid organizations what they wanted, namely some "civil society" organizations. The genocidaires realized how far they could misuse aid without triggering a withdrawal or public denunciation. As Terry noted, "It was strongly in the interests of the former regime to quell the violence in the camps, to avoid jeopardizing the presence of the aid organizations and precipitating a deteriorization of camp services."[88]

Humanitarian organizations were aware of the militarization but took few actions to counter it and did not publicize it. A UNHCR spokesperson admitted, "The involvement of the aid agencies in the camps makes accomplices of us, helping [the militias] consolidate power."[89] Some UNHCR officials excused the passive response to militarization by claiming that such activity took place out of sight of the aid agencies. One official explained that her driver warned her to leave the militarized camps at two in the afternoon so that she would not observe the military training there.[90] As USCR noted at the time, "given the realities of the refugee camps in Goma, NGOs cannot easily claim that their relief programs there are nonpolitical."[91]

After the Rwandan invasion, militants continued to misuse humanitarian aid. The Hutu extremists gathered thousands of refugees at Tingi-Tingi camp and controlled the distribution of aid to the refugees. The Rwandan-backed rebel forces also manipulated humanitarian aid. Human rights organizations reported that the ADFL used humanitarian aid as "bait" to lure refugees out of the forest. As the desperate refugees approached the aid convoys, ADFL officials would block the delivery of aid. By the time aid workers were allowed access, the refugees would have disappeared, increasing suspicions of deliberate massacres. A U.S. Committee for Refugees observer recommended: "Relief agencies must regularly re-examine . . . whether they should suspend operations until they are able to function independently and fulfill their humanitarian mandate without doing inadvertent harm."[92]

Alexander Cooley and James Ron convincingly argue that organizations were wary of exposing militant activity that might reduce donations and result in a termination of aid contracts.[93] The passivity of both governments and humanitarian organizations contributed to the spread of civil war and led to heated debate about the role of aid in conflict. Chapter 6 addresses the policy implications of the Rwandan refugee crisis for future humanitarian interventions.

Unconvincing Socioeconomic Explanations

"The camps were thriving and those that were thriving most were those most opposed to return as the wealthiest refugees were those who had generally emptied the coffers of Rwanda on their way out."

—Joel Boutroue, UNHCR official in Goma, "Missed Opportunities: The Role of the International Community in the Return of the Rwandan Refugees from Eastern Zaire," *Rosemarie Rogers Working Paper Series* (1998)

At first glance, many characteristics of the Zaire camps confirm the socioeconomic explanations presented earlier. In Zaire, the huge camps were situated within walking distance of the Rwandan border. Aid workers claimed that the population included a disproportionate number of young men.[94] Media accounts of the crisis stressed the dire living conditions in the camps. According to the socioeconomic explanations, the size and location of the camps, the supposedly disproportionate number of young men, and the supposedly poor living conditions should have caused violence. Closer scrutiny reveals that those factors did not lead to the spread of the Rwandan civil war. Furthermore, some of the reports about the socioeconomic conditions proved completely inaccurate.

Advocates for refugee protection often argue that large camps are harder to control and protect, allowing militants to blend in and find recruits. Therefore, observers ascribed the militarization of the five huge camps around Goma, which housed over 700,000 refugees, to the size of the camps. The camps spread out for miles in a chaotic pattern that stymied international efforts to impose order.

Two comparisons demonstrate that the size of the Goma camps was not the main factor that led to the violence. First of all, smaller camps also existed in eastern Zaire, primarily in the Bukavu area. The twenty-three camps around Bukavu housed nearly 400,000 refugees. Surprisingly, the smallest camps fell under even tighter control by the militants.[95] Médecins Sans Frontières (MSF) was one of the few NGOs to realize the irrelevance of camp size: "While some believed that in smaller camps the leaders would have less power over the refugee population, this proved to be a mistake. The leaders, some of whom have been identified by other refugees as well-known Interahamwe, wielded considerably more power over the small camp population of 15,000 than their counterparts in the larger camps."[96]

[93]

A second comparison contrasts the Zaire camps to other large camps. The Rwandan Hutu in Tanzania also lived in massive camps of over 100,000 refugees, but these camps experienced a much lower level of violence. These comparisons reveal the irrelevance of camp size in the spread of civil war.

The next factor that observers often blame for cross-border violence is the location of camps near the border of the sending state.[97] Contravening UNHCR guidelines, the Rwandan camps in Zaire were located very close to the Rwandan border, often within walking distance (see map 4.1).[98] UNHCR warned: "The location of camps containing hundreds of thousands of Hutus associated with a bloody genocide a few weeks earlier, virtually on the border of the country their leaders had destroyed, was a formula for inevitable conflict."[99] In a similar vein, Amnesty International reported that "the presence of these refugee camps so close to the border continues to pose a significant security threat, both for residents living in Rwanda and for the refugees themselves."[100]

Comparison with other border camps helps determine that the location of the camps did not provide the primary impetus for violence. The camps in Tanzania contained a similarly violence-prone population and were also located within walking distance of the border. However, those border camps remained much more peaceful than the Zairian camps, despite their similarities. The receiving state's ability and willingness to control the border played a greater role in preventing violence than the location of the camps.[101] Zaire was unable to secure its border and unwilling to allow an external party to provide security. In Tanzania, the tight border security meant that the location of the camps did not facilitate the spread of civil war.

An additional point, one often ignored by humanitarian organizations, is the political nature of camp location. Although presented as a socioeconomic explanation for conflict, border camps exist because they meet political goals of receiving states and, often, the refugees themselves. Thus it is not possible to consider camp location as a purely logistical issue. Even if border camps prove a necessary—if not sufficient—condition for cross-border violence, one cannot separate the demographic from the political aspects of camp location decisions.

A third component of the socioeconomic explanation blames bored young men for the violence. This theory predicts violence when a large number of young men live in the camps. Evaluating this somewhat hazy explanation is complicated by the difficulty in obtaining reliable demographic data.[102] Accurate data on the Rwandan refugees is even more elusive because the militants strongly resisted attempts to register and count the refugees. By presenting higher numbers, the refugees could obtain a greater amount of aid and also cause greater embarrassment to the Rwandan government. The available data suggests that the refugee population in Zaire did not have a higher percentage of men than usual. In fact, the U.S. Center for Disease Control estimated that children under five years old constituted 25 percent of the refugee population in 1994, a larger percentage than sub-Saharan Africa as a whole.[103]

Another related explanation for refugee-related violence claims that refugees are more vulnerable to recruitment by militants if their living conditions are poor and not easily improved. For example, a World Bank mission to Zaire advocated the creation of refugee associations for technical and agricultural training, arguing that, in addition to the economic benefit of such skills, the training would affect the political climate of the camp: "It would mean the participants would have less time for exposure to extremist propaganda. They would also be mentally predisposed to going home."[104] Comparisons over time and with other refugee populations discredit this "material incentives" explanation.

Comparisons over time actually show the opposite effect; the period of scarcity correlates with the lowest level of cross-border violence. The worst living conditions occurred in the early months of exile, when the United Nations was caught unprepared and before the militant leaders consolidated their grip on the camps.[105] As of August 1994, NGOs considered conditions in the camp to be extremely poor. One humanitarian assessment found only one latrine available for every 10,000 people.[106] During this time, between July and October 1994, few cross-border attacks occurred, as the militants were busy establishing their control over the camps.

Mortality rates from the camps demonstrate that conditions rapidly improved after the cholera epidemic ended in autumn 1994. Data collected on three camps in eastern Zaire and Goma town (using the UNHCR estimate of 600,000–800,000 refugees) reveals a crude mortality rate ranging from 34.1 to 54.5 deaths per 10,000 people per day in August 1994. This is one of the highest crude mortality rates ever documented during a refugee emergency.[107] Between 6 and 10 percent of the July arrivals died within a month of arriving in Goma. By September the crude mortality rate had drastically dropped to 2.5 per 10,000 people per day and to 0.2 per 10,000 per day in November. In developing countries, the usual crude mortality rate is between 0.5 and 0.6 per 10,000 per day. Thus, by November 1994, refugees actually had better mortality rates than average, even for nonrefugees in developing countries.[108]

[95]

Malnutrition was also low, measuring at less than 10 percent of the population. A USCR observer noted that "any food shortages that occurred in the Zaire camps appear to be caused by improper or dishonest food distribution by camp leaders, rather than due to a real shortage of food."[109] Another USCR observer commented that "markets in the refugee camps are so well stocked with vegetables, Western manufactured commodities, and beef from cattle rustled from Masisi that many Zairians head to the camps to do their own shopping."[110]

In addition to nutrition and mortality, the refugees' other living conditions improved over time. Refugees found employment and managed to move relatively freely in the region. Locals viewed the refugees as a profitable source of cheap labor. A UNHCR official found that "refugee movements were relatively easy for those who could afford to pay the multiple 'tolls' at the check points set up by the Zairian armed forces." Additionally, entrepreneurial refugees and Zairian army officers ran shuttle services that linked the North Kivu camps. Mobutu gave the former Rwandan government officials and soldiers no trouble when they decided to live outside the camp. The leaders used access to these resources to pursue their goal of toppling the Rwandan government.[111]

After many months of fruitless attempts at repatriation, aid officials and Zairian government leaders concluded that the living conditions discouraged return to Rwanda.[112] In a desperate attempt to encourage repatriation, relief officials worsened living conditions in the camps. Officials closed down refugee businesses and limited movement, in the hopes that declining conditions would lead to a peaceful return. The attempt was halfhearted, however, and failed to break the power of the refugee leaders. Despite the fact that material conditions in the camps had worsened, the refugees refused to return home.[113]

The socioeconomic explanations do not stand up to scrutiny in the Zairian refugee crisis.[114] A more plausible reason for the violence is the political motivations of the refugees and their ability to achieve a high level of political and military organization. The weakness of the socioeconomic explanation becomes even clearer when the refugees in Zaire are compared with those in Tanzania. In Tanzania, similarly good socioeconomic conditions were unrelated to the low levels of violence.

Zaire in Context

The refugee crisis in Zaire is often regarded as an anomaly among humanitarian emergencies. Aid workers have strenuously argued that eastern Zaire was a unique and incomparable situation. Sadako Ogata,

UN High Commissioner for Refugees at the time, claimed that "probably never before has my Office found its humanitarian concerns in the midst of such a lethal quagmire of political and security interests."[115] However, the Zaire crisis was far from unique and can be fruitfully compared to other situations. Treating the Zaire situation as an aberration obscures the true causes of the violence there and distorts the decades-long history of refugee-related violence around the globe.

Zaire was not the only or even the most extreme instance of a refugee crisis leading to civil war. It is merely the most extreme case outside the framework of Cold War politics. Throughout the Cold War, UNHCR tolerated militarized refugee areas in Pakistan, Southern Africa, Central America, and the Thai/Cambodia border. In the case of the Afghans in Pakistan, the scale of the violence perpetrated by the refugees far surpassed events in Zaire. This history of violence makes it possible to compare the Zairian situation with other refugee crises over time.

In addition to denying general comparisons, aid workers balk at the specific comparison of the crises in Zaire and Tanzania.[116] In fact, such a comparison is an ideal way to assess the impact of the political environment on the spread of civil war. Both refugee groups fled the same conflict as states in exile. Thus they were both prone to violence. The Tanzanian and Zairian camps also shared similar geographic and demographic conditions, as well as similar living conditions. The ability to hold so many factors relatively constant allows for a clearer focus on the role of the receiving state and the international influences on the crisis.

Chaos Contained: Rwandan Hutu Refugees in Tanzania

A Thwarted State in Exile

> "In most of the camps, the Rwandans came as a state . . . and as a state, started operating as a state, and managing things as a state, and the NGOs had to operate within this state within the camps."
>
> —Odhiambo Anacleti, Oxfam official, quoted in *Summary Report from the International Workshop on Refugee Crisis in the Great Lakes Region* (August 16–19 1995)

> "We will fight our way home if we have to."
>
> —Refugee Jean-Baptiste Uniragiye, quoted in "Hutu Refugees Train to Invade Rwanda," *Times* (April 10, 1995)

[97]

In April 1994, at the height of the Rwandan genocide, nearly 200,000 Hutu poured across the narrow Rusumo bridge into Tanzania over a period of thirty hours. Taken by surprise, UNHCR and the Tanzanian authorities struggled to impose order on a population containing thousands of genocidal killers. As the refugees crossed the border, an overwhelmed Tanzanian guard instructed them to leave their machetes in an enormous pile.[117] The size and speed of the refugees' unexpected arrival frustrated any additional attempts to prevent militarization.

Once in Tanzania, the leaders reestablished their rule, making no secret of their intention to destabilize Rwanda. Even before the RPF victory and the massive refugee flows to Zaire, militant Hutu leaders publicly proclaimed their intent of using refugee camps as "a staging ground for future attacks."[118] By fleeing, the refugees and the genocidal killers among them had escaped the advancing Rwandan Patriotic Army and retribution for the massacres.

Many characteristics of this crisis suggested that it would spark international conflict between Rwanda and Tanzania. Like Zaire, the massive border camps hosted thousands of unrepentant genocidaires who hoped for a victorious return to Rwanda. Yet despite the similarities between the two situations, Tanzania did not become involved in an international war during the refugee crisis. The crisis resolved in 1996 when the Tanzanian army expelled the refugees. Although the Tanzanian situation was not completely peaceful—the camps were militarized and the refugees were forcibly returned—it compares favorably to the chaotic bloodbath in Zaire.

The primary explanation for the relatively low level of violence is the attitude and capability of the Tanzanian state. The government (for the most part) did not sympathize with the refugees' military goals and had the capability to enforce border control and maintain a semblance of order in the refugee-populated areas. As a relatively stable, democratizing state, Tanzania hoped to avoid involvement in the regional conflict, especially in an election year. Tanzania also has a long history of generous offers of asylum to both Hutu and Tutsi refugees. The government's attempt to maintain stability limited the scope for external actors to aid the militants. Thus, a potentially explosive situation remained under control.

The nature of the Rwandan population marked it as a state in exile. Although the Rwandan refugees appeared to have fled the Rwandan Patriotic Front (RPF) advance, in actuality the Hutu leaders orchestrated the refugee movement. Prunier reported that the refugees "were not fleeing massacres, as their leaders tried to pretend, but on the contrary they were the people who had just killed between 25,000 and 50,000 Tutsi."[119] As the RPF forces descended from the north, many Hutu in internally displaced person (IDP) camps and local villages moved toward Tanzania in orderly processions headed by their communal leaders. One refugee testified that his family left their home due to pressure from the Hutu thugs allied with the government.[120] The Hutu militias (*Interahamwe*) convinced civilians that any stragglers would be executed by the RPF.

As in Zaire, the refugees quickly reproduced the same political and social structures that existed in Rwanda. Immediately upon their arrival in Tanzania, the leaders approached overwhelmed UNHCR officials and offered to organize the camp.[121] One UNHCR staff person observed that "it seemed they were prepared to come. . . . They came with food, jerrycans of water, blankets."[122] Within twenty-four hours everyone had moved around and settled according to commune. Commune leaders supervised first the layout of the camp and later the food distribution, which allowed them to inflate the population numbers presented to the aid agencies.[123]

The camp organization reflected a conscious choice by UNHCR to work with the refugee leaders rather than disrupt their mechanisms of control. One official admitted that "UNHCR was obliged from the first day to cooperate with the leaders" because the influx was too large to do otherwise. Initially, UNHCR even paid the leaders (about $15 per month) to coordinate the camps.[124] Due to the high level of organization, the refugees in Tanzania avoided large-scale outbreaks of epidemics or disease, such as the cholera that killed thousands in Zaire.

From the beginning, extremist political leaders controlled the refugee population. Although the Tanzanian authorities made a desultory effort to separate some of the intimidators in the camps, most of the extremist leaders remained among the refugees. The "intimidators" consisted mainly of politicians and militia members. The bulk of the armed forces (ex-FAR) escaped to Goma, Zaire, in July 1994. As they crossed the border, Tanzanian authorities arrested fourteen known leaders of the genocide. However, the authorities decided they had nothing with which to charge the men and released them from the Ngara police station on June 15, 1994. The men then took up residence in the refugee camps.[125] Those and other militants were suspects in a number of killings within the camps.[126]

The fact that the bulk of the armed forces fled to Zaire does not explain the different levels of violence between Zaire and Tanzania. Although not as many as in Zaire, Tanzania still hosted thousands of armed elements, mostly militia members, and hundreds of former political leaders. Hutu leaders in Tanzania repeatedly attempted military training and organization. The ex-FAR went to Zaire for reasons of military necessity and the Hutu leaders' rapport with the Zairian government. Due to the direction of the RPF advance, it was most expedient for the Rwandan army to flee westward to Zaire. Also, the French-protected zone in the southwest offered a haven for the ex-FAR.

Startling proof of the militants' power in Tanzania occurred when a UNHCR protection officer asked Jean-Baptiste Gatete, one of the released genocidaires and the former *bourgmestre* (mayor) of Murambi commune, to leave Benaco camp in June 1994. Later that afternoon, Gatete organized 5,000 refugees with machetes and pangas to surround the UNHCR compound.[127] The standoff lasted for several hours. The arrival of the Tanzanian police finally dispersed the crowd with shots in the air.[128] After the Gatete incident, UNHCR withdrew services from the camp for three days. The violent episode convinced UNHCR that "they had effectively lost control of the camp or that the reality was that control had always rested with some of the leaders."[129] Rather than wresting control from the militants, the NGOs withdrew their headquarters to a more militarily defensible hilltop but continued to provide humanitarian aid.

The Gatete confrontation was only the most flagrant of multiple examples of aggressive behavior among the refugees. Numerous incidents alerted UNHCR officials that military training occurred, although the militants did make some effort to avoid detection.[130] According to Western security analysts and UN observers, 10,000 militiamen were training in Ngara in preparation for an invasion of Rwanda.[131] One observer noticed groups of men at Kagenyi camp jogging in formation at dawn.[132] In Kitali camp, refugee leaders told UNHCR that suspected militants were actually just training for soccer practice.[133] In similar situations at Benaco camp, a camp official noticed groups of young men that acted as lorry loaders or soccer teams. These groups of about twenty men worked with complete precision and were in excellent physical condition. UNHCR officials assumed the young men were training for the invasion that their leaders hoped would take place, although there were no guns in evidence.[134] When pressed, the refugee leaders responded that they were helpless to halt the training and added that the military style training kept the young men occupied.[135]

In addition to training, refugees had access to weapons, although the arms were fewer in number and more hidden than in the Zaire camps.

A Tanzanian official in the Ministry of Home Affairs suspected that "most of the refugees came with arms and ammunition," but he admitted that due to the nature of the influx, border guards did not have time to search the refugees for weapons.[136] Unlike Zaire, Tanzanian authorities did not allow heavy weapons inside the camps.[137] Between April 1994 and June 1995, police confiscated weapons and ammunition from the refugees, including grenades, pistols, machine guns, and 1165 rounds of ammunition.[138] To avoid confiscation, exiles hid many small arms in the bush. One Tanzanian official claimed that Rwandan militia and soldiers had brought light and heavy weapons, hiding them outside the refugee camps.[139]

From their positions in the camps, the leaders created a climate of fear that discouraged return and increased support for military activity. The refugee masses believed that return meant certain death at the hands of the new Tutsi-led government. In addition to social pressure, militants used physical intimidation, including death threats, to prevent refugee return. In August 1994, militants killed nineteen refugees in Benaco camp suspected of attempting return.[140]

Real injustices occurred in Rwanda that deterred refugee return and gave credence to the horrible stories spread by the militants. One UN official confirmed that "the fear of intimidators is only part of why refugees do not return."[141] For example, when the RPF captured Iwawa Island in Zaire and killed 300 ex-FAR camped there, versions of the incident became so distorted by the time it reached Tanzania that refugees believed that the victims were defenseless Hutu refugees.[142] Enough retaliation occurred by the new Tutsi-dominated government to lend credibility to even the most outlandish propaganda spread by the Hutu militants in the camps. Refugees in the Ngara area camps could see bodies—apparently Hutu victims of the RPF—floating down the Kagera river.[143] One observer claimed that "most camp dwellers would be afraid to leave even if there were no para-military in the camps."[144]

Leaders also presented their own version of Rwandan history to stoke the refugees' fear. In creating an aura of victimhood, the refugee leaders argued that the press unjustly focused on the 1994 genocide only. The militants claimed that the Tutsi had perpetrated many injustices against the Hutu before the 1990s and that one needed to use a historical viewpoint to understand the current situation. The international press unwittingly helped legitimate the leaders by conflating the civil war and the genocide, painting the refugees as victims in need of aid. One eye-catching headline read: "Refugees Swim Past Corpses to

Safety," neglecting the fact that the corpses were victims of the genocide and not ill-fated Hutu refugees.[145] Despite UNHCR efforts, militants remained the main source of information in the camps.[146] The NGO International Rescue Committee noted that "information available to refugees is partial, and tends to be slanted towards bad news. . . . Even accurate news is subject to the worst interpretation in circumstances of fear and restricted information."[147]

As in Zaire, the refugees in Tanzania refused to repatriate to Rwanda despite extensive recruitment campaigns by international agencies and the Rwandan and Tanzanian governments. By refusing to return, the refugees provided support for the militant leaders, who could then claim that they ruled a state in exile. Facing forcible return by the Tanzanian army, refugees declared that "we would rather die in Tanzania than go back and be killed in Rwanda."[148]

Despite Tanzanian border security, the refugees in Tanzania and Zaire maintained contact with each other and many of the militia based in Zaire entered Tanzania via Burundi.[149] In September 1994 a number of ex-FAR forces moved from Zaire to Tanzania to "join their families."[150] Médecins Sans Frontières (MSF) confirmed the occurrence of militant coordination across borders: "MSF believes that the leaders in the camps around Ngara meet and communicate with leaders in the Karagwe district and in Zaire. . . . It is widely known that the Interahamwe has close ties with the Hutus in Burundi and that segments of these groups regularly cross over the border between Tanzania and Burundi."[151] In one incident, six hundred young men arrived suddenly from Zaire.[152] Some of the men claimed to be looking for their families but their clothes were of decent quality and they had visas. UNHCR found it difficult to prevent the entry of such supposed refugees. There were so many entrances and screening points, the rejected people usually just came back later.[153] The infiltration from Zaire ended when the Tanzanian government closed the border with Burundi in March 1995 to prevent the entry of 70,000 Rwandan Hutu refugees massed on the border.

In the end, the state in exile could not fulfill its hegemonic goals. Tanzanian border security contained the sporadic incidents of cross-border violence that occurred throughout the crisis by closing the border and reinforcing camp security.[154] To end the crisis, the Tanzanian army—a much stronger force than the militant refugees—pushed the refugees back across the border to Rwanda. Thus, strict Tanzanian policy thwarted the Hutu extremists' plan for a two-front attack on Rwanda.

A Capable and Willing Receiving State

"We don't allow people to cross into Rwanda and carry out killings."
—Tanzanian Brigadier Sylvester Hemedi, quoted in "Rwanda-Politics:
Defeated Troops Prepare for War," Inter Press Service
(September 9, 1994)

"[Refugees] should surrender all arms or face the music."
—Augustine Mrema, Tanzanian deputy premier, quoted in "Rwanda-
Refugees: Tanzania Sends Troops to Quell Unrest," Inter Press Service
(October 4, 1994)

From the beginning of the influx, the Tanzanian government attempted to enforce security at the camps and prevent the spread of violence—both to Rwanda and the local villages.[155] Government officials hotly refuted Rwandan suggestions that they had encouraged Hutu rebels to invade Rwanda. As Kassim Mwawado, an official in the Ministry of Foreign Affairs and International Cooperation, asserted, "We have never supported the killers."[156] For the most part, the army maintained border control and regulated the refugees' entry. For example, when 70,000 Rwandan refugees congregated at the Burundi-Tanzania border in March 1995, Tanzania deployed the army and closed the border, much to the distress of UNHCR.[157]

In 1994 the huge numbers of Rwandan refugees posed political, economic, and security problems for Tanzania. The government of Tanzania repeatedly expressed concern that the refugee presence and the known militant goals of the leaders would lead to the spread of civil war.[158] After the April influx, the Home Affairs Minister worried that "many Rwandans have crossed at places other than the official entry and are armed. . . . This is very dangerous and may cause untold harm to our people."[159] In late 1994, Radio Tanzania reported that "the security situation of citizens of [northwestern Tanzania] remains worrying because of the entry of large numbers of armed Rwandan refugees."[160] For many Tanzanian officials, the Rwandan refugees differed from the past influxes, which had been met with generosity. Jenerali Ulimwengu, a member of parliament in Tanzania, described the new attitude toward the refugees: "We're not dealing with refugees, we're dealing with a whole new phenomena of people who are committing crimes in their country of origin, and who, before they can be apprehended, way in advance of the war that was advancing on them . . . they had all the time to move from their place of origin and go and resettle in other areas and

[103]

baptize themselves as refugees and we accept this! . . . We have people who are not refugees and who we treat as refugees."[161]

Deputy Minister for Home Affairs E. Mwambulukutu explained that "protecting and assisting refugees has brought new risks to national security, exacerbated tensions between states and caused extensive damage to the environment." Despite the threat, he maintained that Tanzania would never let the situation deteriorate to the level of eastern Zaire.[162]

The government attempted to separate the "intimidators" from the rest of the refugees, but the efforts fell short due to lack of both funding and will among Tanzanian authorities. One policy involved constructing a separate camp, Mwisa, to contain intimidators, but few militants were sent there.[163] The decision to build a camp rather than prosecute the militants and genocidaires in the courts reflects the ambivalence of the Tanzanian government toward the refugee leaders. As of 1996, Tanzania had not arrested anyone responsible for the genocide.

In theory, Tanzanian refugee law grants the government wide powers in dealing with refugees. At the time of the Rwandan influx, the 1966 Refugee (Control) Act shaped refugee policy. Section 10 of this law allowed detention of any refugees who the authorities deemed were acting in "a manner prejudicial to peace and good order or were prejudicing the relations between the government of Tanzania and any other government."[164] Although the judicial system did not have the capacity to enforce the law in a systematic way, a structure did exist within which to make policy.

Tanzania relied on UNHCR to boost the government's capability in the refugee-populated areas. In western Tanzania, UNHCR funded the deployment of hundreds of police officers, providing incentives, equipment, and training. Early in the crisis Tanzania deployed about 300 police, which it later increased to 500. Even so, insufficient resources meant that the police were woefully overstretched. For example, in Benaco camp thirty Tanzanian officers policed 350,000 refugees.[165] UNHCR set up an unarmed refugee security force called "guardians," which patrolled the camps and adjudicated conflicts among the refugees.

Three factors explain why Tanzania allowed the refugees to enter and then discouraged military activity. These were: 1) positive past experiences with asylum seekers, 2) relatively neutral relationships with the combatants (Hutu and Tutsi), and 3) domestic political pressure to contain the refugees' activity. Tanzania's history as a generous provider of asylum continued in the Rwanda crisis. Since its independence in 1961,

Tanzania had welcomed waves of both Hutu and Tutsi refugees from Rwanda and Burundi. In many cases the state permitted refugees to engage in productive activity and to obtain citizenship as part of the government's development strategy.[166] However, the combination of the Burundi refugee crisis of 1993 and the Rwandan influx strained Tanzania's hospitality to the breaking point.

At the time of the genocide, Tanzania did not have a strong alliance with either Hutu or Tutsi parties in Rwanda. Prunier noted: "Unlike . . . the Zairian government which was involved in a very complicated political game with the remnants of the old Rwandese regime, the Tanzanian government was probably the most neutral and fair of those who were forced to shelter thousands of refugees at the time of the genocide."[167] It was no secret, though, that some Tanzanians, especially those in the western part of the state, felt more sympathy toward the Hutu.[168] Many perceived an ethnic kinship between the Hutu and some Tanzanian groups. Anti-Tutsi sentiment hardened when thousands of long-term Tutsi refugees returned to Rwanda after the RPF victory, taking with them their cattle and other wealth. Tanzanians viewed the Tutsi returnees as ungrateful for the support that had enabled the refugees to integrate into Tanzanian society. Although they strongly opposed the spread of civil war, Tanzanian authorities did not confiscate every weapon or imprison all suspected genocidaires, due in part to some level of sympathy for the Hutu.[169]

On a national level, however, domestic politics provided an impetus for strict treatment of refugees. In 1994, Tanzania was in the process of democratization and elections were approaching. Most voters did not support leniency toward the refugees. In many areas, the refugees far outnumbered the local population and contributed to increased crime, banditry, and environmental degradation. Local leaders resented the burden of the refugee crisis and demanded more resources from the central government. As democratization progressed, refugee policy became subject to political maneuvering and pressures.[170] The refugee issue provided a convenient scapegoat that campaigning politicians used to explain Tanzania's problems.

The accumulation of political, economic, and security threats related to the crisis precipitated the forcible return of the refugees back to Rwanda. Following the massive repatriation from Zaire to Rwanda in November 1996, Tanzania strongly encouraged its own refugee population to leave. In early December, the government (in conjunction with UNHCR) issued an ultimatum ordering the refugees to depart by December 31, 1996. Camp leaders attempted to circumvent the ultimatum by leading the refugees further east into Tanzania, toward Kenya or Malawi. Refugee leaders convinced their charges that they would be executed immediately upon crossing the border to Rwanda. On December 12, 1996, Tanzania deployed soldiers around the camps to force the refugees home and prevent them from moving further east. The soldiers then pushed the refugees out of the Ngara camps toward the border. From Benaco camp, a line of hundreds of thousands of refugees stretched on the twelve-mile highway to the border. Despite the army cordon, aid workers reported that many of the hard-core militants separated from the refugees and continued to move east. In a matter of days, hundreds of thousands of Rwandan refugees returned to their country, ending the perceived threat to regional and local security.[171]

International Humanitarian Aid and Militant Organization

"There were no security problems. We were extremely well organized."

—UNHCR official involved in the Tanzania operation (July 20, 1999)

Unlike Zaire, Tanzania avoided an uncoordinated NGO free-for-all during the crisis. At the beginning of the influx, the Tanzanian government appointed UNHCR to coordinate the humanitarian response. UNHCR approved only a handful of NGOs to work in the camps.[172] Paradoxically, the international humanitarian organizations' bias for imposing order increased the militants' power, enabling the genocidaires to retain their influence over the population.

During the early stages of the refugee emergency, UNHCR and other agencies followed the path of least resistance and allowed the self-proclaimed refugee leaders to organize the camps. An influential evaluation of the crisis confirmed that "initially, most agencies appear to have paid little attention to the genocide, the presence of the militia and the implications for the power structures in the camps."[173] The smooth functioning of the camps had two effects, one intentional and one not. First, the organization efficiently helped the refugees avoid major epidemics, such as the cholera that killed thousands of refugees in Zaire. Second, the camps' organization inadvertently consolidated the power of the genocidal leaders and militia members. These leaders oversaw food distribution and controlled the information passed to the refugees. In some instances, UNHCR actually hired genocidaires to maintain security in the camps, further boosting their power.

Since militant leaders controlled the distribution process, they inflated population figures and misappropriated huge quantities of food. At first aid organizations distributed food for 350,000 refugees. A formal registration in July 1994 adjusted the refugee numbers down to 230,000. This enormous difference in estimated and actual population allowed leaders to divert and sell large amounts of maize and other food. Jaspers reported that "food effectively became a political weapon, which perpetuated the instability that refugees had experienced in Rwanda, and reinforced the power imbalance that caused the conflict."[174]

Later, to counter the power of militant refugee leaders, UNHCR attempted an alternative method of organization when it opened Kitali camp in February 1995. UNHCR organized camp settlement by date of arrival rather than commune, which reduced the power of the traditional leaders. One NGO observer viewed this as a detriment to the "community spirit" of the camp, whereas the UNHCR official who organized Kitali viewed its unique structure as an asset. Even the NGO observer admitted that "ex-leaders/administrators in the camp do exist but according to several sources have lost their power since they do not actually have any power to act." Because it did not rely on militant refugee leaders to coordinate the population, UNHCR never achieved the same level of organization in Kitali as it did in the earlier established camps.[175]

In retrospect, international aid agencies viewed the response to the Tanzanian crisis as a model operation.[176] In making this judgment, aid workers focused on the efficient humanitarian response to the crisis, the avoidance of epidemics, and the absence of visible military elements in the camps. The international aid agencies ignored the political effects of the camp organization and the power ceded to genocidal refugee leaders. There was also an implicit assumption that hidden militarization posed less of a threat than overt military activity. This assumption was due to the fact that hidden militarization posed less of a threat to aid distribution—the main concern of many relief workers—regardless of its effects on regional instability or the spread of civil war. Considering the negative impact of the camp organization, the refugee crisis in Tanzania was not a model operation. Indeed, the Tanzanian camps only appeared in such a favorable light when compared to the bloody mayhem in Zaire.

Overall, the genocidaires and *Interahamwe* militias benefited greatly from the implicit "don't ask, don't tell" policy of the international agencies and NGOs. As long as the militants conducted their activities out of plain sight, the humanitarian aid continued to flow. From the point of view of the aid agencies, the militarization presented few problems since it usually did not directly impinge on aid delivery. Thus, while serving a militarized state in exile, NGO observers—with a limited scope of concern—could claim that "security in the camps is generally good."[177]

Socioeconomic Similarities to Zaire

"It's OK here. We're not hungry."

—Jean Bosco Sarambuye, refugee in Benaco camp, quoted in "Better-Run Camps in Tanzania Threatened by New Influx and Violence," Associated Press (September 2, 1994)

"The urban-style idleness so near the Rwandan border made credible, at least to some refugees, plans to violently retake Rwanda. This was why the militia groups were able to flourish in the camps, at least for a time."

—Tony Waters, NGO worker in Tanzania, *Bureaucratizing the Good Samaritan* (2001)

Like the camps in Zaire, the Tanzanian camps contravened all the UNHCR recommendations regarding location and composition of the camps. From the sprawling camps, refugees could easily walk to the border with Rwanda. Each camp housed many more than the recommended 20,000 inhabitants and each was filled with idle young men. Despite their similar geographic and demographic characteristics, the Tanzanian camps experienced a much lower level of violence than those in Zaire. According to the socioeconomic explanations, one would expect much better living conditions in Tanzania than in Zaire since the refugee situation was much less violent. However, camps in both Zaire and Tanzania experienced relatively good conditions. In general, the camps had better nutrition and mortality figures than neighboring Tanzanian villages.

According to the socioeconomic explanation, the large number of refugees housed in huge border camps created a security threat in Tanzania. The massive camps presented an opportunity for offensive mobilization against the sending state and provided a target for the avenging RPF. Indeed, the influx of Rwandans nearly overwhelmed western Tanzania. As of mid-June 1994, UNHCR estimated that 410,000 Rwandan refugees lived in Ngara and Karagwe districts, where they vastly outnumbered the local population.[178] During the initial influx in Ngara, 200,000 refugees descended on a village of 6,000 Tanzanians.[179] Tanzania managed to prevent this large population from becoming an offensive weapon in the hands of the genocidal leaders.

Like Zaire, the size of the camps varied widely. Ngara district hosted the largest camps, Benaco and Lumasi, which held between 100,000 and 200,000 refugees. Populations in the eleven smaller camps in Ngara and Karagwe districts numbered anywhere from a few hundred to eighty thousand refugees.[180] Although the evidence is not conclusive, the size of the camps did not visibly affect the level of militarization.[181] All the camps fell under the control of the former leaders, regardless of size. But none of the camps served as rear bases for cross-border military activity.

Proponents of the socioeconomic explanations also cite the location of the camps so near the Rwandan border as dangerous. By 1995, 430,000 of the refugees resided in five camps less than 20 miles from the Rwandan border (see map 4.1). This occurred because UNHCR and Tanzania had designated Benaco as a potential refugee site for a Burundian influx—partly because it was considered a safe distance from the Burundi border (over 30 miles). The officials had not considered the possibility of a Rwandan influx. Benaco filled quickly and by June a second site opened at Lumasi, 3 miles away. Kitali was located nearly 50 miles from the border, whereas most of the larger camps were less than 20 miles from Rwanda.[182]

The ease of crossing did not lead to cross-border attacks by Rwanda or the refugees. Clearly, a factor other than camp location caused the violence in Zaire, since Tanzania's border camps remained relatively peaceful. A more significant factor is that Tanzanian border guards were much more effective than their Zairian counterparts. Because of Zaire's weakness and connivance with the Hutu militants, the militants used the border camps as rear bases and the Rwandan government could easily attack the camps.

Information shortages make it difficult to determine the number and proportion of young men among the Rwandan refugees. The UNHCR statistical report covering 1995 omits demographic information on Rwandan refugees in Tanzania.[183] One source claims that the population was not typical of an African society in that the refugees had more teenagers than usual and fewer small children. (Thirteen percent under five years old in one camp, compared to 20 percent in rural Tanzania and Rwanda.)[184] Without better data it is not possible to evaluate the gender balance explanation for Tanzania. There is no suggestion of a drastic shortage of men in the Tanzanian refugee population, however, which suggests that a gender imbalance did not cause the low levels of violence.

According to one socioeconomic explanation for the spread of civil war, material incentives encourage refugees to support military activity. Desperate refugees, especially young men, will become fighters to improve their living conditions. For aid workers, this means that higher levels of assistance can forestall the spread of civil war, regardless of the political motivation of the refugees and potential fighters.

The material incentives explanation would assume that there were terrible living conditions in Zaire and good conditions in Tanzania, since Zaire experienced such high violence and Tanzania did not. Evidence from the camps flatly contradicts that explanation. Once the initial cholera crisis subsided in Zaire, camps in Zaire and Tanzania experienced similar living conditions. In both regions, the refugee camps enjoyed adequate food, shelter, and health care, relatively speaking, due to massive international expenditures.[185] In March 1995, the International Federation of Red Cross and Red Crescent Societies reported that "the general health situation in the [Tanzanian] camps is excellent."[186] Mortality rates in the camps roughly equaled the average mortality rate of 0.5 per 10,000 people per day found in most developing countries.[187]

In theory, Tanzanian law restricted refugees' movement and right to employment; in reality the refugee-populated area provided economic opportunity for both refugees and locals. Like the camps in Zaire, the Tanzanian camps resembled small towns with markets, shops, bars, and other businesses. One observer noted, "Tanzanian hosts established extensive social relations with refugees, particularly in areas close to the camps."[188] In Benaco camp alone, five markets operated, enabling the refugees to supplement the monotonous diet provided by international donors.[189] Refugees produced food, such as bananas and beans, for sale to other refugees and local residents. The charity CARE estimated that over 10,000 hectares of land had been cultivated by refugees as of 1996.[190] Rwandan refugees also provided cheap labor for the local peasants.

In Tanzania, the relatively good living conditions did not blunt the political goals of refugees. Despite the existence of informal employment, markets, agricultural land, and social interaction, refugees continued to attempt military organization. Statements and actions of refugees and their leaders indicated a desire to engage in violence, regardless of the material opportunities in exile. The response of the Tanzanian government to the militants explains the low levels of violence, not material incentives.

Two years into the crisis, aid workers abandoned the idea that better conditions would promote return and reduce violence. One UNHCR official even claimed that refugees resisted repatriation from the Tanzanian camps because conditions there were "better and more secure."[191] In 1996, the Tanzanian government and aid agencies curtailed social services, such as secondary education, in an attempt to encourage repatriation. UNHCR cut food rations from 2000 to 1500 calories/person/day. Some UNHCR officials claimed that "refugees were reluctant to leave the camps as they believed they were leading a more comfortable life there than they could in Rwanda or Burundi."[192]

The evidence does not support aid workers' predictions that lowering rations would lead to widespread violence. One NGO memo pleaded that "to avoid a possible outbreak of mass violence and uncontrollable instability urgent food supplies are needed now." Yet despite several weeks with only half-rations, refugees remained calm and relied on other sources of food within the local economy. Refugees' resistance to repatriation, especially on the part of the leaders, did not change with fluctuations in rations. As the situation in Tanzania became less attractive, resistance to repatriation remained unyielding. Later that year, the Tanzanian army, not economic incentives, finally effected the refugees' return to Rwanda.[193]

Border Battles: Burundian Refugee Insurgents in Tanzania

"Geo-political considerations . . . explain the government of Tanzania's greater tolerance toward the Burundian refugee caseload, and possibly a more ambivalent attitude towards the involvement of this caseload in 'political' activities."

—Jean-Francois Durieux, "Preserving the Civilian Character of Refugee Camps. Lessons from the Kigoma Refugee Programme in Tanzania," *Track Two* (November 2000)

A brief examination of the Burundian refugees in Tanzania emphasizes the importance of the receiving state policy in whether or not civil war spreads. Whereas Tanzania repressed militarization among the Rwandan refugees, the government tacitly accepted the rebel activity based in and around the Burundian camps. Without Tanzanian sympathy, the Burundian rebels, with few resources or external sympathizers, could not have operated so effectively. The different outcomes for the Rwandans and Burundians show that Tanzanian willingness to control the spread of war depended on the political context of the crisis.

Ever since the 1972 genocide in which Tutsi leaders targeted educated Hutu, Tanzania has hosted waves of Burundian refugees fleeing ethnic violence. During the 1990s, two waves of Hutu refugees arrived. In October 1993, Tutsi army officers assassinated the elected president of Burundi, Melchior Ndadaye, a Hutu. Following the assassination, fifty thousand people died in reciprocal massacres between Hutu and Tutsi. To escape ethnic persecution by the Tutsi-led army, 700,000 Burundian Hutu crossed into Rwanda, Tanzania, and Zaire.[194] When the situation in Burundi stabilized in March 1994, most of the refugees returned home. Another large influx of 200,000 Hutu occurred in 1996 after General Pierre Buyoya's coup displaced the elected Hutu government with Tutsi military rule. Despite ongoing mediation led by former Tanzanian President Julius Nyerere and former South African President Nelson Mandela, the conflict remained intractable. Some of the parties signed a peace accord in November 2001, which inaugurated a multiparty transitional government, but the two main armed rebel groups refused to sign.

The origin of the crisis reveals that the Burundian refugees in Tanzania constituted a persecuted refugee group, rather than a state in exile like the Rwandans. The 1993 and 1996 refugee flows stemmed from the brutal ethnic conflicts between Hutu and Tutsi in Burundi in which over 250,000 people died. One refugee described the reason for his flight: "Soldiers came to our village. We heard gunshots. We started running. . . . We passed dead women and children on the way."[195] As a strategy to deny the rebels a sympathetic population base, the Tutsi government corralled Hutu into crowded, unsanitary 'regroupment' camps, causing many civilian deaths. The army also forcibly conscripted Hutu citizens and sent them to the front lines against the rebels. The refugees shared the coalescing experiences of persecution by a Tutsi government. A former UNHCR official observed: "Newly arriving refugees were not only a bitter reminder of the continuing violence in Burundi, they were also rich material for anti-government, anti-Tutsi propaganda."[196] Although the Hutu who left did not do so alongside a defeated army, as the Rwandans did, it was clear that the Hutu rebel leaders encouraged the creation of a large population of refugees, sometimes forcibly.[197]

Statements by refugees made clear that, unlike a state in exile, they did not require a complete victory to return. Their goals of peace, security, and ethnic integration contrasted sharply with the genocidal aims of the Rwandan refugee leaders. The Burundian refugees expressed fear of the Tutsi-dominated army and a desire for stability. One refugee explained his preconditions for return: "If the rebels were integrated in the army, we believe that all of us would be able to repatriate."[198]

Over time, militarized rebel groups and political parties developed within the Burundian refugee camps and enjoyed high levels of refugee support. Some of the groups even gained official recognition during the peace negotiations at Arusha, Tanzania. A number of Hutu parties, including Conseil National de Défense de la Démocratie (CNDD), Palipehutu, Frolina, and Frodebu, conducted illegal meetings in the camps.[199] Political leaders traveled from Burundi to address the refugees and recruit fighters. The parties also enforced a war tax on refugees, either in food or cash.[200] The leaders manipulated information available about Burundi to discourage return, although the situation in Burundi was generally so dire that little propaganda was needed to discourage the refugees.[201]

Despite Tanzania's denials, analysts generally accepted that Hutu rebel groups operated from Tanzanian soil. Privately, UNHCR officials and internal documents admitted that refugees were involved in military activity. The most common activities were military recruitment among the refugees and cross-border raids against the Burundian government.[202] The rebels conducted military activities in the forest and on the Burundi border, evading direct observation by international aid workers. Rebels also entered the camps to rest and recuperate after battle. The refugee camps themselves did not function as military bases, but they were highly politicized. When a UNHCR team assessed the security situation, it found a high level of political activity and meetings.[203] Similarly, an official at the Tanzanian Ministry of Home Affairs admitted that fanatical and extremist parties were meeting "secretly" on Tanzanian soil.[204]

Tanzania and Burundi repeatedly clashed at the border and in diplomatic exchanges. The Burundian government complained that Tanzania allowed militants to use the camps and launch cross-border raids. Burundian President Buyoya warned that "the presence of Burundi refugees in neighboring countries contributes to the creation of social crisis."[205] Tanzania consistently denied any involvement in the rebel activity.[206] The border tensions escalated with each successive attack, including Burundian reprisal raids into Tanzania.[207] Some of the Burundian army's hot pursuit raids killed Tanzanian citizens as well as Burundian refugees. This led to a Tanzanian military buildup on the border and threats of full-fledged war.[208] Extremist Burundian Tutsi groups threatened to bomb refugee camps in Tanzania.[209] Tanzania issued strongly worded threats that any attack on the refugee camps would be considered an attack against Tanzania and would meet with military retaliation.[210]

Tanzania had a history of sympathetic ties with the Burundian refugees dating from the Burundian genocide in 1972 and the subsequent influx of

Hutu refugees escaping the genocide. After the 1972 influx, cross-border attacks occurred between refugees and the Burundian military, including Burundian bombing raids against Tanzanian villages. Unlike the Rwandan Hutu refugees, who were associated with the perpetrators of a genocide, the Burundian refugees were victims of genocide. Ideologically, the Tanzanian government, especially President Julius Nyerere, supported the Hutu position.

The Tanzanian government strongly condemned Buyoya's 1996 coup and pressed successfully for regional economic sanctions against Burundi's new military government. Members of the Tanzanian government initially viewed the Hutu rebellion against Tutsi domination with the same sympathy as they had for African liberation movements of the 1980s.[211] The Tanzanian government did not overtly support the Hutu rebels against Buyoya, but it was common knowledge that political parties operated in the camps and that various rebel groups based in western Tanzania conducted cross-border raids into Burundi. As a former UNHCR official explained, Tanzania "was happy to allow them to exert enough pressure on the Burundi regime so as to force political concessions out of the latter."[212] Another high-ranking UNHCR official confirmed that "Tanzania will go quite far to support an alternative to Buyoya."[213]

Tanzania's need to enhance its international legitimacy through its handling of the refugee crisis conflicted with Tanzania's distaste for Buyoya. The desire for legitimacy was especially acute considering Tanzania's active involvement in the Burundian peace process convened in Arusha, Tanzania. The government wanted to appear capable and neutral regarding both the refugee situation and the peace negotiations. Thus Tanzania did not overtly aid the rebels and ensured that the refugee camps themselves showed no outward signs of militarization.

The strain of the refugee presence—economically, politically, and socially—also contributed to Tanzania's reluctance to support the rebels openly. International and domestic pressure shaped Tanzania's decision to round up thousands of Burundian refugees from villages in 1997 and confine them in camps. The restrictive policies were aimed at silencing the critics from Burundi and elsewhere who accused Tanzania of harboring rebels. The roundups also satisfied domestic complaints that the refugees committed crimes, contributed to environmental degradation, and sucked resources away from Tanzanian citizens.

To control the security situation, Tanzania entered into an agreement with UNHCR whereby UNHCR funded the deployment of nearly 300 police officers in the refugee-populated areas. The security arrangement with UNHCR provided a visible way for the government to demonstrate its commitment to law and order, without requiring much change in the status quo. A former UNHCR official observed that "in practice, the policemen lack time, resources and knowledge to do more than scratch the surface of 'hard' security issues such as military recruitment, subversive propaganda, power struggle between rebel factions or infiltration of combatants."[214] In isolated instances, the Tanzanian authorities seized arms caches in the camps and intercepted new refugee recruits on their way to fight in Burundi. Even when the Tanzanian police arrested suspected militants, they had no formal mechanism to deal with the detainees. In one instance, the police arrested forty-three refugees who had volunteered as rebel fighters. Within days, thirty-two of them had escaped, and the others appeared unlikely to face any charges.[215]

Humanitarian aid to the refugees benefited the militants in a number of ways. Refugee leaders extorted a portion of the income earned by refugee employees of international agencies. A Tanzanian researcher reported that "Refugees who refused [to contribute] were forced to resign from their jobs or false allegations were made against them so that they could be sacked by the agencies employing them and their positions filled by those prepared to make contributions."[216] The political parties, especially CNDD and Palipehutu, forced all refugees to pay a war tax out of their rations. In addition, wounded fighters relied on the health services in the camps to recover from their injuries.[217]

UNHCR publicly ignored the militarization of the refugee-populated area, taking solace in the fact that the refugee camps themselves were not openly militarized. When UNHCR and the government of Tanzania conducted a joint mission to assess the security situation in 1997, they reported no signs of militarization.[218] The assessment mission did not examine the security situation around the camps and limited itself to looking for arms in the camps. The mission ignored issues of military recruitment or rebel political activity (including 'food taxes') within the camps. Those public reports contradict internal UNHCR memos on military activity. Following two rebel raids into Burundi, a UNHCR International Security Liaison Officer in Tanzania surmised that "these raids indicate the existence of a well coordinated political/military organization operating in and around the camps," adding that "it can also be safely assumed that there must be arms hidden around the camps, particularly within the adjoining forests."[219] A UNHCR legal official later emphasized that the role of UNHCR was to maintain the civilian nature of the camps, not to stop the armed attacks on Burundi.[220]

[115]

POLITICAL RESPONSES TO REFUGEE CRISES IN THE GREAT LAKES REGION

The three-way comparison among the Rwandan refugees in Zaire and Tanzania and the Burundian refugees in Tanzania provides a unique study of the conditions under which civil war spreads. In Zaire, the refugee crisis sparked international and civil wars that devastated millions of lives. Among the Rwandans in Tanzania, similar dynamics between the refugees and the sending state did not result in the spread of civil war, largely because of political considerations on the part of the receiving state. By contrast, Tanzania discreetly supported the spread of civil war involving Burundian refugees. In all three crises, the internationally supported refugee camps provided vital resources for the militants.

The political explanation for the spread of the civil war suggests radically different policy prescriptions than those currently championed by governments and aid workers. Ever since the Rwanda crisis, there have been calls to locate camps far from borders, reduce camp size, and demilitarize refugees. The proponents of these policy ideas imply that the problem of refugee-related violence is more logistical in nature than political. Yet the Rwandan refugees in Zaire and Tanzania experienced similar socioeconomic factors but very different levels of political violence—and were forced to behave very differently.

In reality, preventing the spread of civil war in refugee crises necessitates a political response, and sometimes a military one. Disarming refugees and separating soldiers and civilians requires a willing receiving state. Often that state needs significant international assistance to demilitarize a refugee area. Faced with a hostile receiving state, preventing the spread of war would require coercion.

The ideal solution is the rapid arrival of international peacekeepers to disarm refugees and secure the border area. Such a force was not forthcoming in the Rwandan or Burundian crises. The United States sent military forces but restricted their mandate to humanitarian tasks such as organizing clean water supplies for the refugees. An evaluation of the international response commented that "the fact that Western military contingents were in Goma to assist with the relief efforts but were not mandated to address the problem of insecurity in the camps appeared illogical."[221] The abdication by states of any political engagement left aid agencies and NGOs with the task of providing humanitarian aid in a highly politicized and militarized environment. Under such circumstances, international aid had great political significance and increased the military capability of the exiled combatants.

In the Rwandan refugee crisis, especially in Zaire, the political context of the crisis made a mockery of the humanitarian efforts on behalf of the refugees. The aid operations run by NGOs and international agencies served as pawns of Mobutu and the Hutu militants. The blatant militarism and genocidal ambitions of this state in exile shocked the international organizations and governments that were providing assistance. In fact, this state of shock seems to have prevented any evaluation regarding the aggressive goals of the refugee leaders until after the refugees had returned to Rwanda. A UNHCR evaluation of the crisis in 1996 admitted its failure in considering the political context of the refugee crisis: "What was especially lacking in the Rwandan situation was an early assessment of the nature of a refugee caseload which was far from straightforward from the point of view of UNHCR's [protection] mandate."[222] Throughout the crisis, the prevailing attitude from states and humanitarian organizations was a mixture of passivity and willful ignorance of the robust and menacing nature of the Rwandan Hutu state in exile ensconced in the refugee camps.

The crisis also highlights the importance of time as a contributing factor towards militarization. The continuation of the refugee crisis clearly was to the advantage of the Hutu militants in Zaire. This conclusion has important policy implications for the humanitarian groups and states that aid refugees. To start with, militants were able to import weapons, train recruits, and siphon off international humanitarian donations from the relative security of Zaire. Further, the two-year refugee crisis so destabilized the region that an international war broke out. Looking beyond the framework of international humanitarian law (which prohibits forced repatriation) suggests that a rapid return might have reduced the violence that eventually engulfed eastern Zaire.

[5]

Demilitarizing a Refugee Army

BOSNIAN MUSLIM RENEGADE REFUGEES

While ensconced in fetid chicken coops and burned-out buildings, a group of Bosnian Muslim refugees drilled for war in fall 1994. Their target was to recapture their hometown—not from the Serbs but from the Bosnian Muslim government. In fact, the breakaway Muslim faction relied on Serb artillery to defeat the Bosnian government forces. The militant refugees also relied on food, shelter, and medical care provided by international humanitarian organizations.

The story of that ultimately unsuccessful Muslim rebellion against the Sarajevo government is often considered a footnote in the overall history of the war in the former Yugoslavia. In the words of one journalist, it was a "bloody fratricidal sideshow."[1] Although the intra-Muslim conflict defies the conventional wisdom about ethnic conflict, it provides a uniquely helpful look at the spread of civil war in refugee crises.

Under the leadership of charismatic businessman Fikret Abdic, a group of about 25,000 Muslim refugees fled their town, Velika Kladusa in the Bihac pocket, twice during the war in Bosnia. The first refugee crisis occurred in late 1994 when the Bosnian government army defeated Abdic's rebel Muslim forces. That crisis ended in early 1995 when the refugees formed an army to retake their hometown from the Bosnian 5th Corps, which was deployed by the Muslim-led government. When the Bosnian 5th Corps pushed Abdic's supporters out of Bosnia a second time in August 1995, the refugees were unable to mobilize militarily. The refugees either returned home peacefully or were resettled to third countries (see table 5.1).

Table 5.1 Timeline of relevant events in former Yugoslavia

1987–1989		Abdic imprisoned for commercial fraud.
1989		Collapse of the Soviet Union. Abdic released from prison.
1989	November	Abdic wins popular vote in Bosnian election.
1991	June	Slovenia and Croatia secede from Yugoslavia.
	July	War between Serbia and Croatia begins.
1992	March	Bosnia secedes from Yugoslavia.
	April	War in Bosnia begins.
1993	March	Muslim versus Croat fighting.
	September	Abdic declares autonomy from Sarajevo.
1994	March	Muslim and Croat alliance, "Washington Framework Agreement."
	August	First refugee crisis—Bosnian Army expels Abdic group to Batnoga and Turanj.
	December	Refugee army attacks Velika Kladusa with Serb assistance.
1995	July	Formal Croat and Muslim alliance, "Split Declaration."
	August	Second refugee crisis—Bosnian army expels Abdic group to Kuplensko. Krajina Serbs defeated in "Operation Storm."
	November	Dayton Peace Agreement signed.
1996		Most Abdic refugees return home peacefully.

By examining the same population twice within a single conflict, this comparison holds constant many factors associated with the refugee crisis, such as culture, history, and leadership. The motivations of the refugees remained the same throughout, but the capabilities of the refugees changed drastically due to shifts in the political context. The comparison over time demonstrates that the existence of a militant refugee group does not always lead to civil war.

Given the militant motivations of the Abdic state in exile, the deciding factor for the spread of war was the policy of the receiving state. In the first refugee crisis, the refugees allied militarily with their hosts, the Serbs, and proceeded to attack Bosnia. The Serb hosts allowed militarization and encouraged the misuse of international humanitarian aid. In the second crisis, Croatia refused to allow any militarization due to its alliance with the Bosnian government.

Throughout both crises, socioeconomic factors—camp size, camp location, living conditions, and percentage of adult males—remained virtually constant. Thus, those factors cannot explain the lack of war in the second crisis. The one socioeconomic difference was that in the second crisis the refugees had better long-term alternatives. Thus, many militants resettled abroad or integrated into Croatian society. This suggests that socioeconomic explanations should focus less on immediate camp conditions and more on viable long-term alternatives for refugees.

Development of the Muslim Rebellion

"Alija Izetbegovic is the biggest Muslim fundamentalist. Fikret Abdic is the best economist and smartest man."

—Refugee, quoted in "Bosnian Army Takes Control in Rebel Pocket," *Christian Science Monitor* (August 24, 1994)

The breakup of the Soviet empire, and the resulting insecurity, contributed to political upheaval and ethnic tension in Yugoslavia after 1989. In 1991, Slovenia and Croatia seceded from Yugoslavia, citing fears of Serb domination of the federation. Their secessions and the perceived mistreatment of the Serb minority in Croatia led to war between Serbs and Croats. In the multiethnic state of Bosnia, wedged between Serbia and Croatia, the majority Muslims felt threatened by the Serb-dominated Yugoslav federation. Against the wishes of Bosnian Serbs, the state government decided to secede from Yugoslavia in 1992. Over the course of the ensuing war, Croatians and Muslims alternately fought each other and allied against the Serb forces. Within the Croat-Muslim-Serb hostility, a small intra-Muslim conflict emerged in northwest Bosnia. This chapter examines the refugees created by that rebellion against the Sarajevo government.

The war created millions of refugees and internally displaced persons. At the height of the displacement crisis, the United States Committee for Refugees (USCR) estimated that "fully half of Bosnia's pre-war population was dead or uprooted."[2] Most refugees did not live in camps but were either privately housed or accommodated in collective centers—schools, hotels, army barracks, and so on.[3] The vast majority of refugees did not engage in military activity while receiving humanitarian assistance.[4] An exception to that pattern was the group of refugees from Velika Kladusa who formed an army while benefiting from UNHCR support.

The town of Velika Kladusa, Fikret Abdic's power base, is nestled in the far northwest corner of Bosnia, in the Bihac region (see map 5.1). After World War II, Bihac was one of the poorest areas in Yugoslavia. Abdic transformed the region into a highly profitable industrial center. Through his company, Agrokomerc, he controlled virtually every aspect of the economy. His empire included local television and radio stations, which proved to be invaluable resources in the war against the Sarajevo government.[5] By providing lucrative employment and a high standard of living, the charismatic Abdic secured the undying loyalty of most of the inhabitants of Bihac, especially those in Velika Kladusa.[6]

In what had seemed a permanent defeat, Abdic spent two years in prison under investigation for commercial crime until his release in 1989.[7] The temporary lack of resources slowed his rise to power but not his popularity. A resilient politician and businessman, Abdic bounced back from prison and bankruptcy to become one of the ten members of the Bosnian presidency in 1991. He actually won more votes than any candidate in Bosnia in the 1991 regional elections. A still-unexplained intraparty deal gave the presidency to Alija Izetbegovic, however.[8]

Observers agree that the residents of Velika Kladusa treated Abdic "like a god" and "were ready to do whatever he said."[9] One vivid image captures the reverence in which his followers held him. After his release from prison in 1989, Abdic desired a triumphal entry into Velika Kladusa. During his return from incarceration supporters lined the main road, chanting "Babo, Babo" ("Daddy, Daddy"). As his white Mercedes car entered town, supporters slaughtered an ox in the road. Perhaps prophetically, Abdic's convoy arrived home splashed in ceremonial blood.[10]

In order to understand the dynamics of the later violence, it is necessary to trace the political and military relationships built by Abdic before the war. When war broke out between Serbia and Croatia in 1991, Abdic's political and economic fortunes were governed by the complex political connections he had forged with the belligerents. Journalist Emma Daly reported: "The Abdic empire, built around Agrokomerc, depended on a dangerous and delicate web of trade links, involving Croatia (which gave Mr. Abdic a free port in Rijeka), its Serbian enemies in Knin, the Bosnian Serb army besieging fellow Muslims in the Bihac pocket, and Belgrade."[11] That history of dealmaking stood him in good stead during the Serb siege of Bihac in 1993. Although other parts of the enclave starved, residents of Velika Kladusa survived on smuggled and black market food. As always, "Babo" took care of his own.

By spring 1992, the Bihac pocket was surrounded on four sides by hostile forces—the breakaway Republic of Serb Krajina (carved out of Croatian territory) to the west and north, Bosnian Serbs to the south and east. Serb-held Croatia included the Krajina area. The Serb-held areas hosted a United Nations Protection Force (UNPROFOR), which renamed them United Nations Protection Areas (UNPAs). UNPA South and North bordered the Bihac region (see map 5.1). The poorly armed

5th Corps of the Bosnian army was stranded in the pocket, unable to defend Bihac in case of attack. A French battalion arrived as part of UNPROFOR in February 1993 but its mandate was limited.[12]

Two reasons explain the continued existence of Bihac under Muslim control, despite its vulnerable position. The large size of the enclave deterred the Serbs from attack for fear of heavy losses. Secondly, as Tim Judah has described, "too many people were making too much money out of it to want it snuffed out." Despite a Serb blockade, the Bosnian 5th Corps successfully fought its way out of the Bihac pocket for a brief period in 1994. Judah also claimed that the secret of the Bosnians' strength was that "the Bosnian Serbs themselves . . . had sold the 5th Corps a good part of its weaponry." The Krajina Serbs even sent food into Abdic's territory for processing by Agrokomerc.[13]

Abdic loyalists managed to profit from both UNHCR and the UNPRO-FOR battalion. When UNHCR ran short of vehicles, it hired eleven trucks and local drivers from Abdic. In February 1993, that scheme ended in embarrassment when Serbs stopped the trucks at a checkpoint and found 700,000 Deutsche Marks hidden in the door of the trucks.[14] Some UNHCR officials suspected that Abdic used the humanitarian convoys to import contraband for a huge profit, but they were never able to confirm this. Abdic also ran his own for-profit convoy by importing food from Zagreb using French military trucks. In an unorthodox bargain, Abdic traded storage space in Agrokomerc warehouses to the United Nations in exchange for UNPROFOR escorts of Abdic's imports.[15]

Some observers speculate that both Croatia and the Serbs tried to use Abdic to meet their own, conflicting, goals. Silber and Little reported that "for the Serbs, Bihac was the missing link needed to join Serb-held land in Croatia and Bosnia to Serbia itself, which is what Croatia wanted to avoid at all costs."[16] Abdic cooperated with both sides, safeguarding his position of power in Bihac. Unconfirmed stories that Abdic was providing intelligence about the Serb positions to the Croatian government could explain Croatian tolerance for Abdic's behavior and his easy acquisition of Croatian citizenship.[17] For tactical reasons, the Croatian government needed Bihac in "friendly" hands during the war.

The war between the Croatians and the Bosnian Muslims in 1993 greatly advanced Abdic's own position and may have spurred him to declare the Autonomous Province of Western Bosnia in September of that year. After the declaration, two brigades of the Bosnian Army 5th Corps defected with Abdic—roughly 2,500 soldiers—but the rest of the Bosnian army now targeted Abdic as a dangerous enemy.[18] A few months after the declaration of autonomy, the Washington Framework Agreement

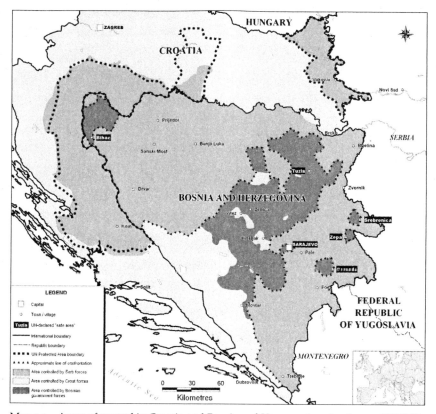

Map 5.1   Areas of control in Croatia and Bosnia and Herzegovina, April 1995. UNHCR, *State of the World's Refugees* (Oxford: Oxford University Press, 2000), 223. Modified by the author.

of March 1994 enforced an alliance on the Bosnian Muslims and Bosn-ian Croats (and their allies, the Croatian government). At least officially, the breakaway Muslim enclave lost Croatia as a source of support.

Prior to Abdic's secession, the area of Bihac contained about 200,000 people.[19] Roughly 50,000 lived in the northern part and were fiercely loyal to Abdic. Further south, loyalty to Sarajevo trumped support of Abdic.[20] Only the northern part of the pocket followed Abdic in the declaration of autonomy. The declaration divided neighbors, even families. The stated reason for secession stressed the radicalization and Islamic fundamental-ism of Sarajevo. Abdic claimed he just wanted to follow western capital-ism free from ideological restrictions. He declared that the enclave enjoyed a more natural linkage with Zagreb than with the rest of Bosnia. As an autonomous territory, he planned to continue dealing with both

[123]

Croats and Serbs. Abdic followers claimed that they enjoyed better food and drink in his army. In addition to practical and self-interested reasons to support Abdic, refugees felt strong loyalty to their leader. After interviewing hundreds of the Abdic refugees, a UNHCR official confirmed that "people had enormous trust in him."[21]

Abdic's defection left the remainder of Bihac in dire straits. The 5th Corps fought on four fronts, with no hope of reinforcements. Starvation loomed because the agricultural industries required imported raw materials in order to produce food. Until the 1993 declaration of autonomy, some aid had arrived by convoy to the southern part of Bihac. After August 1993, Abdic and the Serbs blocked all aid to the beleaguered south. As UNHCR sources reported, "the Bihac pocket, where until recently activities ran very smoothly, has become another source of serious concern: local authorities in Velika Kladusa informed UNHCR and UNPROFOR that convoys would not be allowed into the area before 4 December [1993]."[22]

The Bosnian Army launched an offensive against Abdic on June 10, 1994, in a desperate attempt to break the blockade on southern Bihac. As UNHCR described, "both sides reportedly impressed civilians into their armed forces, and detained others whose sympathies were suspect (many families have members on both sides of the conflict)."[23] Daly reported that the Croatian government, pushed into an alliance with Bosnia, "regretfully sacrificed Mr. Abdic—and his cash."[24] With a force of 20,000 soldiers, the 5th Corps overran Velika Kladusa after Abdic refused to recant his declaration of autonomy.[25]

A RENEGADE STATE IN EXILE, 1994–1995

"When we left Velika Kladusa last August, we did not flee. . . . We only tactically withdrew to avoid fighting and destruction."

—Refugee, quoted in "Rebel Muslims: Fighting for Return," *Associated Press* (November 27, 1994)

"A sizeable portion of the Abdic exiles . . . fled in uniform with arms."

—Carol J. Williams, "Muslim's Drive for Fiefdom Ends in Chaos," *Los Angeles Times* (August 10, 1994)

The Abdic supporters who escaped the Bosnian Army constituted a state-in-exile refugee group. Unlike most refugee populations, the group fled as an organized political entity in the face of impending military defeat. The crisis was engineered not by the victorious Bosnian government forces but by the retreating rebel leaders. The rebels used the refugee crisis as a strategic escape that allowed them to regroup for battle. Consistent with the group's status as a state in exile, the refugees refused to return home peacefully, despite credible guarantees of safety, as long as the Bosnian government remained in power. In the refugee camps, the militant leaders openly prepared to fight and used international humanitarian assistance as a resource of war.

By August 21, 1994, over 25,000 people had fled Velika Kladusa in front of the advancing Bosnian Army, creating a stream of refugees that stretched for thirty miles.[26] They traveled in cars, buses, and tractors, bringing along herds of cattle and dozens of horses. Individual motives for flight varied, but observers agree that political leaders orchestrated the refugee movement. During the exodus, UNHCR observed that Abdic's supporters "sought to pressure others to leave, and are pressuring them not to return. They exercise effective control over the camps. There are those who fled fearing for their lives as the [Bosnian] army advanced, often reacting to false rumors spread by the first group, a propaganda campaign that began well before the final advance. Others, as witnessed by UNHCR, did not want to flee but were pressured to do so. And there were those who had long intended to leave and saw this as an opportunity."[27]

The receiving "state" for the refugees' first exile was the Republic of Serb Krajina, Croatian territory that had been seized by the Serbs. The Krajina was nominally under the protection of the United Nations and was known as a United Nations Protected Area (UNPA). A demilitarized no man's land separated the Serb-controlled territory from Croatia.

The refugees ended up in two locations, both in Serb-held Krajina (see map 5.2). To the west, about 16,000 people stopped at Batnoga, a disused chicken farm owned by Abdic, only a few miles from Velika Kladusa. To the east, 7,000 refugees went to Staro Selo, an area of open ground. UNHCR reported that after three or four days, "just as assistance was becoming organized, these refugees moved to Turanj at the instigation of the local authorities and Abdic followers, who were encouraging the refugees to force an entry into Croatia proper, and preventing some from returning home." Twenty-five hundred refugees traveled directly to Turanj, bypassing Staro Selo.[28]

As the refugees moved north, the Croatian government stopped them at Turanj, a destroyed, heavily mined area between the front lines of Croatia and Serb-held Krajina. Turanj was a depopulated strip of land

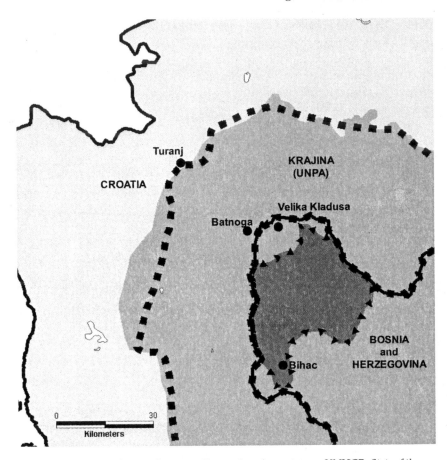

Map 5.2 Velika Kladusa and surrounding region, August 1994. UNHCR, *State of the World's Refugees* (Oxford: Oxford University Press, 2000), 223. As modified by author.

a few miles wide that had been demilitarized when UNPROFOR negotiated a pull back between Serb and Croatian forces. The Serbs allowed
the refugees into Turanj at their checkpoint. On their side, Croatian
police blocked the border with armored personnel carriers and water
cannon, trapping the refugees in the no man's land and crushing
Abdic's hopes of reaching Croatian territory.[29]

In addition to the political desire to gain international attention, pragmatic considerations governed the direction of the refugees' flight. Serb-
held Krajina was not the refugees' first choice for an asylum area. As
former migrant workers in Croatia, many of the refugees knew they
would find better economic opportunities there. Serb-held Krajina, on

the other hand, was practically without water or electricity and suffered 90 percent unemployment. However, the refugees found themselves stuck in Krajina.

The refugees' utter reliance on Abdic's propaganda encouraged hardline attitudes toward return. As one refugee explained, "We all would rather go home, but not without our Babo."[30] Another refugee confirmed, "All the people want to go home—but only under Abdic. . . . There is no other option whatsoever."[31] Since the Bosnian government considered Abdic a dangerous traitor, a peaceful return with him was not a feasible option. UN negotiators, pressing Abdic to support return, reported, "all talks on the political level with leaders of the refugees have been unsuccessful so far."[32] Negotiators sensed that Abdic and his allies were willing to hold out for a long-term political solution, using humanitarian aid to support the refugees indefinitely. Refugees claimed that they would return if UNPROFOR controlled Bihac and installed Abdic as head of state.[33]

According to UNHCR reports, refugees had few alternatives other than to go along with Abdic's plan: "The likely level of political manipulation against return was so high that a free and informed choice on their future might be impossible in these circumstances."[34] Abdic's strategy was to keep the refugees concentrated. He wanted to force entry into Croatia and used the international attention on the terrible conditions in Turanj to embarrass Croatia. A few refugees managed to escape to live with relatives in Croatia, and UNHCR resettled nine families who did not want to fight with Abdic. In order to protect those refugees from retaliation, UNHCR had to spirit them out of the camp.[35]

Throughout the crisis, refugee leaders rejected the UN plans for repatriation; instead they organized for a military comeback in their hometown. During the time that the refugees prepared for a military return, it was difficult to determine the extent of their access to weapons. The refugees entered the camp with some small arms but stored heavy weapons, including six fifty-year-old Soviet-built tanks donated by the Serbs outside the camp in Serb-held territory. One press report described "Serbian soldiers . . . standing over a huge pile of assault rifles and other military detritus turned over by Abdic's fleeing troops."[36] Later, the refugees were able to buy additional weapons from the Serbs to facilitate the return to Velika Kladusa.[37] Observers noted that young men were recruited from the camp but trained in Serb-held territory. UNHCR was unable to disarm the refugees or control their movements between the camp and Serb-held Krajina.[38]

In the second week of November 1994, the refugees and their Serb allies prepared to advance on Bihac and fight the Bosnian 5th Corps, led by General Atif Dudakovic. UNHCR reported that Abdic and the Serb police "began mobilizing draft age men in the camps to participate in the offensive." Despite UN protests, Abdic mobilized an estimated 10,000 refugee men.[39] The Abdic/Serb offensive began in December 1994. The refugees attacked Bihac using the camps as a rear base. With Serb support, the refugee army attacked the 5th Corps from the rear, opening a second front in the battle.[40] The besieged enclave was weakened by the continued blockade of aid convoys. By early 1995, the refugee army, relying on Serb logistics, had regained control of Velika Kladusa. With invaluable Serb assistance, Abdic reestablished the front line at its July 1994 position. Over a period of five days, Batnoga and Turanj camps emptied their refugees, who returned to Velika Kladusa in the same buses that had carried them out.[41]

Demilitarizing a Refugee Army, 1995

Eight months later, in August 1995, Abdic's followers fled Velika Kladusa for a second time as a state in exile. This time, the Croatian army had completely defeated the Krajina Serbs, which changed the equation in favor of the refugees returning home peacefully. As Misha Glenny wrote, "as soon as the Krajina Serbs were attacked by the Croats, Abdic's defenses collapsed."[42] The loss of their patron Serbs, combined with Croatian reliance on American support (which mandated an alliance with Sarajevo), left the Velika Kladusa refugees no opportunity to engage in political violence. The political shifts weakened Abdic's influence in the region, even though his people remained fiercely loyal. Eventually, most refugees returned home peacefully, while the remaining hardline militants were resettled abroad.

After he retook Velika Kladusa in early 1995, Abdic's continued manipulation of humanitarian assistance led to further conflict with the Bosnian Army 5th Corps. UNHCR relied on Krajina Serb cooperation to reach the Bosnian-held Bihac pocket, but the Serbs required the convoys to detour through Velika Kladusa in order to benefit Abdic.[43] He and his Krajina Serb allies repeatedly denied clearance to UN convoys destined for the starving residents of Bihac, which was under Bosnian government control. As the only entrance for the convoys passed through Abdic-controlled territory, UNHCR depended completely on Abdic, even though the organization complained that he "was demanding a larger allocation of aid going into [Velika Kladusa] than UNHCR considered justified." In many cases, UNHCR agreed to provide Abdic with a large portion of the aid in order to secure clearance. In March 1995, after months of frustrated attempts to assist Bihac residents and beleaguered Bangladeshi peacekeepers, UNHCR cut food aid to Krajina Serbs and Abdic's enclave. The food ban lasted about 10 days, until Abdic and the Serbs agreed to allow convoys to reach Bihac.[44]

At the end of July 1995, Abdic and Krajina Serb troops launched an offensive on southern Bihac and made significant gains. The Croatian government, while sympathetic to Abdic, did not want Bihac to fall to the Serbs. The Croatians and the Bosnian Muslims had agreed in the "Split Declaration" of July 1995 to unite in repelling Serb aggression. Once again, larger political interests overruled Croatian sympathy for Abdic (and the desire to do business with him).[45]

The Croatian Army began an offensive to retake Serb-held Krajina in the summer of 1995. "Operation Storm" first attacked Serb forces in Krajina (UNPA North and South).[46] The offensive lasted two or three days in the South and a bit longer in the North. When Krajina collapsed, the Croatians crossed into Bosnia and, with the Bosnian 5th Corps, advanced on Abdic's position. In the face of certain defeat, Abdic quickly surrendered and his followers fled north out of their hometown.

The refugees crossed the border into the Krajina just after the Serbs fled and before the Croatians established border guards. Croatian Special Police stopped the 25,000 refugees on the road near the village of Kuplensko, only twelve miles from the Bihac border. The Croatians established a checkpoint and fenced in the area, as thousands of people set up camp on a stretch of roadside of less than three miles. The whole situation was very chaotic since the territory had just been liberated from the Serbs and 150,000 Serbs had been driven out of the Krajina (UNPA North and South).[47] Croatian police did not completely disarm the refugees but effectively prevented the group from entering any further into Croatia or engaging in military activity. Croatian police also forcibly repatriated at least fifty refugees after a violent confrontation within the camp.[48]

Despite the changed political circumstances, UNHCR still found it difficult to communicate with the refugees due to the strength of Abdic's propaganda. The refugee leaders accused the United Nations of bias when it tried to distribute accurate information. The hard-core leaders, about five hundred of them, controlled the camp and violently discouraged attempts to return or speak to outsiders. The refugees made decisions based on the incomplete and biased information provided by Abdic and his supporters.[49]

The majority of the refugees stayed in Kuplensko from August to December 1995. As winter approached, UNHCR focused on repatriating people from the ill-equipped camp. Refugee militants stopped the first group of returnees by surrounding the bus and threatening to blow it up. Croatian police accompanied later buses with a convoy of five cars to deter intimidation.[50]

Refugees began to return home when the influence of their leaders weakened. Once he lost Serb backing, Abdic lacked the capability to mobilize an army to retake Velika Kladusa. The signing of the Dayton Peace Accords in November 1995 further weakened Abdic's position. Within Kuplensko, Abdic maintained the loyalty of the refugees but was unable to capitalize on that loyalty as he had done in 1994. Without the assistance of the Krajina Serbs, who had armed the refugees and policed the camps, Abdic's henchmen could not compel unswerving obedience from the refugees for any extended period of time. Some of Abdic's leaders left the camps because they had connections in Croatia or Germany. A UNHCR official reported that others were recruited into the Croatian army into "key positions." In general, people became discouraged and desired return. The presence of the Croatian police finally put an end to intimidation against return by Abdic supporters.[51]

By June 1996, between ten and fifteen thousand refugees had repatriated peacefully to Velika Kladusa. Women, children, and the elderly usually returned first. Once they reported that the situation was safe, the former soldiers returned to their families. Few violent incidents were reported, although the returnees did face some harassment by political opponents and local police.[52] Five thousand hard-core followers of Abdic remained at Kuplensko, refusing to return. UNHCR admitted that those refugees saw "the camp, which was very close to the border with [Bosnia]—as an effective base for recruiting DNZ (Abdic) party support."[53] As one UNHCR official recalled, "they were a difficult bunch of people."[54]

In order to break the political organization of the refugees living perilously near the Bosnian border, Croatia relocated the remaining refugees. The refugee leaders, showing their clout, refused to relocate unless ensured of the refugees' right to vote in the 1996 Bosnian elections.[55] Once the United Nations negotiated voting rights, many refugees went to Gasinci camp in eastern Croatia. They lived in a former army barracks while awaiting resettlement to third countries. Croatian authorities transferred about 1,200 of the refugees to Obonjan collective center on a rocky, desolate island.[56] Both locations allowed the government to limit the refugees' movements and contacts with possible militants in Velika Kladusa.

After the war, Abdic did not return with his followers to Velika Kladusa, since he faced certain arrest by the Sarajevo government on war crimes charges. Instead he found refuge in Croatia, which refused to extradite him to Bosnia. Abdic continued his opposition to the Sarajevo government and regularly called for its overthrow from his radio station, Velkaton.[57]

Despite the refugees' peaceful return home, intracommunal tensions occasionally flared in Velika Kladusa after the war ended. The Islamic Community of Velika Kladusa issued a *fatwa* against Abdic followers, branding them as heretics. Isolated incidents of violence occurred between government supporters and Abdic followers. Remarkably, Abdic loyalists continued to wait patiently for his victorious return from exile.[58]

Abdic's fortunes took a turn for the worse in summer 2001 when Croatian authorities confined him to the Rijeka prison to await trial for war crimes. After the downfall of Croatian President Tudjman, Abdic lost many of his allies in the government. The Croatian court found him guilty in July 2002 and sentenced him to 20 years in prison. Ever resilient, Abdic announced that he planned to lead his campaign for membership in Bosnia's collective presidency from prison. Despite a strong turnout in Velika Kladusa, Abdic won only one percent (nearly 5,000 votes) in the election.[59]

SAME TERRITORY—TWO RECEIVING STATES

In both crises the refugees fled to the area of Croatia called the Krajina. But this territory changed hands between the first and second refugee crises. The first time the territory was controlled by Serbs, who had taken it from the Croatians and called it the "Republic of Serb Krajina." By the second crisis, the Croatian government had retaken the Krajina. The different political contexts in the Krajina radically changed the refugees' ability to militarize. The Krajina Serbs had the capability and the willingness to encourage the militarization of the refugees. The Serbs and the Abdic refugees shared a history of economic cooperation and the goal of defeating the Bosnian government. When the refugees came to the Krajina the second time, in 1995, the political context was entirely different. The Croatians had routed the Serbs, the Bosnian army had expelled Abdic's forces, and the Americans were pressing for a settlement along the new battle lines. The Abdic forces—now friendless—were no match for the Croatian Special Police. Although the refugees still clung to their militaristic goals, they had no way to achieve them.

In the first crisis, the Krajina Serbs exercised strict control over the camps. Unlike the Croatian government, however, the Serbs used their power to encourage political violence and shield the refugees from international interference. Abdic's planned offensive against the Bosnian army required the active support of the Krajina Serbs. The Serbs also prevented UNHCR or any other external force from disarming the refugees. The Krajina Serbs ostensibly protected the refugees, but also restricted their movement and access to information. Serb and Abdic police guarded the camps in a joint effort to control the inhabitants.[60]

The Serbs aided the militant refugees for a number of military, political, and economic reasons. Most importantly, the refugees provided a military advantage to the Krajina Serbs in the Serbian war against the Bosnian Muslim government. The Serbs outgunned the Bosnian Muslims but faced a severe disadvantage in the infantry because Serb forces stretched across an impossibly long front-line through Bosnia and Croatia. The Bosnian 5th Corps had between 14,000 and 20,000 soldiers in Bihac.[61] Abdic's ability to raise an army of 10,000 men complemented the needs of the Serb forces, which were more than willing to provide artillery support. The close economic ties between Abdic and the Serbs before and during the war also facilitated their military cooperation.

In addition to the "Republic of Serb Krajina" quasi-state, there was also another entity that could claim authority in the 1994 refugee crisis—UNPROFOR. The UN Security Council authorized UNPROFOR in February 1992 and charged it with maintaining demilitarization in Serb-occupied Croatia. In theory, UNPROFOR controlled the Krajina Serb territory. The Bosnian government was galled by the fact that the attacks on Bihac came from Muslim rebels who were operating out of UN-controlled territory. Rasim Delic, commander of the General Staff of the Bosnia-Herzegovina army, complained, "Bihac is being attacked not from Bosnia-Herzegovina but from the UNPROFOR territories in Croatia that should have been under the control of the blue berets."[62] The passivity of the UN forces in the face of the military activity in this so-called demilitarized zone marginalized the role of UNPROFOR in the conflict.

By contrast, Croatia demonstrated a hard line against the refugees from the beginning of the first crisis in 1994. In the first refugee crisis, Croatia refused to allow the refugees to move from the Krajina no man's land to Croatia proper. At the time of the refugee exodus, Croatia and Bosnia were trying to patch up their split. When Bosnia defeated Abdic in 1994, the United States and Germany pressured Croatia to remain loyal to Sarajevo. Despite Croatian sympathy for Abdic, he was still a relatively minor player in the war. Politically, Croatia could not risk international support and the alliance with Sarajevo for the sake of Abdic's 25,000 refugees.[63]

In the second crisis, Croatia possessed both the ability and the willingness to secure the camp. Croatian Special Police guarded the makeshift camp at Kuplensko and restricted the movement of the refugees, not hesitating to shoot at escapees. Although combatants lived among the refugees, they were too afraid of the Croatians to organize. Former soldiers removed their uniforms and tried to blend in with the other refugees. Only their combat boots gave away their military status.[64] The police also forcibly repatriated some of the men to Bihac. UNHCR reported that its efforts to winterize the Kuplensko camp were hampered by the "extremely strict control imposed by the Croatian Special Police."[65] Croatia's willingness and capability to prevent the spread of civil war determined the relatively peaceful outcome of the second crisis.

HELPLESS AND PASSIVE HUMANITARIANS

International humanitarian assistance benefited the Abdic state in exile three ways.[66] First, and most obvious, the humanitarian organizations provided food, shelter, and medical care directly to active combatants. Abdic's forces numbered up to 10,000 and they quartered in the camps while preparing for war. This meant they received the benefit of medical care for war wounds and other life-sustaining support.

Secondly, the humanitarian assistance also freed the militants from the burden of supporting their dependents. Although Abdic styled himself the leader of his people, once in exile he did not provide the goods and services that a state provides its citizens. Instead, international humanitarian organizations provided the infrastructure, poor though it may have been, that sustained the Abdic followers.

Thirdly, the presence of international humanitarian organizations imparted legitimacy to Abdic's movement. The establishment of refugee camps transformed the defeated, retreating army into a population of so-called victims. The mixing of civilians and fighters obscured the reality that the refugees constituted a belligerent state in exile. Paradoxically, the humanitarian organizations had an interest in presenting the Abdic group as needy refugees. Publicizing the presence of 10,000 soldiers among the refugees would have damaged the legitimacy of the relief program in the eyes of potential donors.[67]

The humanitarian aid operation also enabled Abdic to bolster his legitimacy among his followers, in addition to the wider international audience. For example, during the first exile when the United Nations set up a food distribution center for humanitarian aid, the refugee leaders hung a huge billboard of Abdic's face over the food tables. The refugees were meant to assume that it was Abdic, not the United Nations, who was taking care of their needs.[68]

The Abdic crises revealed two problems in the refugee-relief regime. The first problem was the lack of control over the issue of militarization among the refugees. UNHCR and other United Nations actors had no power to disarm or coerce the refugees during the Abdic crises. In each situation, the humanitarian organizations had to work within the constraints imposed by the receiving state policy. The second problem was the narrow way in which humanitarian organizations viewed their responsibilities. UNHCR ignored militant activity that occurred outside of the camps and refused to address the fact that humanitarian aid was sustaining Abdic's refugee army. In this way, the humanitarian organizations perpetuated their own helplessness.

During the initial refugee crisis in 1994, the international presence had neither the mandate nor the capability to prevent militarization of the refugees. UN personnel powerlessly observed as uniformed Serbs and Abdic leaders drafted people in the camps. Serbs positioned their artillery very close to the Batnoga camp, near the Bihac border. UNHCR protested but could not compel a halt to the militarization.[69] When wounded refugee men entered Turanj, UN personnel could not ascertain how or where they had been wounded.[70] In vain, UNHCR appealed to the Serbs to ensure that "the refugees receive objective information, have a free choice on return, are not subject to manipulation, and do not engage in acts incompatible with their status."[71]

Abdic relied on propaganda to obscure the UN message in a number of ways. With Serb support, Abdic broadcast to the refugees from his radio station Velkaton in nearby Vojnic.[72] A UNHCR spokesman complained of an "orchestrated campaign to prevent refugees getting independent analyses of the situation in Kladusa."[73] The relationship between Abdic and the refugees ensured that they trusted implicitly the information produced by his radio station. International organizations could not develop such a high level of trust, as refugees suspected outside information as biased.

Despite the refugees' intransigence, UNHCR pressured both the Bosnian government and the leaders of Serb-held Krajina to facilitate a return of the refugees. The Sarajevo government agreed to offer an amnesty to the refugees and a six-month respite from military service. UNHCR reported difficulty communicating the Bosnian government's amnesty offer because "the climate of intimidation and the scope for the leadership to manipulate and interpret to the refugees both information and events required caution."[74]

On October 1, 1994, the Krajina Serbs agreed to allow distribution in the Turanj camp of a UNHCR note explaining the amnesty offer. The letter, dated September 30, 1994, reminded refugees of their duties under international law: "We also need you to understand that refugees must not engage in any hostile acts against either the authorities in their home country or those where they are refugees." The note ended with the plea, "Please remember that UNHCR is a humanitarian organization, with no political objectives."[75] UN workers were unprepared for the violent reaction to the note. Aid workers recounted that "distribution started peacefully with the refugees reading the note, but then the situation rapidly degenerated, as some refugees violently objected to the contents of the note, which they prevented others from reading."[76] Abdic's supporters protested the note's condemnation of the military preparations for return and the suggestion by the United Nations that a peaceful return to Bihac—interpreted as surrender to the Bosnian government—was possible. Angry refugees flipped over UN Civilian Police cars, and UNHCR workers hid in fear for their lives. Polish UN troops quelled the riot by firing in the air, wounding two refugees.[77]

Although UNHCR tried to ignore the military activity involving refugees, it could not credibly claim ignorance of the overt militarization in 1994. The refugees arrived at Turanj and Batnoga as a retreating fighting force. Since the receiving state abetted the militarism, UNHCR faced the difficult decision of providing aid to the militants or depriving nonmilitant refugees of assistance. There is no evidence of debate over this issue within UNHCR, rather the agency immediately provided assistance to the refugees despite their status as a militant state in exile.

The situation of Turanj camp highlights how narrowly the humanitarian agencies perceived their mandate. Based in Turanj, militant refugees stored mortars and artillery with the Krajina Serbs and then crossed to Turanj to sleep and eat with their families. UNHCR observers claimed that Turanj camp posed no security problem because there were no arms in the camps, even as one official admitted, "the Serb territory was the depot."[78] From the point of view of the beleaguered Bosnian 5th Corps in Bihac, of course, the location of the arms in the camp or on the borders was a purely academic distinction. The end result—an internationally supported refugee army—was the same.

As in Turanj and Batnoga, UNHCR lacked any means to disarm or control the refugees in Kuplensko during the second exile. The only military support extended to UNHCR was the UN Military Liaison Officer (UNMLO). The UNMLO acted purely in an advisory capacity. The officer could explain to UNHCR about the capability of certain weapons or how, in theory, military maneuvers might be carried out. Any disarmament procedures relied on voluntary compliance and brought in few weapons.[79] Because of strict Croatian policing, however, the refugees did not engage in military activity in Kuplensko.

MINEFIELDS AND CHICKEN COOPS: SOCIOECONOMIC EXPLANATIONS

"The situation for the Abdic refugees was much worse than for the average refugee in Croatia."

—Tanvir Shahzada, UNHCR official (July 1998)

"The people say they don't care what kind of conditions they are living in as long as they don't have to go back."

—ICRC official Michael Frey quoted "Babo's Lost Tribe Is on the Road to Nowhere," *The Independent*, Aug. 24, 1995.

Current explanations for the spread of conflict in refugee crises focus on the socioeconomic aspects of the refugee situation. Proponents of these explanations argue that large camps—over 30,000 inhabitants—are more prone to violence and are more difficult to control. They also argue that camps near the border of the sending state create instability because of the ease of border crossing. A third argument is that a disproportionate number of men in the population will increase levels of violence, especially if the men are young and bored. Finally, poor living conditions are thought to induce political violence, as refugees find no other means to improve their situation.[80]

None of the socioeconomic explanations explain the militarization and subsequent demilitarization of the Abdic refugees. For the most part, socioeconomic characteristics remained constant throughout both crises. The camps were small and located near the Bosnian border. There was an unusually large proportion of men in the refugee population. Living conditions in the camps were awful. The socioeconomic explanation would predict a lower level of conflict based on the small camp size. However, it would also predict higher risks of violence from the other three factors. Because of their constancy over time, the socioeconomic predictions do not account for the different levels of violence that occurred in the two crises.

The Abdic refugee crises strongly contradict the prevailing conceptions about the size of refugee camps. UNHCR recommends establishing small camps of about 20,000 to 30,000 refugees on the assumption that small camps are more manageable and create fewer social problems than massive camps of hundreds of thousands of people. The Abdic group, at 25,000 refugees, fit the ideal perfectly. Despite its small size, the refugee group was highly militarized and caused the spread of civil war.

The crises also counter the idea that the location of the camp near the border is a cause of the spread of civil war. In both crises, the camps were located within walking distance of the Bosnian border. Batnoga camp practically straddled the border and Turanj was just a few miles away. Kuplensko camp was around twelve miles from the border. In the first crisis, the refugees invaded across the border. In the second crisis, the Croatian Special Police effectively controlled the border crossing. The most one could claim is that border camps are a necessary but not sufficient cause of conflict.

The Abdic followers differed from most other Bosnian refugee populations in the relatively larger proportion of men among the refugees. The mass of Bosnian refugee populations consisted of women, children, and the elderly. For refugee men, militarization took the form of forced conscription into a state army and did not directly affect the provision of assistance to other refugees. For example, in late 1992 and 1993, Croatian officials forcibly repatriated draft-age Bosnian males to fight in the Bosnian army as part of a friendship agreement between the two states.[81] When the alliance between the Muslims and Croats collapsed in 1993, Croatia forcibly repatriated Bosnian Muslim men to Bosnian Croat prison camps rather than to the Bosnian Army.

In the Abdic crises, the fighting-age men remained in the refugee camp. Most of the male refugees had experience as soldiers; some even fled in uniform. However, this factor does not explain the spread of civil war because the number of men remained constant from the first crisis to the second. The policy of the receiving state determined whether or not the men mobilized for military action.

The "living conditions" explanation predicts that both refugee crises would have resulted in violence, due to the poor conditions. In the first crisis, living conditions in both Turanj and Batnoga camps were awful. Refugees lived in chicken coops in Batnoga and in a mined no man's land in Turanj. At Batnoga, the chicken coops had no electricity, little clean water, and insufficient shelter from the cold. In Turanj, 60 percent of the refugees lived in destroyed and mined buildings, 30 percent lived in vehicles, and 10 percent slept in UNHCR tents.[82] Although UNHCR warned that the effects of the oncoming winter posed "major health, fire, and security hazards," the refugee leaders still discouraged a peaceful return.[83] The harsh conditions, combined with the impossibility of crossing into Croatia proper, encouraged thoughts of return. However, one UNHCR official noted that "a quiet return was not acceptable . . . and people started to envisage a military solution."[84]

Conditions in Kuplensko were also quite harsh, especially by the standards of other Balkan refugee settlements. One observer described "streams filled with excrement and litter, the sun broiling, the flies swarming."[85] The camp was not an organized settlement, but a motley collection of tents and vehicles along a couple miles of road. In comparison, most other Bosnian refugees lived with host families or in public buildings, schools, and hotels that provided better shelter and amenities. The Croatian government refused to allow the construction of weather-resistant structures at Kuplensko. These poor conditions did not lead to violence, however, which negates the idea that the militarization in the first exile stemmed from living conditions.

The comparison between the two crises reveals a difference in the long-term options—resettlement, local integration, or return—available to the refugees in each crisis. Refugees' long-term options in 1994 were limited by their leaders' refusal to countenance a peaceful return, the international community's resistance to resettlement abroad, and the condition of the host state as an impoverished, war-torn, renegade territory. The refugee leaders met with many European representatives and pleaded unsuccessfully for resettlement abroad. All the European officials stressed the hopelessness of gaining asylum in Europe. Despite Abdic's alliance with the Serbs, there was no question of the Muslim refugees settling permanently in the Serb-held territory.

From Kuplensko, dismal as it was, the refugees' choices were not as circumscribed. After the war, international willingness to resettle Bosnian refugees offered a nonviolent option to the five thousand refugees who refused to return home peacefully.[86] During the second crisis, the Abdic refugees eagerly accepted offers to resettle in the United States and other western countries. The militant refugees found these peaceful alternatives more attractive than attempting military activity with the weakened Abdic. The peaceful resolution of the 1995 crisis demonstrates that the spread of civil war is not inevitable, even when dealing with a state in exile. The essential factor is a capable and willing receiving state which demilitarizes the refugees and secures the border.

IMPLICATIONS FOR REDUCING VIOLENCE

The Abdic refugee crises were far from typical, compared to other Bosnian refugee situations. The atypical nature of the crises does not make them unsuitable for systematic study, however. The Abdic situations are actually ideal for examining the causes of violence because so many factors remained constant throughout the comparison. Disregarding Abdic's unusual motivation for violence—intra-Muslim hostility—the findings remain generalizable to other refugee crises. The analysis of the receiving states and external interveners, including humanitarian organizations, does not hinge upon whether or not Abdic was a typical rebel. Clearly he was not. The remarkable thing about these comparisons is that, given the militant motivations of Abdic's followers in both refugee crisis, the spread of war occurred only once.

This small case of 25,000 refugees confirms the findings of the larger Afghan and Rwandan cases presented earlier. Given the presence of a militant state-in-exile refugee group, the most important factor in determining the spread of civil war is the attitude and capability of the receiving state. In the first Abdic crisis, the receiving "state"—the Republic of Serb Krajina—was hostile to the sending state and willingly armed the refugees. In 1995, Abdic's surrender to the Bosnian 5th Corps and the Croatian rout of the Serbs left the Muslim rebels with no strong external supporter. Although defeat did not dull the intense loyalty of the refugees to Abdic, the Croatian Special Police limited the extent of possible manipulation and mobilization. Strong security measures by the receiving state, in this case backed up by pressure from the United States, limited the threat posed by the hardline refugee leaders. The loss of external support encouraged the refugees to demilitarize and accept a peaceful return or resettlement to a third country.

The Abdic crises refute the idea that the socioeconomic conditions of the refugee camps cause the spread of civil war. The socioeconomic conditions remained nearly constant from the first crisis to the second. The small size of the camps should have prevented military activity but, during the first crisis, it did not. The location of the camps on the border should have led to violence but, during the second crisis, it did not. The relatively high proportion of men in the camps should have encouraged military mobilization but, during the second crisis, it did not. The poor living conditions should have increased violence among the refugees but, during the second crisis, they did not.

One socioeconomic condition emerged in the Abdic cases that differs from the Afghan or Rwandan crises. This condition is a peaceful long-term alternative to refugee status, namely resettlement to a third country or integration into the receiving state. During most refugee crises, especially large-scale ones, refugees have virtually no alternative to camp life or return home. In the usual case, it is not politically or logistically feasible to resettle or integrate hundreds of thousands of refugees. With the 25,000 Abdic refugees, long-term options became available at the end of the second crisis. In order to break the stalemate in the camps, western states offered to resettle thousands of refugees. Croatia also welcomed a few militant leaders and even integrated them into the Croatian army. By luring about 5,000 militants away from the camps, Croatia was able to repatriate peacefully the remaining refugees.

Although long-term alternatives have a significant effect on reducing militarism, the provision of such alternatives is generally beyond the mandate of humanitarian organizations. Only receiving states and third-party states can offer local integration, in the form of citizenship or permanent residency, or resettlement. Thus the efficacy of this condition depends on the willingness and capability of the receiving state or a powerful third party to offer alternatives.

The Abdic crises echo the serious qualms raised in the Afghan and Rwandan crises about international humanitarian assistance to militant refugee groups. In 1994, humanitarian organizations were helpless to prevent military activity among the rebel Bosnians and they expressed little interest in doing so. The UN agencies and NGOs did not address the ethical dilemma of feeding a state in exile as it prepared for war. Clearly, however, the assistance benefited Abdic's army and its Serb allies as they planned their offensive. Even as the militants brazenly recruited soldiers within the Abdic camps, UNHCR continued to provide assistance. Fighters trained outside the camps and then returned for food, shelter, and medical care. Numerous aid workers claimed that militarization was not a problem because the military activity did not impede the distribution of aid. Nonetheless, the fact remains that internationally supported refugee camps succored thousands of soldiers and camouflaged their aggressive activities, even as the humanitarian workers professed their neutrality in the conflict.

[6]

Collateral Damage

THE RISKS OF HUMANITARIAN RESPONSES
TO MILITARIZED REFUGEE CRISES

> *"To deliver humanitarian assistance in a no-questions asked, open-ended manner is to deliver the extremists their strongest remaining card."*
>
> —African Rights, *Rwanda: Death, Despair, and Defiance* (1995)

The unintended negative consequences of humanitarian aid indicate an urgent need to alter traditional responses to militarized or potentially militarized refugee crises. Most reactions ignore the militarization. Governments avoid political and military action by treating the crisis as purely humanitarian, especially if the situation does not present a global security threat. For example, western governments did not regard war in eastern Zaire as a threat to international security and thus refused to disarm the genocidal killers among the refugees. Fiona Terry argues that "the international response to the Rwandan crisis . . . suggests that humanitarian action in the post–Cold War period has been transformed from a tool with which governments pursue foreign policy objectives to a tool with which to avoid foreign policy engagement."[1] But in reality, so-called humanitarian crises often require a political or military response to prevent the spread of civil war.

Humanitarian organizations ignore the political implications of crises due to their perceived helplessness, as well as myopia about their humanitarian mandate. Many organizations view attention to the political context and physical protection issues as a threat to their neutrality, impartiality, and independence. However, the unintended negative consequences of a myopic humanitarian policy question the wisdom of the current status quo. In the extreme case of Zaire, the spread of civil war that followed the refugee crises left millions dead and millions more displaced. In such cases, governments and humanitarian organizations must re-examine the existing policies in light of the political context of the crisis.

The ideal response to a militarized or potentially militarized crisis is the deployment of a security force to separate noncivilians and provide physical protection in the refugee-populated area. Such a force could be supplied by the receiving state (army or police) or by international donors (e.g., UN peacekeepers). The ease of providing adequate security depends on the attitude and capability of the receiving states. Weak states will require extensive security assistance from donors. Demilitarizing refugees in hostile receiving states will necessitate the use of force.

In the cases presented earlier—Afghan refugees in Pakistan, Rwandan refugees in Zaire, Burundian refugees in Tanzania, and Bosnian refugees in Serb-held Krajina—states and international organizations failed to uphold international refugee law. Third-party states either ignored the military aspects of the crisis or actively abetted the cross-border attacks. Pakistan enjoyed the support of external donors, including the United States, who approved of the military activity. Zaire lacked the capability to provide security in the refugee-populated areas. Tanzania turned a blind eye to militarism on its borders. The Krajina Serbs joined forces with the refugees to attack Bosnia. Donor states and the UN Security Council failed to prevent the spread of civil war. This left the humanitarian organizations alone to contend with these situations.

In each situation, the humanitarians mostly ignored the military activity associated with the refugee population. Throughout the Afghan, Rwandan, and Bosnian crises, humanitarian aid flowed unimpeded to the state-in-exile refugee groups. Humanitarian organizations contributed to the spread of civil war by feeding militants and their dependents, contributing to the war economy, and boosting the legitimacy of the armed elements. The militants' consolidation led to increased cross-border attacks against the sending states and retaliation against the refugee camps.

In evaluating their actions during militarized refugee crises, humanitarian organizations usually focus on the states' negligence in implementing international law. Transferring blame to states, even where rightfully placed, does not solve the difficult issue of a militarized refugee crisis, however. Even if states and the UN Security Council fail to act or act in a way to encourage violence, refugee relief agencies still bear responsibility for their actions. Ignoring the militarization affects the situation every bit as much as confronting it.

Whether actively or passively, the refugee relief regime can contribute to the spread of conflict.[2]

To avoid contributing to the spread of conflict, humanitarian organizations, such as UN agencies, the International Committee of the Red Cross (ICRC), and non-governmental organizations (NGOs), cannot approach their work in isolation from the political and military context surrounding it. Despite the desire for neutrality, it is virtually impossible for material assistance to have a neutral effect in a conflict situation. Recognizing that fact, aid organizations should pressure the receiving state, the UN Security Council, and major donors for quick police action to demilitarize the refugees and protect international borders. These organizations can publicize the need for security and engage in partnerships with security-providing entities. Even without external assistance, it is possible to counter militarist propaganda and support non-militarist leaders among the refugees. In extreme situations where the negative effects of assistance outweigh the benefits, humanitarian agencies must consider withdrawing or reducing assistance.

ESSENTIAL CONCEPTS

Before proceeding further, this chapter explains the terms "humanitarian organization" and "refugee protection," as they are used here.

Although this chapter uses the phrase "humanitarian organizations" to discusses a broad spectrum of groups, it is important to bear in mind the many differences among these organizations. One difference is intergovernmental versus non-governmental organizations (NGOs). UN agencies such as UNHCR are not independent from the member states of the United Nations and rely on funding from donor states. NGOs are more able, in theory, to operate independently of state direction. There are hundreds of humanitarian NGOs, many of which work in refugee crises. There are often sharp differences among these NGOs, as well as between them collectively and the intergovernmental agencies.

Under the broad umbrella of refugee relief, organizations have different missions and agendas. Some organizations have a mission to protect and assist refugees, for example the International Rescue Committee (IRC) and UNHCR, whereas other agencies limit their activities to material assistance. NGOs such as Médecins sans Frontières (MSF) combine advocacy on behalf of victims with the provision of material assistance. In addition to formalized differences (e.g. in funding, mission, etc.), frictions occur due to turf battles and personality conflicts, just as in any organizational context. The result of these different agendas and missions can be conflict and chaos—as occurred in eastern Zaire—especially if there are insufficient mechanisms for coordination. The variations among humanitarian organizations also mean that any generalizations about them include many exceptions.

The traditional understanding of the term "refugee protection" refers to the legal protection afforded refugees, especially asylum. UNHCR defines its primary protection role as ensuring implementation of international refugee law, including the right of non-*refoulement* (no forcible return) and the right to apply for asylum.[3] "Refugee protection" has not usually included issues of physical safety. Physical protection and security issues have been left to the receiving state. That separation of legal and physical protection obscures the link between the two concepts—that is to say, physical protection is a prerequisite for successful legal protection.

Recent failures by receiving states have led some humanitarian organizations to widen the protection concept to include physical protection and security issues. There is a growing realization that legal protection activities cannot progress in an atmosphere of insecurity and militarization. Yasushi Akashi, former special representative of the secretary general of the United Nations Protection Force for the former Yugoslavia, explained in 1997 that "when people are forcibly uprooted and pushed from their houses, and the aim of warfare is to inflict maximum pain, then 'protection' requirements are quite different to what was needed in more traditional humanitarian assistance operations."[4] There is also a greater willingness among the humanitarian organizations to include protection of human rights as a goal of their activities.

This chapter uses the term "physical protection" to distinguish this aspect of protection from legal protection. Physical protection entails safeguarding refugees from attacks or threats of attacks against their life or well-being. The attacks could emanate from militants among the refugees, the sending state government, or other parties to the conflict. The chapter uses the term "security" to denote a broader concern with threats to the territory and citizens of a state.

Forestalling Militarization

"Relief workers on the ground should be alert to the political and social climate in which they're operating."

—UNHCR, *Protecting Refugees, A Field Guide for NGOs* (1999)

"For UNHCR staff, the general tendency is to perceive emergencies in terms of logistics and not as failures of politics, the development process, or ethnic relations."

—Gil Loescher, *The UNHCR and World Politics* (2001)

Despite the shortages of resources and influence that plague most humanitarian organizations, ignoring militarization is not the only option. Humanitarian organizations can help prevent refugee militarization. One mechanism for prevention is to separate the militants from the refugees at the outset of a crisis. Early action is essential to stunt the growth of a state in exile. Finding peaceful alternatives such as resettlement or local integration in protracted refugee crises will stall militarization. State support will facilitate the separation of militants and other long-term solutions, but even state passivity does not entirely doom humanitarian efforts.

A prerequisite to preventing the spread of civil war is identifying violence-prone situations as early as possible. As described in chapter 2, there are three categories of refugee groups based on the cause of their flight. Situational refugees flee generalized violence and have little propensity for militarization. Persecuted refugees escape targeted violence or oppression based on group characteristics such as ethnicity, religion, or language. They are more easily organized for military purposes. Lastly, a state in exile flees defeat in a civil war and uses the refugee crisis as an opportunity to regroup for battle. Obviously this group is the one with the highest propensity for violence.

Prevention depends on accurate identification of the cause of the crisis. With limited resources, humanitarian organizations and governments should use security forces in the most violence-prone situations. If the refugees flee as a state in exile or from targeted persecution, military activity is more likely. Such refugee groups may organize an offensive or may be victims of attack by the sending state. Although the distinctions between situational, persecuted, and state-in-exile groups are not always clear cut and are better regarded as falling on a continuum, it is still possible to identify aspects of a crisis that predict later violence.

The importance of the cause of the crisis forces aid agencies to look beyond the immediate crisis to its precursors. Usually the provision of emergency assistance consumes all the attention of the aid groups, leaving little room for political analysis, which is seen as the purview of policymakers and academics. One NGO report admits: "Once the team is in the field, the intensity of the medical work it faces prevents it from making a true analysis of the society in which it is operating, of the surrounding conflict, its roots, or its impact on a national and regional scale. This is why a real analysis, based on a conceptual framework which takes into account the complexity of the situation, is indispensable."[5] Similarly, a UNHCR evaluation of the Rwanda crisis condemned the agency's "lack of understanding of the social, cultural and political background of the refugees."[6] That crisis made painfully clear the need to identify violence-prone situations as early as possible. These analytical deficits suggest a necessity for more partnerships between aid organizations, governments, and academics to integrate refugee aid, protection, and political understanding in a crisis.

Separate Noncivilians from Refugees

> *"After the genocide, we failed to push hard enough to expel genocidal killers from the refugee camps, and we shrank from the truth that it was worth risking bloodshed to force a separation between killers and legitimate refugees."*
>
> —Roger Winter, U.S. Committee for Refugees, "How Human Rights Groups Miss the Opportunity to Do Good," *Washington Post* (February 22, 1998)

The best way to prevent the spread of war, after identifying a potentially violent crisis, is to separate the noncivilians from the refugees as quickly as possible. As UNHCR has put it: "In certain situations, . . . there may be no other option than to deploy international police or military forces to effect the separation and exclusion of people who do not qualify for international protection as refugees."[7] The longer the separation takes, the more entrenched the militants become among the population. The time factor underlines the need for early identification of potential state-in-exile groups.

Many obstacles hinder screening and separation of militants. Problems include prohibitive costs (political, military and economic), logistical difficulties, and ethical dilemmas. Currently, no humanitarian organization has the resources or mandate to identify and separate militants during a refugee crisis. Effective separation of militants will require state cooperation or increased security roles for humanitarian organizations.

A major obstacle to separation and disarmament is the need for coercion. In situations where the militants are organized and capable, disarming and separating them will require the use of force. In 1994, a U.S. Committee for Refugees (USCR) mission to the Rwandan refugee camps in Zaire warned that "any disarmament effort would probably require a mini-war for several weeks or months against a desperate regime that has already proven its willingness to employ brutally extreme tactics to survive."[8] Such action clearly falls beyond the purview of humanitarian organizations and would require a political and military commitment from external forces.

In eastern Zaire during the Rwanda crisis, wealthy states refused to pay the political and military price of separating the Rwandan militants from the refugees. The Zairian government, the United Nations, and major donors ignored or watered down numerous appeals by humanitarian organizations. In November 1994 Boutros Boutros-Ghali, then UN secretary general, offered the Security Council four options to address the security problems in the camps: a UN peacekeeping operation, a UN force to separate the militants from the refugees, a non-UN multinational military force, and the use of foreign police and military to train local forces. The Security Council rejected all but the weakest option—using foreign forces to train Zairian forces. Looking back on the failure to separate and contain the militants, Sergio Vieira de Mello, then UN Assistant High Commissioner for Refugees, noted bitterly: "It should be remembered that the 1994 proposals to [separate and exclude militants] were rejected partially for financial considerations. Meanwhile, a far larger sum has been spent on care and maintenance to maintain refugee camps for longer than was justified, not to speak of the human suffering involved."[9]

Even if the use of force is not required, the cost and time of identifying nonrefugees is enormous. A small screening project in Tanzania illustrates the prohibitive costs of individual refugee screening. In 1998, UNHCR began individually assessing the 12,000 Rwandans in Tanzania to determine which Rwandans merited refugee status. UNHCR projected a cost of $350,000 to screen 12,000 refugees. The screening was estimated to take a few hours per person.[10] At that rate, it would cost nearly $3 million to screen 100,000 refugees and would take months, if not years, to complete. The time and money involved in individual screening of refugees suggests that the process is not feasible for large, rapid outflows.

In the Rwanda crisis, initial plans to separate the militants from the refugees fell through when aid agencies realized that they would have to move 60,000 to 100,000 militia and army members (with their families) at an estimated cost of $90 million to $125 million. The Zairian government refused to assist UNHCR in separating armed elements from the refugees. The government put the onus on UNHCR to gather a list of names of intimidators, but UNHCR could not convince the Zairian army to arrest any militants. UNHCR itself had no mechanisms in place for excluding militants. One official noted that two years into the exile, during summer 1996, UNHCR was still discussing the proper criteria for exclusion from refugee status.[11]

Even given the existence of a screening process, the aid workers still have to determine who the militants are—usually with scant evidence. Many humanitarian organizations cite the difficulty of identifying militants and war criminals, especially in a chaotic emergency situation.[12] For example, in Zaire, many of the Rwandan Hutu soldiers shed their uniforms. Additionally, "the top ex-FAR officers and other Rwandans with past high positions were highly mobile."[13] UN observers concur that "the identification of armed elements leads to enormous problems."[14]

A related problem is the treatment of the militants once they are identified. Refugee relief agencies rarely have the mandate to assist nonrefugees, especially noncivilians. However, humanitarian organizations would oppose their forcible return to the sending state. One solution would be some sort of detention center in the receiving state. War criminals could be prosecuted under international law. Soldiers could have the option of demobilizing and returning to the refugee camp or returning home. Soldiers who refused to demobilize would stay in detention until they could safely return home.

In addition to logistical, political, and cost issues, humanitarian organizations face ethical dilemmas regarding separation of militants. UNHCR officials with experience in Zaire have concerns about this: "One problem with the separation proposal is that many people inciting trouble in the camps are accompanied by innocent family members. Separating leaders and soldiers from their families would be controversial under international guidelines for treatment of refugees."[15] Humanitarian organizations also would want to avoid a situation where they became responsible for detaining nonrefugees.

So far, the assessment of separating militants from refugees is not encouraging. This does not mean the idea should be abandoned. In a large, rapid influx, there are ways to shorten the process of demilitarization. Rather than in-depth individual screening, a peacekeeping force could disarm entering refugees and detain obvious soldiers or known war criminals. Such a broad sweep might not find every militant and every weapon, but it would prevent the coalescing of an organized military and political entity. Hindering the militants' organization would go a long way toward reducing the spread of conflict.

With a willing receiving state, the issue of separation of militants is less of a problem for humanitarian organizations. Recent instances of separation and demilitarization show that a committed receiving state or a welcome international force can succeed, especially when the number of militants is small. In October 2001, United Nations peacekeepers in the Democratic Republic of Congo (DRC) separated 1,000 Central African Republic (CAR) soldiers from 24,000 UNHCR-assisted refugees camped on the CAR/DRC border. The peacekeepers transferred the soldiers and their families to a site 90 miles away from the border. Once the soldiers were separated, UNHCR provided assistance to the ex-combatants on "extraordinary humanitarian grounds," even though they were not refugees. Throughout the operation, the local security forces (the rebel Congolese Liberation Movement, or MLC) supported the separation and disarmament of the fighters.[16]

Despite the patent need to demilitarize, especially when facing a state in exile such as the Rwandan Hutu, international support is not usually forthcoming. To increase support, humanitarian organizations can publicize the need for security measures and lobby governments for assistance in separating militants from refugees. One selling point of an international demilitarization force is that the operation is likely to be of short duration, especially compared to most peacekeeping operations.

Avoid Protracted Crises

"Time was reinforcing extremists within the refugee population."
—Joel Boutroue, UNHCR official in Goma, "Missed Opportunities: The Role of the International Community in the Return of the Rwandan Refugees from Eastern Zaire," *Rosemarie Rogers Working Paper Series* (1998)

State-in-exile groups generally gain strength over time. Finding a quick and durable solution to a crisis can thwart the plans of potential militants. For example, Croatia dissipated the influence of the militant Abdic followers by facilitating resettlement abroad or local integration for 5,000 hard-core militants in 1995.

The two years in eastern Zaire clearly helped the Rwandan Hutu state in exile consolidate its military capability and organization. For the first few months after the Rwandans arrived in Zaire, chaos and cholera reigned in the camps. During the early period of confusion (July through September 1994), thousands of refugees willingly returned home. By November 1994, virtually no refugees returned voluntarily; in fact, a number of would-be returnees were beaten to death by extremists.[17] Observers suggest that the period of chaos was a tragic missed opportunity for the international refugee-relief effort to organize a mass repatriation. UNHCR complained that the UN Security Council did not even debate the issue of camp security until October 1994.[18] In the time lag between July and October, the genocidaires improved their organization, gathered more resources, and exerted complete control over the refugees.[19]

Similarly, the Afghan refugees in Pakistan evolved into a state in exile over the first months of that crisis in early 1980. When the Soviets invaded Afghanistan in December 1979, most of the Afghan resistance parties were newly established. Initially they did not constitute a state in exile. As millions of persecuted refugees poured into sympathetic Pakistan, the resistance parties used the refugee crisis as an opportunity to recruit followers and consolidate their power. With massive external humanitarian and military assistance, these persecuted refugees hardened into a state in exile. Those early months after the Soviet invasion would have been the best time to impede militarization among the refugees, had that been a desired option.

The three generally accepted durable resolutions to a refugee crisis are repatriation, resettlement to a third country, and local integration into the receiving state. Resettlement or local integration will blunt the militant goals of the refugees and reduce their ability to organize militarily. These options also reduce the threat perceived by the sending state. By accepting a durable solution, refugees sever, to some extent, the ties with their homeland.

Third-country resettlement probably offers the most desirable nonviolent resolution for refugees who feel they cannot return home. The increasingly rare option of resettlement usually entails permanent residence in an industrialized country. A second attractive option consists of local integration into the receiving state. In this option, the refugee receives the right to own property, hold employment, and eventually attain citizenship or permanent residence in the country of asylum. Like resettlement, this coveted option rarely occurs.[20]

Recent trends in refugee policy have favored return to the sending state as the optimal outcome. Former UN High Commissioner for Refugees Sadako Ogata confirmed the emphasis on repatriation: "When refugee outflows and prolonged stay in asylum countries risk spreading conflict to neighboring states, policies aimed at promoting early repatriation can be considered as serving prevention."[21] However, for a persecuted or state-in-exile group to return to the sending state usually requires coercion or a subordination of refugees' political goals.

In many crises, a quick and durable solution is not possible. In the Afghan case, return to the Soviet-occupied country was not a feasible solution. The refugees could not return to such an unsafe environment. The sheer size of the refugee population in Pakistan (two to three million) made resettlement impossible and local integration unpopular with local residents. The Palestinian refugee crisis has also endured for decades without a durable solution. Israel blocked the refugees' return following the 1948 war. For the most part, the refugees and the receiving states resisted resettlement and local integration, using the continued crisis as a source of political pressure on Israel. As in the Afghan case, the size of the refugee population (nearly four million) limits the solutions to the crisis.

In cases that defy peaceful resolution, aid agencies and governments must take into account the added negative effect of a long refugee crisis. For a state in exile or persecuted refugee group, a long exile will aid those among the refugees who seek to engage in organized military activity. Humanitarian aid will have a higher likelihood of reinforcing the state in exile during protracted crises.

REDUCING THE SPREAD OF CIVIL WAR

Preventing the spread of civil war is an expensive, risky undertaking that requires timely political and military cooperation from the receiving state or other parties intervening externally. Because of those obstacles, humanitarian organizations with inadequate security resources often find themselves facing an actual or potential state in exile. In this situation, humanitarian organizations can either ignore the militarization or attempt to reduce it. For reasons detailed earlier in the chapter, humanitarian organizations often ignore militarization. However, reducing the spread of conflict has long-term benefits for refugee protection and regional security.

Assuming humanitarian organizations want to reduce militarization, there are three useful policies they can follow. The first is to develop security partnerships with entities that will help demilitarize the refugee area. Possible partners include the receiving state police or army, UN or regional peacekeeping forces, international police, and private forces. Second, humanitarian organizations can support non-militant leaders among the refugees. And third, aid agencies can implement information campaigns to counter militant propaganda. As in prevention, the success of security partnerships, leadership development, and information programs will depend on the cooperation and capability of the receiving state.

Create Security Partnerships

Refugee crises in Zaire and Tanzania offer two models of security partnerships between states and humanitarian organizations, both of which fell short of demilitarizing the refugee areas. In 1994, Secretary General of the United Nations Boutros Boutros-Ghali asked sixty countries for help in providing a security force for the Zaire camps; only Bangladesh responded positively. The Security Council's lack of action pushed the issue into UNHCR's lap. As a last resort, UNHCR hired fifteen hundred elite soldiers from Mobutu's Presidential Guard. The Zairian force, called the *Contingent Zairois pour la Securité dans les Camps* (CZSC), was deployed in February 1995. The objective of the force was to ensure security in the camps for refugees and relief workers. The force had no mandate to disarm the militants. UNHCR paid the soldiers $3 per day plus food, lodging, and clothes.[22]

The Zairian force received mixed reviews. The first contingent of soldiers that arrived in early 1995 was relatively well disciplined. Later contingents of soldiers actually contributed to insecurity as their discipline and morale broke down. The soldiers became involved in crime and extortion, victimizing the refugees rather than protecting them. When the Rwandan forces invaded in 1996, many of the Zairian soldiers fought with the Hutu militias against the Tutsi attackers. The Zairian experience suggests that an ill-disciplined force may be worse than no force at all. Throughout the crisis, UNHCR had little or no control over these forces, even as it footed the bill for their presence.

A second, more promising, model for security provision was undertaken in Tanzania in the late 1990s to deal with security threats associated with over 500,000 Burundian and Congolese refugees. Security problems included military activity by Burundian rebel groups, violence among rebel factions, and criminal activity within and around refugee camps. The violence strained Tanzanian relations with Burundi and stoked discontent among local citizens. Under the arrangement, known as the "security package," UNHCR agreed to train, equip, and pay nearly three hundred police officers to work in the refugee areas. UNHCR paid the officers a stipend of about $280 per month—about three times their normal wages. The Memorandum of Understanding signed between UNHCR and Tanzania outlined the goals of the package: "It is expected that the additional police presence will considerably reduce the level of insecurity, criminality, and safeguard the civilian and humanitarian character of the refugee camps."[23] The mandate of the police included reducing criminal activity, decreasing gender-based violence, and separating armed elements from the refugees. Police also confiscated weapons and arrested rebel recruiters in the camps but did not deal with any rebel activity occurring outside the camps.

Inappropriate police behavior and inadequate capability bedeviled the Tanzanian security package. Refugees and humanitarian workers noted a lack of discipline among some officers, including public drunkenness and the failure to patrol the camps. At higher levels of management, there was also noncompliance with aspects of the security package. A police report for Ngara district noted that between January 1998 and June 1999, 120 members of the police force were dismissed and 132 reassigned for taking bribes.[24] Police rotations usually did not last the agreed-upon six months, resulting in many inexperienced and untrained officers who stayed only a few months in the camps. The police were singularly unsuccessful in separating militants from the refugees. In 2001, for example, 40 percent of detained militants absconded from detention.[25]

Although refugee crises rarely allow much lead time for planners, security partnerships do not have to be created from scratch when a crisis occurs. Planning activities can occur beforehand. In this spirit, UNHCR has developed the concept of a ladder of options for providing security.[26] The options vary in the level of force needed and the actors necessary for implementation. The lowest level, implementable by humanitarian organizations, includes mass information systems and dispute resolution mechanisms. The most forceful measure is a Chapter VII peace enforcement operation. Agencies can also assess the likelihood of receiving state cooperation when a crisis seems imminent. Humanitarian organizations can press for a quick response by the UN Security Council to send peacekeepers. At a minimum, organizations can seek funding for security partnerships, so that financing will be in place to implement an improved version of the Tanzania security package.[27]

The capability and intentions of the receiving state determine the success of a security partnership. Tanzania was a stable, peaceful country that sought international recognition for assisting refugees.[28] Chaotic or hostile receiving states will further complicate attempts at security partnerships. Such inhospitable environments would require more external security assistance, and perhaps coercion, to implement security programs. With a hostile or collapsed receiving state, a security partnership would be impossible and a peace enforcement force would be required instead. That is a completely different undertaking, one not suited to humanitarian organizations.

Cooperation from external actors or donors also determines the success of a security package. UNHCR does not have sufficient funding or appropriate personnel to implement security on its own and requires cooperation from donor states. If money and personnel are not forthcoming, a security partnership is unlikely to succeed. In January 2003, the government of Canada responded to violence in Guinean refugee camps by seconding two officers from the Royal Canadian Mounted Police to train Guinean security forces. The Canadian-UNHCR partnership served as a pilot project to assess cooperative measures for improving refugee protection. The initial assessment was only cautiously optimistic, noting that the Canadian contingent was hampered by insufficient equipment, an unclear mandate, and lack of support from the Guinean government.[29]

Among humanitarian organizations, attitudes toward security partnerships are varied and volatile. Some agencies express qualms that security partnerships will violate their neutrality. UNHCR warns that "using force to protect humanitarian assistance may compromise the foundation of those activities, since the actual use of force, by its nature, will not be neutral."[30] Refugees and combatants may not distinguish between UN relief workers and UN peacekeepers, reducing the perception of humanitarians as neutral. There is also a fear that external military forces will act as a magnet for refugees hoping for physical protection. Military units may also increase security risks by drawing fire from opponents of demilitarization.[31]

In addition, some organizations have a philosophical antipathy to relying on armed security. For example, the International Committee of the Red Cross (ICRC) stresses that "humanitarian work must be disassociated from military operations aimed at ensuring security and restoring law and order in regions affected by conflict."[32] Most NGOs do not have the capacity to deploy their own security, yet they jealously guard their autonomy and are wary of UN domination. No hierarchy exists among organizations, meaning that each makes its own decisions regarding security issues.

Influence Refugee Leadership Structure

Aid workers often rely on existing leadership structures among refugee populations to run the camps. This is done in part to maintain community, encourage self-reliance, and avoid paternalism. UNHCR mandates that refugees "should always participate in determining the needs of their community and planning and designing programmes to meet those needs."[33] Aid agencies work with the local leaders, even if they are not democratically chosen. As a result, refugee leaders wield great influence and can easily gain access to resources, especially via food distribution.

In general, the instinct to maintain refugees' communities improves stability and organization in the camps. However, maintaining the refugees' original leadership structure backfires when the potential for a militarized crisis exists. A nascent state in exile will gain legitimacy and power if humanitarian organizations funnel resources through established channels. In a militarized crisis, the benefits of a close-knit and organized refugee community become distorted because militants misuse the social structure and humanitarian resources for their own ends.

In the Rwandan refugee camps, the UNHCR attitude toward camp leadership had the unintended effect of strengthening the genocidaires. Immediately after their arrival, the refugees reconstituted themselves into their pre-flight social and political structures. The overwhelmed humanitarian organizations were initially grateful for the orderly and rapid arrangement of the population. With their power established, the genocidaires blatantly recruited fighters and intimidated the refugees in the camps. By the time the agencies realized the power of the militants, it was too late to change the established situation.

In theory, UNHCR understands the potentially dangerous influence of refugee leaders. Its *Handbook for Emergencies* warns aid workers to "be aware that some new power structures might emerge, for example through force, and may exercise de facto control over the population, but may not be representative."[34] During an actual crisis, however, the path of least resistance is to work with the existing leaders, even if they have militant tendencies. In Tanzania and Zaire, many genocidaires ended up on NGO payrolls because they were educated and spoke English. This sent an unintentional message to the refugees about the humanitarian organizations' attitude toward the leaders. Another UNHCR official noted that the tendency to hire English-speakers undermined the role of traditional elders, who often are not as hot-headed as the young, educated leaders.[35]

Humanitarian organizations cannot single-handedly mold the leadership structure of refugee populations. Nevertheless, aid agencies can avoid propping up war criminals, militants, and genocidaires. UNHCR and NGOs can promote new leadership in their hiring patterns and by organizing the selection of new leaders. Some Tanzanian camps held elections for leaders in which UNHCR stipulated a certain number of women must stand for election. Humanitarian organizations can also more carefully screen their refugee employees to avoid supporting militants. As with other aspects of demilitarization, accurate intelligence is essential to identify and neutralize militant leaders.

Improve Information Flows

Information is an essential, but often overlooked, aspect of the physical protection of refugees. Refugees constantly seek information about their home country. They want to know about the political situation and whether it is safe to return. This knowledge greatly influences whether the refugees will return peacefully or whether they will actively sympathize with a rebel group.

Powerful militant leaders expertly control and distort the information received by the refugees. Using propaganda, leaders manipulate the refugees' perception of past and current events. Leaders often greatly exaggerate the threats from the sending state, convincing refugees that a return home would be suicidal and that their only hope is to support the militants. Leaders also convince reluctant refugees that their military activity is defensive, whereas the militant actions of the refugees may in reality constitute an offensive threat and precipitate an attack by the sending state on the camp. Tools used to spread information include word of mouth, radio, newspapers, and community meetings.

In the Rwandan Hutu camps, militant leaders quickly realized the value of controlling the information available to the refugees. Refugee leaders circulated leaflets that described the horrors endured by Hutu who had returned to Rwanda. The militants operated radio stations from eastern Zaire and propagated the idea that Hutu were the main victims of the genocide. The calculated strategy of manipulating information effectively sidelined humanitarian organizations and the international media. The refugees considered the aid agencies as a biased and inaccurate source of information.

Humanitarian organizations face two obstacles in providing information to refugees. First, agencies must obtain accurate information. This is not an easy task in war-torn regions with poor communications capabilities. In a few instances, humanitarian organizations have not received information in a timely fashion or have unknowingly disseminated erroneous reports. These errors damage the reputation of aid agencies as unbiased and reliable sources of information.

Secondly, the aid workers must convince the refugees that the information is accurate. This is difficult if militant leaders are also sending powerful and contradictory messages to the refugees. Refugees generally mistrust information from aid agencies and rely on their own sources as well as on international news (such as BBC). Humanitarian aid workers are often seen as allied with the sending or receiving state, rather than with the refugees. One successful NGO information program was the Jesuit-funded radio stations that broadcast in some areas of western Tanzania.

Information failures often result from lackadaisical planning and execution. Insufficient resources and attention are given to the important task of disseminating information and gaining the refugees' trust. In some camps, there are no organized channels for sharing information between refugees and humanitarian organizations.[36] Successful information campaigns must start early and must be tailored to the refugees' needs. Countering militants' control of information will reduce the likelihood of conflict and increase the chances for voluntary repatriation.

When All Else Fails: Humanitarian Aid as Leverage

Humanitarian Dilemmas

"Sometimes we just shouldn't show up for a disaster."
—Roy Williams, International Rescue Committee, quoted in "Aid Dilemma: Keeping It from the Oppressors; U.N., Charities Find Crises Make Them Tools of War," *The Washington Post* (September 23, 1997)

Recent crises, such as the Rwandan refugee crisis in Zaire, have demonstrated the colossal failure of state actions to prevent militarization. In such contexts, indiscriminate humanitarian assistance becomes a building block for successful rebel movements. Unconditional assistance worsens the security situation for refugees, local residents, and relief workers by enriching and legitimizing militant elements. The negative impact of humanitarian assistance in militarized refugee crises raises the question of when aid should be reduced or withdrawn. Even with only minimal state support, humanitarian organizations can use their resources as leverage to improve security. In some hostile and chaotic crises, however, the least harmful outcome may involve the withdrawal of humanitarian assistance.

Humanitarian organizations have two assets, or forms of leverage, with which they can affect outcomes. They have the moral clout that comes from the charitable, altruistic nature of their work. They also have the tangible asset of material resources. Organizations have these assets in different amounts, varying according to reputation, wealth, and mandate. Aid agencies can leverage these assets to attain a more secure environment for refugees, local inhabitants, and aid workers. For example, humanitarian organizations can demand a basic set of security preconditions so that their work does not contribute to conflict. This involves negotiations with the receiving state, rebel groups, external donors, and potential third-party actors. The need for adequate security should be highly publicized and clearly communicated to all of the parties involved. Using aid as leverage can prevent future loss of life if war can be prevented.

Moral clout enables humanitarian organizations to lobby policymakers and use the media to gain support for their positions. Currently, organizations use their moral clout to publicize the need for material assistance in a crisis. Newspapers regularly report on the quantity of tents, food, and medicine that humanitarian organizations need for a crisis. Issues of physical protection receive much less attention, from both UNHCR and the media. By directing more resources toward issues of physical protection of refugees and aid workers, aid agencies can increase public awareness of the issue. Analyst Kathleen Newland concurs: "UNHCR, other states, and refugee advocates must rely on diplomatic pressure, persuasion, and incentives to encourage reluctant states to implement provisions for international protection."[37] Humanitarian organizations can trade on their altruist credentials to emphasize the need for security measures in refugee crises.

The idea of using moral clout to encourage intervention by the Security Council or another external party is not without precedent. In the lead-up to the military intervention in Somalia in 1992, NGOs explicitly demanded better security for humanitarian operations. In a press conference, a group of prominent American NGOs threatened to withdraw from Somalia unless security was improved.[38] In the late 1990s, a number of NGOs encouraged the NATO intervention in Kosovo. Médecins Sans Frontières received criticism for championing the Kosovo intervention but later withdrawing from Kosovo due to abuses of aid there.[39]

Within the NGO community, debate rages over the appropriateness of advocating military intervention. NGOs fear losing their moral clout by advocating intervention and appearing to identify with one of the warring parties. But moral clout is also eroded when humanitarian organizations stay silent and implicitly acquiesce to militarization. Both inaction and action have political consequences and neither can be rationalized as neutral. Terry cautions that "the best that aid organizations can hope to do is *minimize* the negative effects of their action."[40]

Humanitarian organizations' second asset, material resources, has a great impact on the war-torn areas that receive assistance. In resource-poor environments, militant leaders depend on humanitarian assistance to sustain their followers. In Angola, rich with oil, or Sierra Leone, rich with diamonds, combatants also fund conflict through smuggling natural resources. Yet even when militants have other resources, humanitarian assistance can provide valuable legitimacy to their cause. Thus, the value of humanitarian assistance provides leverage for humanitarian organizations to improve the security situation.

Using humanitarian aid as leverage entails making aid contingent on security improvements. Possible security requirements include disarmament of refugees, separation of militants, and adequate police protection of the refugee-populated area. Adequate border security also prevents cross-border attacks by the sending state or the refugees. A Médecins Sans Frontières official cautions that humanitarian organizations should take action to preserve "humanitarian space" but not to enforce a respect for human rights in the society at large.[41] The leverage would not be used to pressure for major changes in the government of the receiving state or the structure of peacekeeping operations. In practice, that means that NGOs should act to prevent situations in which aid is diverted or used to endanger the recipients.

Conditionality is not necessarily an all-or-nothing proposition. There are gradations in the levels of assistance and the numbers of agencies involved. In extreme cases, all humanitarian organizations may withdraw; in other situations, only certain organizations will do so. Sometimes essential life-saving services might remain, like hospital workers and emergency feeding centers. For example, in the 1990s the World Food Programme scaled back its services in Afghanistan to the bare minimum in an attempt to pressure the government to respect human rights.[42]

As a last resort, humanitarian organizations can consider shutting down the refugee camps altogether. This drastic step might occur when the harm caused by the camps overwhelms the benefits of refugee assistance. As refugee studies scholar Myron Weiner warned, "Sometimes it may be necessary to close refugee camps because they are used by warrior refugees intent on pursing armed conflict." According to Weiner, conditions for forcible return include when "camps are used by military forces as a staging area for resuming the war (by recruiting boys and young men in the camps, extracting resources from camp refugees, and using camps as a safe haven) and . . . refugees have become hostages to warriors and are therefore unable to choose whether or not to repatriate."[43] UNHCR also recognizes that, in extraordinary circumstances, forced return and camp closure may be the least harmful policy. UNHCR reasons that, in forced returns, "the risk of undermining the principle of voluntariness must be weighed against the ability to save people's lives."[44]

Ethical and Practical Challenges

A logical requirement for refugee relief is that the assistance must do more good than harm, yet putting that into practice is difficult for many reasons.[45] First of all, aid organizations cannot easily determine the harm being done or the probable outcome in the absence of humanitarian assistance. Thus they face an ethical dilemma involving an uncertain tradeoff between alleviating short-term suffering and providing long-term benefits. As a practical matter, humanitarian organizations fear losing funding if they withdraw from a crisis.

Aid workers' greatest fear is that people will suffer and perhaps die if aid is withdrawn or reduced. In the short term, organizations often view making assistance contingent on physical protection as an unacceptable tradeoff because it punishes legitimate refugees for the behavior of the militants. Aid workers see the denial of immediate assistance to people in need as a violation of humanitarian principles. Terry challenges that objection to conditionality, noting that "the idea that withholding aid is doing evil presumes that external aid is indispensable to the survival of the refugees." She suggests that aid workers have a psychological (and practical) need to portray assistance as essential to the recipients' survival.[46]

Part of aid workers' concerns about withdrawing assistance arise because the benefits of physical protection are less tangible than those of assistance. It is easy to see that providing food and medicine prevents deaths. It is less easy to demonstrate (especially to the public back home) how demilitarization will prevent deaths. Donors want to provide food and medicine to needy children, not train local police. Also, physical protection is perceived as more political than material assistance. Donors and humanitarian organizations often fail to admit the political implications of material assistance. This misperception of physical protection as a secondary or irrelevant goal is not an insurmountable obstacle, but it requires a concerted effort to educate governments and the public about the importance of security during a refugee crisis.

In militarized crises, the culture of relief agencies may impede conditionality policies. Humanitarian organizations closely guard their independence and each agency reserves the right to act as it sees fit, hindering coordination during a crisis. Some analysts question the value of this independence when taken to extreme levels: "Is a point reached where the right of each agency and donor government to make its own ethical judgment in fact makes the impact of the system 'dysfunctional'? To what extent do different mandates justify different compromises?"[47] The lack of coordination and competition between agencies does not lend itself to a clear-headed analysis of the situation. Ideally, there would exist some overarching coordinating body that could guide organizations facing these difficult decisions.[48]

A humanitarian organization's attitude toward conditionality also depends on its mission. Organizations that focus purely on material assistance generally view their actions as separate from the political sphere. The sentiments of one aid worker in eastern Zaire illustrate this attitude: "I know some of them have killed a lot of people. But I don't care about the past. My job is to feed everyone irrespective of the past."[49] Other organizations have multiple (and sometimes conflicting) missions. Médecins sans Frontières (MSF) provides medical assistance and also acts as a vocal witness to human rights abuses. The ICRC describes its mission as helping victims and promoting respect for international humanitarian law.[50] Agencies whose missions include refugee protection or promotion of human rights are more receptive to using some limited form of conditionality.

If all relevant organizations came to the conclusion that their actions were causing more harm than good, not even this would necessarily lead to withdrawal. Agencies are still faced with a coordination problem because each organization does not know what the others will do. Each organization assumes that if it pulls out of a crisis, it would lose "market share" because other organizations would stay. An individual organization may see it as futile and self-defeating to withdraw since, as in most past cases of withdrawal, a replacement organization will quickly take over. For example, before MSF withdrew from Ethiopia in the 1980s due to government abuses of aid, the organization negotiated for a replacement NGO to step in. In practical terms, if one agency withdraws and others do not, then the withdrawing agency has lost its contracts and may lose funding. The ethical gesture may doom the organization in the long run. Thus, it is easy for an organization to rationalize its passivity on both ethical and pragmatic grounds.

UNHCR faces additional obstacles to withholding assistance because it is beholden to the governments that finance it. Amnesty International noted: "This dependence on governments can sometimes constrain

UNHCR from taking a strong and public stance on protection issues and may affect the vigor with which it discharges its protection mandate."[51] By sending UNHCR to the crisis, governments claim to take action while avoiding the political and military commitments needed to resolve the crisis. This means that UNHCR could face stiff resistance from donors if it demands a peacekeeping force to demilitarize the refugee situation. UNHCR also has concerns about losing its relevance and status as the preeminent refugee relief agency.[52]

Past Precedents

The initial reaction of many humanitarian organizations to suggestions of making aid contingent on physical protection is that such actions are unethical and contrary to the humanitarian imperative of impartiality.[53] However, organizations have used aid as leverage in many instances in the past when faced with unacceptable security risks. Most of these decisions were made on an ad hoc basis rather than in compliance with a formalized policy. For UNHCR, the decision to withhold assistance often rested with the UNHCR officials in the field. The withdrawals were not long-term or complete, but were designed to gain compliance from the militant leaders in the camps.

In the Great Lakes, aid agencies used assistance as leverage on several occasions. In Goma, Zaire, the UNHCR official in charge of the camps banned machetes in a camp after militants threatened inhabitants and aid workers. Humanitarian organizations cut off food aid to the camp and withdrew personnel until the camp leaders gave a security guarantee. It took ten days before the refugee leaders agreed to put away their weapons. During that time, NGOs chafed at the strict measures used by UNHCR.[54] In another instance, humanitarian organizations temporarily suspended their activities when militants shot at aid workers who were trying to conduct a census.

Individual NGOs, such as MSF France, pulled out of the Rwandan refugee camps completely to protest the militarization. MSF director Jacques de Milliano claimed, "In refugee camps there are killers walking around making plans for new attacks. We don't want to be part of that system."[55] Tellingly, however, not all country chapters of MSF withdrew from the camps. Even within an organization there are different understandings of its mandate.[56] The charity CARE withdrew from Katale camp in October 1994 after former Hutu soldiers took over the camp. The takeover led to five hours of talks between Zairian authorities, UNHCR, and 150 representatives of the refugees.[57] In these small ways, aid workers made assistance contingent on demilitarization. On the whole, however, billions of dollars of humanitarian assistance sustained the militant Hutu state in exile during the refugee crisis.

Another example occurred after thousands of Kurdish refugees fled Turkey and moved to northern Iraq in 1993 and 1994. UNHCR eventually withdrew from the Atroush camp in northern Iraq due to rampant militarization and cross-border violence. The Kurdish Workers Party (PKK) firmly controlled the Atroush refugee camp, which housed around between 10,000 and 20,000 refugees. At one point, Kurdish militants held thirteen humanitarian workers hostage. Turkey protested the militarization and conducted cross-border attacks against the camp. This expansion of the civil war occurred despite the small number of refugees and the location of the camp more than forty miles from the Turkish border. In 1996, the Turkish government pressured UNHCR to close the camp. UNHCR complied in early 1997, citing the unacceptable level of politicization and militarization in the camp.

Conditionality has occurred in other types of humanitarian crises, as well. ICRC withdrew assistance from rural Liberia in 1994 when it found that "the level of diversion by the factions had reached a systematic and planned level, that it was integrated into the war strategy. . . . It had become obvious that the factions were opening the doors to humanitarian aid, up to the point where all the sophisticated logistics had entered the zones: cars, radios, computers, telephones. When all the stuff was there, then the looting would start in a quite systematic way."[58] During the mid-1990s, armed elements looted 20 million dollars' worth of equipment from humanitarian agencies in Liberia.[59]

MSF withdrew its presence from North Korea in 1998 after determining that the organization was too constrained to fulfill its mandate. The North Korean government refused to provide the aid agency with independent access to famine victims; instead the government attempted to control all aid distribution.[60]

The Need for Humanitarian Leadership

Humanitarian organizations have many disincentives to confront the problem of militarized refugee crises. One problem is the fractured nature of the humanitarian response, which makes it difficult for any one organization to prevent the spread of conflict. Organizations fear losing funding to competing NGOs if they protest militarization. One solution to this coordination problem is stronger humanitarian leadership.

In the refugee relief regime, UNHCR is the dominant actor. Despite the constraints described above, UNHCR could coordinate humanitarian action in situations where most organizations agree that their efforts are worsening conflict. UNHCR leadership in protesting abuse of aid is likely to bring about a somewhat unified response. Because of the coordination problems afflicting NGOs, they will not be able to encourage change among donor governments or refugee receiving states without UNHCR leadership. It is probable that agencies that feel too helpless to seek change might follow the UNHCR lead, were it to do so.

In the past, UNHCR's lack of humanitarian leadership has hindered a coherent response to militarization. For example, Human Rights Watch noted that UNHCR passivity in the face of abuses in Guinea inhibited smaller organizations from protesting: "UNHCR generally plays an intermediary role between international nongovernmental humanitarian agencies and the authorities of the refugee-hosting country; but in Guinea UNHCR appeared unwilling to do so, creating a climate in which aid workers were also unwilling or unable to speak out. UNHCR's failure to press for access to the border region in particular posed a major obstacle to the work of its partner agencies."[61] During the Rwanda crisis in eastern Zaire, NGOs implored UNHCR to address the violence in the camps. The NGOs were told that they would be replaced if they left.[62] UNHCR contributed to the coordination problem afflicting NGOs rather than take a leadership role in publicizing and combating militarization.

Although independence remains an essential value for many NGOs, that does not mean that these organizations prefer to operate in a leadership vacuum. In January 2003, the International Rescue Committee (IRC) appealed to UN Secretary General Kofi Annan regarding the dilemmas about humanitarian action in Iraq. The letter from IRC asserted, "the UN is the only banner under which the majority of aid agencies, donors, and border states can work together effectively and independently of the military forces involved in the conflict."[63]

Critics of a UNHCR leadership role suggest that UNHCR can easily be replaced if donors become dissatisfied. The usual example is Kosovo in 1999, where NATO stepped in to care for the Kosovar refugees. It is misleading to claim that the Kosovo situation could ever be the norm in most of the world, however. In most areas affected by refugee crises, NATO has no desire to engage. Crises in Europe are the exception. In reality, there is little alternative to UNHCR as the main actor in refugee relief.

CONCLUSION

The foregoing analysis assumes that refugee relief agencies do not ignore militarization in refugee crises. As explained earlier, there are many incentives for them to do so. These include aid agencies' powerlessness, narrow mandates, dependence on donors, and institutional self-interest. Militarization is often perceived as a phenomenon beyond the control of the humanitarian sphere. Given these perverse incentives, what is the likelihood that humanitarian organizations will take some of the measures described in this chapter to prevent or reduce the spread of civil war in refugee crises?

The ideal situation is a convergence of purpose among the refugees, the receiving state, donors, and humanitarian organizations to reduce militarization. Usually this does not occur; the militarization may be in the strategic interest of the receiving state or external powers, or it may be of no concern to major powers. Either way, the refugee relief organizations are left to deal with the issue on their own.

In this worst-case situation, organizations have two possible motivations to pursue demilitarization. First, a humanitarian organization is more likely to act if its mandate includes both protection and assistance. Such organizations include UNHCR, the International Committee of the Red Cross, and various NGOs, including MSF and the International Rescue Committee, among others. The severity of the situation also drives motivation. If the militarization threatens the security of aid workers and hinders agencies' abilities to fulfill their humanitarian tasks, refugee relief organizations are more likely to pursue demilitarization. Essentially, aid agencies are likely to reduce or prevent militarization based on ethical norms to protect refugees and on the practical need to safeguard their own resources, including staff members.

Despite the many differences among NGOs, the ICRC, and United Nations agencies, they all can benefit from accurate political analyses of crisis situations. Humanitarian organizations generally recognize that humanitarian crises are part of a larger political and military context. However, to move beyond a surface acceptance of that fact, humanitarian organizations must improve their analytical capabilities. Understanding the political context and origins of the crisis will enable organizations to predict potential militarized situations. At the extreme, political analysis will provide warning of a state-in-exile movement, such as the Rwandan Hutu in Zaire and Tanzania.

Given an accurate understanding of the situation, humanitarian organizations can use their moral clout to publicize the desperate need for security assistance. Western policymakers and citizens already understand the benefits of material assistance, such as food, medicine, and shelter. Less understood is the equal need for physical protection and demilitarization in refugee crises. Humanitarian organizations must bring this to the fore and make a concerted effort to raise funds for security—both for refugees and aid workers.

With adequate political and military support, humanitarian organizations can pursue strategies of prevention. This requires military or police intervention to disarm entering refugees and separate militants from the refugees. Prevention also requires a determined political effort to find a durable, quick, and peaceful solution to the crisis. The longer the crisis drags on, the more likely that persecuted or state-in-exile groups will turn to military activity.

Even without external support, agencies can reduce the effects of militarization. One way to do this is to enter into security partnerships. This is commonly done with local receiving state forces, especially police. This type of partnership requires a financial commitment from donor states, but not necessarily a military one. Security partnerships have the potential to reduce militarization and crime in the refugee-populated areas. Thus far, security partnerships, such as the one between UNHCR and the Tanzanian police, have been partially successful. Their ultimate success relies on adequate external funding and cooperation from the receiving state government. In the absence of a security partnership, humanitarian organizations can attempt to reduce the influence of militants by promoting alternative leaders and engaging in information campaigns that counter militarist propaganda.

Current humanitarian responses to militarized refugee crises generally ignore the political context of the crises. By doing so, humanitarian organizations all too often contribute to the spread of conflicts. The numerous excuses for ignoring militarization may seem legitimate, but they provide little consolation when humanitarian aid exacerbates violence. In the long run, if agencies do not leverage their resources to improve security, they risk losing their moral clout when humanitarian assistance contributes to conflict. The humanitarian fiasco in the Rwandan refugee camps highlighted the urgent need to design refugee relief programs with a better understanding of their political and military impacts. In militarized refugee crises, purity of intention cannot prevent the spread of conflict.

Notes

Chapter 1. Refugee Crises as Catalysts of Conflict

1. African Rights, *Rwanda: Death, Despair, and Defiance* (London: African Rights, 1995, revised edition), 1094.

2. International Rescue Committee, "Mortality in the Democratic Republic of Congo: Results of a Nationwide Survey" (New York: IRC, April 2003).

3. In this book, the term *refugee* includes people designated as refugees according to the criteria of either UNHCR or the U.S. Committee for Refugees (USCR). It is necessary to use definitions from both organizations because there are a few areas in which they do not overlap. For example, USCR counts Palestinians as refugees, whereas UNHCR does not. For discussions of the definition of refugee, see Jennifer Hyndman, *Managing Displacement* (Minneapolis: University of Minnesota Press, 2000), 6–14; Aristide R. Zolberg et al., *Escape From Violence: Conflict and the Refugee Crisis in the Developing World* (New York: Oxford University Press, 1989), 3–33; and Susanne Schmeidl, "From Root Cause Assessment to Preventive Diplomacy: Possibilities and Limitations of the Early Warning of Forced Migration" (Ph.D. diss., Ohio State University, 1995), ch. 2 and appendix B.

4. The term *sending state* refers to the country from which the refugees fled. *Receiving state* describes the country that hosts the refugees.

5. James Jay Carafano, "An Ill-Considered Notion: Eisenhower's Volunteer Freedom Corps" (Washington, DC: undated manuscript), quotation 6.

6. Myron Weiner, "The Clash of Norms: Dilemmas in Refugee Policies," *Journal of Refugee Studies* 11:4 (1998), 9.

7. Courtland Robinson, "Case Study: The Thai-Cambodian Border," Paper presented at the Workshop on Physical Security and Protection of Refugee Populated Areas, Massachusetts Institute of Technology, Cambridge, MA, October 29–30, 1999. See also Fiona Terry, *Condemned to Repeat: The Paradox of Humanitarian Action* (Ithaca, NY: Cornell University Press, 2002), ch. 4; Zolberg et al., *Escape from Violence*, 170–73, 275–78.

8. William Stanley, "Blessing or Menace? The Security Implications of Central American Migration," in Myron Weiner (ed.), *International Migration and Security* (Boulder, CO: Westview Press, 1993), 245.

9. Terry, *Condemned to Repeat*, 83–113; and Zolberg et al., *Escape from Violence*, 204–24.

10. National Intelligence Estimate, "Growing Global Migration and Its Implications for the United States," NIE 2001–02D, March 2001, 25, 4.

11. The term *militarization* describes noncivilian attributes of refugee-populated areas, including military training, recruitment, and the inflow of weapons. Militarization also includes actions of refugees and/or exiles who engage in noncivilian activity outside the refugee camp, yet depend on assistance from refugees or international organizations. The term *exiles* refers to people, including soldiers and war criminals, who leave their country of origin but do not qualify for refugee status. *Demilitarization* involves the separation of a refugee-populated area and military actors and activity; demilitarization occurs when all parties (i.e., refugees, receiving state government, and any external interveners) respect international law relating to the protection of refugees.

12. On forced repatriation, see Anne Bayefsky and Michael W. Doyle, *Emergency Return: Principles and Guidelines* (Princeton, NJ: Center for International Studies, Princeton University, 1999).

13. For a similar argument about military intervention in general, see Richard K. Betts, "The Delusion of Impartial Intervention," *Foreign Affairs*, November/December 1994.

14. On the perverse effects of humanitarian aid, see Alexander Cooley and James Ron, "The NGO Scramble: Organizational Insecurity and the Political Economy of Transnational Action," *International Security* 27:1 (Summer 2002), 5–39; Terry, *Condemned to Repeat*; Stephen John Stedman and Fred Tanner (eds.), *Refugee Manipulation: War, Politics, and the Abuse of Human Suffering* (Washington, DC: The Brookings Institution, 2003); Neil S. MacFarlane, "Humanitarian Action: The Conflict Connection" (Providence: Brown University, Thomas J. Watson Jr. Institute for International Studies, Occasional Paper #43, 2001); Mary B. Anderson, *Do No Harm: How Aid Can Support Peace—or War* (Boulder, CO: Lynne Rienner, 1999); Alex de Wall, *Famine Crimes: Politics and the Disaster Relief Industry* (Bloomington: Indiana University Press, 1998); and Tony Vaux, *The Selfish Altruist: Relief Work in Famine and War* (London: Earthscan, 2001).

15. David Rieff, *A Bed for the Night: Humanitarianism in Crisis* (New York: Simon and Schuster, 2002), 184.

16. Quoted in ibid., 54.

17. Lucy Hovil, "Refugees and the Security Situation in Adjumani District" (Kampala, Uganda: Refugee Law Project, June 2001), 13.

18. Anderson, *Do No Harm*, 49; see also Kathleen Newland, "Refugee Protection and Assistance," in *Managing Global Issues: Lessons Learned* (Washington DC: Carnegie Endowment for International Peace, 2001), 522; and Terry, *Condemned to Repeat*, 45–46.

19. Cooley and Ron, "The NGO Scramble," 30–31.

20. Human Rights Watch, "Liberian Refugees in Guinea: Refoulement, Militarization of Camps, and Other Protection Concerns" (New York: November 2002), 20.

21. MacFarlane, "Humanitarian Action," 17; and Terry, *Condemned to Repeat*.

22. ICRC, "ICRC Conditionality: Doctrine, Dilemma and Dialogue," in Nicholas Leader and Joanna Macrae (eds.), *Terms of Engagement: Conditions and Conditionality in Humanitarian Action*, Report No. 6 (London: Humanitarian Policy Group, Overseas Development Institute, 2000), 25.

23. MacFarlane, "Humanitarian Action," 23.

24. Cooley and Ron, "The NGO Scramble," 5–39.

25. Integrated Regional Information Network (IRIN), "Angola: IRIN Interview with Eugenio Manuvakola," March 14, 2002.

26. Rieff, *A Bed for the Night: Humanitarianism in Crisis*, 330.

27. On the non-neutrality of famine aid, see David Keen, "Engaging with Violence: A Reassessment of Relief in Wartime," in Ken Wilson (ed.), *War and Hunger: Rethinking International Responses to Complex Emergencies* (London: Zed Books, 1994), 209–21.

28. These explanations are discussed further in chapter 3. For a discussion of the conventional explanations, see United Nations Security Council, "Report of the Secretary-General on Protection for Humanitarian Assistance to Refugees and Others in Conflict Situations," S/1998/883, New York, September 22, 1998, section E; and International Council of Voluntary Agencies, "Refugee Camps on the Border: A Recipe for Disaster in West Africa," December 22, 2000.

29. Myron Weiner's classification of refugee-related security threats is an exception. See Weiner, "Security, Stability, and International Migration," *International Security* 17:3 (Winter 1992/93), 103–20.

30. For more on this, see Sarah Kenyon Lischer, "Refugee-Related Political Violence: When? Where? How Much?" Rosemarie Rogers Working Paper Series (Cambridge, MA: MIT, Center for International Studies, December 2001). Found at http://web.mit.edu/cis/www/migration/pubs/rrwp/10_lischer.html.

31. For more examples, see Elly-Elikunda Mtango, "Military and Armed Attacks on Refugee Camps," in Gil Loescher and Laila Monahan (eds.), *Refugees and International Relations* (Oxford: Oxford University Press, 1989), 87–121. On Cambodia, see Terry, *Condemned to Repeat*, 114–54.

32. Human Rights Watch, "Liberian Refugees in Guinea: Refoulement, Militarization of Camps, and Other Protection Concerns."

33. Hovil, "Refugees and the Security Situation in Adjumani District."

34. Mark Tessler, *A History of the Israeli-Palestinian Conflict* (Bloomington: Indiana University Press, 1994), 456–64.

35. On these instances of violence, see country reports for Burma, Uganda, and Hong Kong in U.S. Committee for Refugees, *World Refugee Survey* (Washington, DC), various years.

36. IRIN, "Ethiopia: 33 Killed in Refugee Camp Violence," Daily selection of IRIN Africa English reports, e-mail list, December 2, 2002. Found at www.reliefweb.org.

37. On the Tanzania-Uganda war, see Anthony Clayton, *Frontiersmen: Warfare in Africa Since 1950* (London: UCL Press, 1999), 104–8.

38. Nicholas Wheeler, *Saving Strangers: Humanitarian Intervention in International Society* (Oxford: Oxford University Press, 2000), 61.

39. Transcript of President Clinton's Radio Address to the Nation, September 17, 1994.

Chapter 2. Political Incentives for the Spread Of Civil War

1. Weiner characterized the causes of refugee flows as inter-state war, ethnic conflict, non-ethnic civil war, and revolutionary and authoritarian regimes. My analysis looks further at what type of violence occurred and which groups were specifically targeted. See Weiner, "Bad Neighbors, Bad Neighborhoods: An Inquiry into the Cause of Refugee Flows," *International Security* 21:1 (Summer 1996), 18.

2. Nigel Marsh of World Vision, quoted in IRIN, "DRC: People Running for Their Lives in the East," November 16, 2000. Found at http://www.reliefweb.int.

3. Sheldon Yett, "Masisi, Down the Road from Goma: Ethnic Cleansing and Displacement in Eastern Zaire," Issue Brief (Washington, DC: U.S. Committee for Refugees, June 1996), 5.

4. Human Rights Watch, "Liberian Refugees in Guinea: Refoulement, Militarization of Camps, and Other Protection Concerns" (New York: November 2002), 8.

5. Burton Bollag, "Destabilization: The Human Cost," *Refugees*, July–August 1988, 20.

6. Interviews with two hundred refugees revealed 96 percent with a "very or somewhat negative" attitude toward RENAMO and 1 percent with a "positive" attitude. Seventy-two percent of refugees expressed "no complaint" about government forces, Frente de Libertação de Moçambique, or FRELIMO, but only 11 percent characterized their attitude as positive. Robert Gersony, "Summary of Mozambican Refugee Accounts of Principally Conflict-Related Experience in Mozambique," report submitted to Bureau of Refugee Programs, U.S. Department of State, April 1988.

7. In one study, 65 percent of respondents cited security as their main priority for return. The other 35 percent cited various economic and social factors. Khalid Koser, "Information and Repatriation: The Case of Mozambican Refugees in Malawi," *Journal of Refugee Studies* 10:1 (March 1997), 5, 11.

8. Sandy Kuwali, "Escape to Nsanje," *Southern African Economist*, February/March 1989, 11.

9. Amnesty International, "Bosnia-Herzegovina: All the Way Home—Safe 'Minority Returns' as a Just Remedy and for a Secure Future," February 1998.

10. Amnesty International, "Bosnia-Herzegovina: All the Way Home."

11. For more on the phenomenon of refugee groups that become militarized after their flight, see Howard Adelman, "Why Refugee Warriors Are Threats," *Journal of Conflict Studies* (Spring 1998), 49–69.

12. Gerard Prunier, "Rwanda: Update to End of July 1995," Writenet Country Papers, Refworld, UNHCR, August 1995, sec. 3.1.

13. Jean-Francois Durieux, "Preserving the Civilian Character of Refugee Camps: Lessons from the Kigoma Refugee Programme in Tanzania," *Track Two* 9:3 (November 2000), 31.

14. Real and perceived persecution fuels the refugees' fears. See, for example, IRIN Update 1,014 for the Great Lakes, "Burundi: Tutsi group threatens to attack refugee in camps in Tanzania," September 19, 2000. Found at www.reliefweb.int.

15. Emile Segbor, UNHCR official, interview by the author, Geneva, Switzerland, July 15, 1998.

16. My concept of a state-in-exile population is similar to what Zolberg et al. term a "refugee-warrior community." They describe these groups as "highly conscious refugee communities with a political leadership structure and armed sections engaged in warfare for a political objective." See Zolberg et al., 275–78. The term *state in exile* is a more accurate description than "refugee-warriors" and does not carry the same pejorative connotation.

17. African Rights, *Rwanda: Death, Despair, and Defiance* (London: African Rights, 1995 revised edition), 1098.

18. The number of refugees is still disputed. At its establishment in 1950, the United Nations Relief and Works Agency for Palestinian Refugees (UNRWA) registered 726,000 Palestinian refugees. See Benny Morris, *The Birth of the Palestinian Refugee Problem, 1947–1949* (Cambridge: Cambridge University Press, 1987), 1; and Yezid Sayigh, *Armed Struggle and the Search for State: The Palestinian National Movement, 1949–1993* (Oxford: Oxford University Press, 1997), 3–4.

19. Yezid Sayigh, "The Politics of Palestinian Exile," *Third World Quarterly* 9:1 (January 1987), 28. The precipitating causes of the Palestinians' flight in 1948 are still controversial.

20. Ibid., 33, 55.

21. Alan Dowty, "Return or Compensation: The Legal and Political Context of the Palestinian Refugee Issue," in *World Refugee Survey 1994* (Washington DC: United States Committee for Refugees, 1994), 26.

22. Helena Cobban, *The Palestinian Liberation Organization: People, Power, and Politics* (Cambridge: Cambridge University Press, 1984), 41–42; Sayigh, *Armed Struggle*, 174–79.

23. Sayigh, "The Politics of Palestinian Exile," 31.

24. Mark Tessler, *A History of the Israeli-Palestinian Conflict* (Bloomington: Indiana University Press, 1994), 456–64.

25. Salim Nasr, "Lebanon's War: Is the End in Sight?" *Middle East Report* 162 (January–February 1990), 5.

26. Cobban, *The Palestinian Liberation Organization*, 128–30; and Mark Whitaker, "The Making of a Massacre," *Newsweek*, October 4, 1982, 24.

27. Randa Farah, "The Marginalization of Palestinian Refugees," in Mark Gibney, Niklaus Steiner, and Gil Loescher (eds.), *Problems of Protection: The UNHCR, Refugees, and Human Rights* (New York: Routledge, 2003), 168.

28. Daniel Pipes, "Demoralizing U.N. Labeling of Palestinians Makes Bad Situation Worse," *Chicago Sun-Times*, August 26, 2003.

29. The Organization of African Unity (OAU) Convention states that "Signatory States undertake to prohibit refugees residing in their respective territories from attacking any member state of the OAU." Organization of African Unity, "Convention Governing the Specific Aspects of Refugee Problems in Africa," 1969, article 3. The Organization of American States (OAS) also urges the institution of "appropriate measures in the receiving countries to prevent the participation of the refugees in activities directed against the country of origin." Organization of American States, "Cartagena Declaration on Refugees," 1984. In a more recent document, the Security Council reaffirmed "the primary responsibility of States to ensure [refugee] protection, in particular by maintaining the security and civilian character of refugee and internally displaced person camps." UN Security Council Resolution 1265, adopted September 17, 1999, UN Doc. S/RES/1265 (1999).

30. Signs of a lack of capability include one or more active rebel groups within the country. The strength of the military and police is also a measure of capability. One can view the receiving state's capability as an absolute measure, as well as relative to the capability of its neighbors.

31. Examples of the spread of civil war where the receiving state had high capability and low willingness include Afghan refugees in Pakistan (1980s), Burundian refugees in Tanzania (1990s), Liberian refugees in the Ivory Coast (1990s), Ugandan refugees in Tan-

zania (1978), Cambodian refugees in Thailand (1980s), Nicaraguan refugees in Honduras (1980s), and Rwandan refugees in Uganda (1990).

32. The extreme case is a "failed" state. A failed state occurs where there is "a weak central authority, challenged by one or more armed groups in control of portions of the country, and where the government lacks the ability to protect its citizens." Weiner, "Bad Neighbors, Bad Neighborhoods," 22.

33. International Council of Voluntary Agencies, "Refugee Camps on the Border: A Recipe for Disaster in West Africa," December 22, 2000. For more on this situation, see Human Rights Watch, "Guinea, Refugees Still at Risk," 13:5 (July 2001).

34. Examples of violence-prone situations that did not lead to the spread of civil war include Afghan refugees in Iran (1980s), Rwandan refugees in Tanzania (1990s), and Nicaraguan refugees in Costa Rica (1980s).

35. Lucy Hovil, "Refugees and the Security Situation in Adjumani District" (Kampala, Uganda: Refugee Law Project, June 2001), 14.

36. Human Rights Watch, "Liberian Refugees in Guinea: Refoulement, Militarization of Camps, and Other Protection Concerns."

37. UNHCR ExCom, "The Security, and Civilian and Humanitarian Character of Refugee Camps and Settlements," Doc. No. EC/49/SC/INF.2, January 14, 1999, par. 11. On camp size and location, see UNHCR, *Handbook for Emergencies*, Geneva, 1999, ch. 6.

38. Ben Barber, "Feeding Refugees or War," *Foreign Affairs* 76:4 (July/August 1997), 14.

39. Bonaventure Rutinwa, "Refugee Protection and Security in East Africa," *RPN* 22 (September 1996), 11–13.

40. As yet, there is no reliable data on the size of all refugee camps, so it is not possible to correlate refugee-related violence with individual camps in a systematic large-N test.

41. Barry Posen argues that in ethnic conflicts, "offensive military capabilities are as much a function of the quantity and commitment of the soldiers [each side] can mobilize as the particular characteristics of the weapons they control." See Posen, "The Security Dilemma and Ethnic Conflict," *Survival* 35:1 (Spring 1993), 29.

42. The data analyzed includes UNHCR annual protection reports for each receiving state, U.S. Committee for Refugees *World Refugee Survey*, and *New York Times* abstracts. See Sarah Kenyon Lischer, "Refugee-Related Political Violence: When? Where? How Much?" *Rosemarie Rogers Working Paper Series* (Cambridge, MA: Massachusetts Institute of Technology, Center for International Studies, December 2001). Found at http://web.mit.edu/cis/www/migration/pubs/rrwp/10_lischer.html.

43. I measure a refugee population as refugees from one sending state in one receiving state—for example, Liberian refugees in Guinea, not all Liberian refugees or all refugees in Guinea. In 1998, there were 117 populations between 2,000 and 100,000 refugees.

44. See Matthews, "Refugees and Stability in Africa," 68, 78.

45. OAU, "Convention," Article 2(6). See also recommendations about camp location in Bonaventure Rutinwa, "The End of Asylum? The Changing Nature of Refugee Policies in Africa" (Geneva: UNHCR), *New Issues in Refugee Research* working paper series, May 1999.

46. UNHCR, *Handbook for Emergencies*, 1999, sec. 6.3.

47. In some cases, refugees return to their homes during the day to farm and then sleep in the refugee camps for safety.

48. Randolph Martin, International Rescue Committee, personal communication to the author. Cambridge, MA, October 30, 1999.

49. IRIN, "Interview with Mark Bowden on Protecting Civilians in Conflict," IRIN Africa-English Service e-mail list, October 21, 2002.

50. Inspection and Evaluation Service UNHCR, "Lessons Learned from the Rwanda and Burundi Emergencies" (Geneva: UNHCR, April 1996), par. 85.

51. I thank Dr. Jennifer Leaning for suggesting this hypothesis to me at the Mellon-MIT Program on NGOs and Forced Migration Brown Bag Seminar, March 2000. See also Simon Turner, "Angry Young Men in Camps" (Geneva: UNHCR), New Issues in Refugee

Research working paper series, June 1999; and Simon Turner, "Vindicating Masculinity: The Fate of Promoting Gender Equality," *Forced Migration Review* (December 2000), 8–9.

52. Tony Vaux, *The Selfish Altruist* (London: Earthscan Publications, 2001), 193.

53. Valerie M. Hudson and Andrea den Boer, "A Surplus of Men, a Deficit of Peace; Security and Sex Ratios in Asia's Largest States," *International Security* 26:4 (2002), 37.

54. Paul Collier, "Doing Well Out of War," in Mats Berdal and David M. Malone (eds.), *Greed and Grievance, Economic Agendas in Civil Wars* (Boulder, CO: Lynne Rienner, 2000),94. Emphasis in original.

55. Accurate measurement of the proportion of men in a camp is not always straight-forward. In many cases, refugees resist attempts to take a census. In the eastern Zaire camps in 1996, the militants strongly opposed a census because they had been inflating camp numbers in order to skim extra aid off the top. The militants shot at aid workers who tried to implement the census. Ann-Sofie Nedlund, UNHCR official, interview with the author, Geneva, July 13, 1999. Systematic data is also elusive. For example, recent UNHCR figures present demographic data on only 5.4 million out of about 13 million refugees. UNHCR, "Refugees and Others of Concern to UNHCR, 1999 Statistical Overview," table III.1.

56. Bela Hovy, UNHCR Statistics Bureau. Personal communication with the author, August 30, 2001.

57. In Africa, 16.3 percent of refugees are children under five, virtually the same as in the nonrefugee population. UNHCR ExCom, "Statistics and Registration: A Progress Report," Doc. No. EC/50/SC/CRP.10, February 7, 2000, pars. 4 and 5.

58. One exception to the demographic similarity between refugees and nonrefugees is when a crisis has an acute emergency phase in which mortality rates rise sharply. In emergencies, young children and the elderly are likely to die, leaving a greater proportion of teenagers of both genders. This pattern is not specific to types of refugee groups and thus is unrelated to the political context of the crisis. The tendency for a bulge of teenagers to emerge over time suggests the interesting hypothesis that violence should be more prevalent in long-term refugee populations. I thank Charles Keely for this insight. Personal communication to the author, August 28, 2001.

59. This research does not examine the impact of the gender balance on crime or other types of violence. It is likely that refugee camps mirror other societies, in which the majority of violent crime is committed by young men.

60. Susanne Schmeidl, "The Quest for Accuracy in the Estimation of Forced Migration," in Stephen C. Lubkemann et al. (eds.), *Humanitarian Action: Social Science Connections* (Providence: Thomas J. Watson Jr. Institute for International Studies, Brown University, 2000), Occasional Paper no. 37, 150–51.

61. "Humanitarian Security and Protection in Refugee-Populated Areas: Operationalizing the 'Ladder of Options,' " unpublished paper presented to UNHCR ExCom, June 2000. Liisa Malkki argues that bored rural Burundian refugees became more politically activist and nationalist than urban refugees who had more options. See Malkki, *Purity and Exile: Violence, Memory, and National Cosmology Among Hutu Refugees in Tanzania* (Chicago: University of Chicago Press, 1995).

62. OAU/UNHCR, "Refugee Protection and Security in the Great Lakes Region," Regional Meeting on Refugee Issues in the Great Lakes, Kampala, Uganda, May 8–9, 1998, 8.

63. UNHCR, *Handbook for Emergencies, Second Edition*, 1999, ch. 2, par. 48.

64. UNICEF Inter-Agency Standing Committee, *Growing the Sheltering Tree: Protecting Rights through Humanitarian Action* (New York: UNICEF, 2002), 112.

65. Testing the effect of living conditions on other types of violence falls beyond the scope of this project.

66. On economics and conflict, see Mats Berdal and David M. Malone (eds.), *Greed and Grievance: Economic Agendas in Civil Wars* (Boulder, CO: Lynne Rienner, 2000); and Karen Ballentine and Jake Sherman (eds.), *The Political Economy of Armed Conflict: Beyond Greed and Grievance* (Boulder, CO: Lynne Rienner, 2003).

67. Paul Collier and Anke Hoeffler, "Greed and Grievance in Civil War," World Bank, January 4, 2001, quotations 2–3.

68. David Keen, "Incentives and Disincentives for Violence," in Berdal and Malone, *Greed and Grievance*, 19–41.

69. In the wake of interventions by numerous states and rebel groups since 1998, the war in the Congo has become deeply intertwined with exploitation of that country's natural resources. It has been persuasively argued that many parties to the conflict are perpetuating war for their own enrichment. See Mahmoud Kassem, "Final Report of the Panel of Experts on the Illegal Exploitation of Natural Resources and Other Forms of Wealth of the Democratic Republic of the Congo" (United Nations Security Council, October 16, 2002).

70. Paul Collier, "Economic Causes of Civil Conflict and Their Implications for Policy" (Washington DC: World Bank, June 15, 2000).

Chapter 3. Afghan Refugees

1. Olivier Roy, *Islam and Resistance in Afghanistan* (New York: Cambridge University Press, 1985), 165.

2. Edward Girardet, *Afghanistan: The Soviet War* (London: Croom Helm, 1985), 104.

3. David Busby Edwards, "The Origins of the Anti-Soviet Jihad," in Grant M. Farr and John G. Merriam (eds.), *Afghan Resistance: The Politics of Survival* (Boulder, CO: Westview Press, 1987), 44.

4. Numerous spellings exist for this word in the Western press, but they all refer to the same concept of Islamic holy warriors.

5. Olivier Roy, *The Lessons of the Soviet/Afghan War*, Adelphi Papers 259 (Brassey's for International Institute for Strategic Studies, 1991), 20.

6. On the provision of Stinger missiles, see Alan J. Kuperman, "The Stinger Missile and U.S. Intervention in Afghanistan," *Political Science Quarterly* 114:2 (1999), 219–63.

7. UNHCR, "Afghanistan Humanitarian Update No. 67," January 3, 2003. Found at http://www.unhcr.ch.

8. Habibulla Tegey and Margery E. Tegey, "Foreword," in Farr and Merriam, *Afghan Resistance*, ix.

9. For more on the Soviet counter-guerrilla strategy, see Benjamin A. Valentino, *Final Solutions: Mass Killing and Genocide in the Twentieth Century* (Ithaca: Cornell University Press, 2004), 217–27.

10. Some have charged that the Soviets deliberately attempted to depopulate the country, but this was not the case. According to American intelligence sources, "charges that the Soviets are deliberately trying to empty the country of the civilian population do not seem to be well founded. The Babrak regime and the Soviets are trying to exploit the refugees as a potentially destabilizing element in Pakistan, but are aware that the enormous refugee population emphasizes the illegitimacy of the Babrak regime. They and the government are trying hard to entice the refugees to return." United States, Department of State, Bureau of Intelligence and Research, "The Afghan Resistance Movement in 1981: Progress, but a Long Way to Go," secret report by Eliza Van Hollen, January 19, 1982. Digital National Security Archive item number AF01310, 10.

11. "Refugees in Pakistan Clamor for Arms," *New York Times*, July 20, 1980.

12. Lawrence Ziring, "Buffer States on the Rim of Asia: Pakistan, Afghanistan, Iran and the Superpowers," in Hafeez Malik (ed.), *Soviet-American Relations with Pakistan, Iran and Afghanistan* (New York: St. Martin's Press, 1987), 111.

13. M. Nazif Shahrani also notes that Mohammed's exile from oppression allowed the formation of a population of refugee-fighters who later reconquered their homeland of Mecca. Qur'an 16:41–42, quoted in Shahrani, "Afghanistan's Muhajirin (Muslim 'Refugee-Warriors'): Politics of Mistrust and Distrust of Politics," in E. Valentine Daniel and John Chr. Knudsen (eds.), *Mistrusting Refugees* (Berkeley: University of California Press, 1995), 187, 191.

14. Tegey and Tegey, "Foreword," in Farr and Merriam, *Afghan Resistance*, x.

15. Roy, *Islam and Resistance in Afghanistan*, 159. The reader should bear in mind that the strong sympathy for the resistance among many Western authors may have led to an exaggeration of the mass support for the resistance. For example, the U.S. government enthused that "the preeminent source of strength for the resistance movement is the support it receives from the Afghan people, regardless of ethnic group or tribal affiliation." United States, Department of State, Bureau of Intelligence and Research, "The Afghan Resistance Movement in 1981: Progress, but a Long Way to Go," secret report by Eliza Van Hollen, January 19, 1982. Digital National Security Archive item number AF01310, 7.

16. Kerry M. Connor, "The Rationales for the Movement of Afghan Refugees to Peshawar," in Farr and Merriam, *Afghan Resistance*, 166–67.

17. Non-Pushtun refugees tended to go to Sind or Punjab provinces. The educated elite generally fled to Europe or the United States and did not become involved in the resistance movement.

18. The size of the refugee population in Pakistan was the subject of much debate. Both the refugees and the Pakistan government had incentives to exaggerate the size of the population to increase aid donations. An undetermined number of refugees exaggerated family size or registered twice. A United States Embassy cable noted that "the reliability of data on registered refugees is open to some doubt" and concluded that the "bottom line is that nobody knows." United States Embassy, Pakistan, "Afghan Refugee Situation in Pakistan's Northwest Frontier Province," (April 23, 1981), confidential cable by Barrington King, Digital National Security Archive item number AF01170, pars. 5 and 7. See also Nancy Hatch Dupree, "The Demography of Afghan Refugees in Pakistan," in Hafeez Malik (ed.), *Soviet-American Relations with Pakistan, Iran and Afghanistan* (New York: St. Martin's Press, 1987), 366–94.

19. Roy, *The Lessons of the Soviet/Afghan War*, 16.

20. Roy, *Islam and Resistance in Afghanistan*, 110.

21. Anthony Hyman, *Afghanistan Under Soviet Domination, 1964–83* (New York: St. Martin's Press, 1982), 133–34.

22. Girardet, *Afghanistan: The Soviet War*, 167.

23. William K. Stevens, "Whose Side is Time on This Time?" *New York Times*, October 3, 1982.

24. "The Crisis of Migration from Afghanistan: Domestic and Foreign Implications," summary of proceedings of an international symposium, report from the Afghan delegation (Oxford: Oxford University Refugee Studies Programme and Department of Ethnology and Prehistory, March 29–April 2, 1987), 12.

25. Sabahuddin Kushkaki, "The Afghan Refugees: Threats Against Their Physical and Spiritual Survival," paper delivered at the international symposium on "The Crisis of Migration from Afghanistan: Domestic and Foreign Implications" (Oxford: Oxford University Refugee Studies Programme and Department of Ethnology and Prehistory, March 29–April 2, 1987).

26. Gowher Rizvi, "The Afghan Refugees: Hostages in the Struggle for Power," *Journal of Refugee Studies* 3:3 (1990), 259.

27. Shahrani, "Afghanistan's Muhajirin," 198.

28. The largest ethnic group is the Pushtun group, which has two major competing tribal sub-groups, the Durranis and the Ghilzays. Pushtun are mostly Sunni Muslims. Other major ethnic groups include Hazaras (mostly Shi'a), Uzbeks, and Tajiks. The many groups do not share a strong concept of unity or loyalty to the central state.

29. Alexander Alexiev, "The War in Afghanistan: Soviet Strategy and the State of the Resistance," The Rand Paper Series (Santa Monica, CA: Rand Corporation, November 1984), 6.

30. Edward Girardet, "Afghan Refugees: The Palestinians of Asia?" *Christian Science Monitor*, July 9, 1982.

31. Randolph Martin, "Regional Dynamics and the Security of Afghan Refugees in Pakistan," paper prepared for a workshop on security in refugee populated areas, MIT, Cambridge, MA, October 29–30, 1999, 6.

32. Figures from Mohammad Yousaf, the former head of the Afghan section of Pakistan's Inter-Services Intelligence. Cited in Fiona Terry, *Condemned to Repeat? The Paradox of Humanitarian Action* (Ithaca, NY: Cornell University Press, 2002), 58.

33. Anthony Hyman, "The Afghan Politics of Exile," *Third World Quarterly* 9:1 (January 1987), 75.

34. For more details, see United States Embassy, Pakistan, "Helicopter Gunships Strafe Afghan Refugee Camp in Pakistan" (October 25, 1980), confidential cable by Arthur W. Hummel Jr., Digital National Security Archive item number AF01065; Department of State, United States Embassy, Pakistan, "Afghan Helicopters Attack Refugee Areas in Pakistan" (November 18, 1981), cable by Ronald Spiers, Digital National Security Archive item number AF01294; Department of State, United States Embassy, Pakistan, "Report of New DRA Gunship Attacks on Afghan Refugees in Pakistan" (December 21, 1981), cable by Ronald Spiers, Digital National Security Archive item number AF01303.

35. United States, Mission to the United Nations, "Pakistan Submits Formal Note to Secretary General on Raids" (November 8, 1980), cable by Donald McHenry, Digital National Security Archive item number AF01077, par. 2.

36. Hasan-Askari Razvi, "Afghan Refugees in Pakistan: Influx, Humanitarian Assistance and Implications," *Pakistan Horizon* 37:1 (1984), 55.

37. United States, National Security Council "U.S.-Iran Dialogue" (May 26, 1986), memorandum of conversation by Howard J. Teicher, Digital National Security Archive item number AF01712.

38. It is important to note that the Pakistani response was not monolithic. Opponents of President Zia's regime resented that the refugee crisis boosted his international standing. They also felt the refugees introduced instability into Pakistani politics. See " The Crisis of Migration from Afghanistan: Domestic and Foreign Implications," summary of proceedings of an international symposium, report from the Pakistani delegation (Oxford: Oxford University Refugee Studies Programme and Department of Ethnology and Prehistory, March 29–April 2, 1987), 10.

39. Camp administrator quoted in Carol Honsa, "Inside a Pakistani Camp for Afghan Refugees," *The Christian Science Monitor*, December 9, 1981. In Pakistan the term *Pathan* is analogous to the term *Pushtun* in Afghanistan.

40. Quoted in Edward Girardet, "Afghan Violence Spilling Over into Neighboring Pakistan?" *Christian Science Monitor*, May 7, 1980.

41. Girardet, "Afghan Refugees: The Palestinians of Asia?"

42. Roy, *The Lessons of the Soviet/Afghan War*, 40.

43. Alexiev, "The War in Afghanistan," 4.

44. Ibid., 5.

45. Roy, *Islam and Resistance*, 122.

46. As the U.S. State Department reported, "There have been several incidents between refugees and local population in the NWFP this year, but what is remarkable is how few there have been." U.S. Department of State, "Afghan Refugee Situation—An Overview," (December 9, 1982), confidential cable, Digital National Security Archive item number AF01408, par. 16.

47. Andrew Hartman, " 'The Red Template': U.S. Policy in Soviet-Occupied Afghanistan," *Third World Quarterly* 23:3 (2002), 467–89.

48. Quoted in Michael T. Kaufman, "Mrs. Kirkpatrick Defends Arms for Pakistan," *New York Times*, August 25, 1981.

49. Craig Karp, "Afghan Resistance and Soviet Occupation," U.S. Department of State, Special Report No. 118, December 1984.

50. Helga Baitenmann, "NGOs and the Afghan War: The Politicisation of Humanitarian Aid," *Third World Quarterly* 12:1 (1990), 63–64; Elaine Sciolino, "U.S. to Keep Up Aid to Afghan Rebels," *New York Times*, February 25, 1989.

51. Roy, *The Lessons of the Soviet/Afghan War*, 35.

52. U.S. Department of State, "Afghan Refugee Situation—An Overview," par. 4.

53. Selig Harrison, "U.S. Policy Toward Afghanistan," transcription of paper delivered at the international symposium on "The Crisis of Migration from Afghanistan: Domestic and Foreign Implications" (Oxford: Oxford University Refugee Studies Programme and Department of Ethnology and Prehistory, March 29–April 2, 1987).

54. Sultan A. Aziz, "Leadership Dilemmas: Challenges and Responses," in Farr and Merriam, *Afghan Resistance,* 69.

55. Mohammad Yousaf, *Bear Trap: Afghanistan's Untold Story* (London: Leo Cooper, 1992), ch. 5.

56. For statistics, see U.S. Department of State, "Afghan Refugee Situation—An Overview," par. 10; Ralph H. Magnus, "Humanitarian Response to an Inhuman Strategy," in Farr and Merriam, *Afghan Resistance,* 205; and Baitenmann, "NGOs and the Afghan War: The Politicisation of Humanitarian Aid," 62–86.

57. Nancy Hatch Dupree, "The Demography of Afghan Refugees," 371.

58. Muhammad Daud, quoted in Carol Honsa, "Inside a Pakistani Camp for Afghan Refugees," *Christian Science Monitor,* December 9, 1981.

59. Yousaf, *Bear Trap: Afghanistan's Untold Story,* ch. 2.

60. Baitenmann, "NGOs and the Afghan War: The Politicisation of Humanitarian Aid."

61. UNHCR, "Review of Assistance to Afghan Refugees in Pakistan" (Geneva: UNHCR, May 1983), pars. 14 and 16.

62. Anthony Dawson, "Review of UNHCR Assistance to Afghan Refugees in Pakistan" (Geneva: UNHCR, April 1987), par. 52.

63. Girardet, *Afghanistan: The Soviet War,* 205.

64. Department of State, United States Embassy, Pakistan, "Visit of WFP Emergency Unit Director to Pakistan" (September 2, 1983), cable by Barrington King, Digital National Security Archive item number AF01494, par. 4.

65. Martin, "Regional Dynamics and the Security of Afghan Refugees in Pakistan," 4.

66. Baitenmann, "NGOs and the Afghan War."

67. Rizvi, "The Afghan Refugees: Hostages in the Struggle for Power," 255.

68. Randolph Martin, International Rescue Committee, personal communication to the author, October 30, 1999.

69. Ewan W. Anderson, "Afghan Refugees: The Geopolitical Context," paper presented at the Fourth International Conference, Refugees in the Islamic World. Bellagio, Italy, October 11–16, 1987, 31.

70. Quoted in William Branigin, "Afghan Refugees Stay Close to the Border," *Washington Post,* January 30, 1980.

71. U.S. Committee for Refugees, *World Refugee Survey: 1987 in Review* (Washington, DC: USCR, 1988), 18.

72. Nancy Hatch Dupree, "The Demography of Afghan Refugees," 381–82.

73. These statistics are not broken down into age categories. Allan Findlay, "End of the Cold War: End of Afghan Relief Aid?" 189; Shahrani, "Afghanistan's Muhajirin (Muslim 'Refugee-Warriors'): Politics of Mistrust and Distrust of Politics," 194.

74. "Refugees in Pakistan Clamor for Arms," *New York Times,* July 20, 1980.

75. Hasan-Askari Razvi, "Afghan Refugees in Pakistan: Influx, Humanitarian Assistance and Implications," *Pakistan Horizon* 37:1 (1984), 57.

76. UNHCR, "Review of Assistance to Afghan Refugees in Pakistan," par. 6.

77. Most of the camp population had rural and/or lower-class backgrounds. Wealthy refugees tended to migrate to urban areas or Western countries.

78. However, living quarters were much more cramped than before the war in Afghanistan. This mainly affected women, who were forced into seclusion by the proximity of so many nonrelatives.

79. A survey found 30 percent malnutrition in children and 200 infant deaths per thousand in Afghanistan compared to 4 percent malnourished and 119 infant deaths per thousand in the refugee camps. The figures for Pakistan are about 20 percent malnourishment, and 200 infant deaths per thousand. Yameema Mitha, "Decision Makers for the Afghan Crisis," unpublished report from the Symposium held at the Refugee Studies Programme, Oxford University, March 29–April 2, 1987.

80. Dawson, "Review of UNHCR Assistance to Afghan Refugees in Pakistan," par. 61.

81. Kathleen Howard-Merriam, "Afghan Refugee Women and Their Struggle for Survival," in Farr and Merriam, *Afghan Resistance,* 16.

82. Ralph H. Magnus, "Humanitarian Response to an Inhuman Strategy," in Farr and Merriam, *Afghan Resistance,* 195.

83. The one restriction on refugee activity was a prohibition on farming, the traditional occupation for most Afghans.

84. Findlay, "End of the Cold War," 190.

85. United States Embassy, Pakistan, "Economic Impact of Afghan Refugees upon Pakistan" (September 8, 1981), confidential airgram by Barrington King. Digital National Security Archive item number AF01260.

86. Sabahuddin Kushkaki, "The Afghan Refugees: Threats Against Their Physical and Spiritual Survival," paper delivered at the international symposium on "The Crisis of Migration from Afghanistan: Domestic and Foreign Implications," (Oxford: Oxford University Refugee Studies Programme and Department of Ethnology and Prehistory, March 29–April 2, 1987), 3.

87. These people (between 500,000 and 600,000 Afghans) were often included in the refugee statistics. Anthony Hyman, "Afghan Refugees in Iran," draft of paper delivered at the international symposium on "The Crisis of Migration from Afghanistan: Domestic and Foreign Implications" (Oxford: Oxford University Refugee Studies Programme and Department of Ethnology and Prehistory, March 29–April 2, 1987).

88. Islamic Republic of Iran, Ministry of Interior, Bureau for Aliens and Foreign Immigrants Affairs, *Statistical Survey on Afghan Refugee Population in the Islamic Republic of Iran,* 1992, 19.

89. United States Embassy, Pakistan, "WFP Mission Studies Establishment of Food Aid Program in Iran" (March 31, 1983), confidential cable by Ronald Spiers, Digital National Security Archive item number AF01445, 3.

90. Population estimates in Islamic Republic of Iran, Ministry of Interior, Bureau for Aliens and Foreign Immigrants Affairs, *Statistical Survey on Afghan Refugee Population in the Islamic Republic of Iran,* 1992.

91. One interview cites a group of 250 young men who worked in Iran and then returned to fight. Chris Kutschera, "Forgotten Refugees: Afghans in Iran," *The Middle East* (August 1986), 45.

92. Tim McGirk, "Iran No Help to Afghans," *Christian Science Monitor,* March 14, 1980.

93. Anthony Hyman, "Afghan Refugees in Iran," draft of paper delivered at the international symposium on "The Crisis of Migration from Afghanistan: Domestic and Foreign Implications" (Oxford: Oxford University Refugee Studies Programme and Department of Ethnology and Prehistory, March 29–April 2, 1987).

94. Some Afghans apparently did fight against Iraq, but Iran never extended more than token support for the resistance parties. There were also reports of forced conscription of Afghans to fight Iraq. In one instance, resistance to forced conscription led to the deaths of ten refugees. See "10 Afghans Killed in Iran," *New York Times,* April 7, 1985, 11; Ivan Zverina, "Iran Accused of Using Afghans in Gulf War," *United Press International,* March 28, 1984; "Soviets Accuse Iran of Arming Afghan Refugees, Using Them in Iraq War," *Associated Press,* August 2, 1983; "Afghan Rebels Offer to Fight for Iran," *United Press International,* October 15, 1980.

95. Leslie Keith, "Iranians Go Out of Their Way to Avoid Provoking the Soviet Bear," *Christian Science Monitor,* July 30, 1980.

96. Federal Broadcast Information Service (FBIS) Daily Report, Middle East and North Africa, Supplement-060, "Afghan MiGs, Helicopters Violate Border," Tehran Domestic Service in Persian, March 1, 1980.

97. "Soviet, Afghan Troops Raid Iran, Pakistanis Say," *Associated Press,* April 7, 1982; "Iran Says Afghan War Is Close to Border," *New York Times,* April 9, 1982.

98. Roy, *Islam and Resistance in Afghanistan,* 191.

99. FBIS Daily Report, Middle East and North Africa, Supplement-052, "EEC Proposal on Afghanistan," Tehran International Service in Arabic, February 27, 1980.

100. Roy, *Islam and Resistance in Afghanistan,* 213.

101. Quoted in United States Embassy, Pakistan, "WFP Mission Studies Establishment of Food Aid Program in Iran" (March 31, 1983), confidential cable by Ronald Spiers, Digital National Security Archive item number AF01445, 6.

102. United States, Defense Intelligence Agency, "Iranian Support to the Afghan Resistance," briefing paper, July 11, 1985. Digital National Security Archive item number AF01634.

103. Tim McGirk, "Iran No Help to Afghans," *Christian Science Monitor,* March 14, 1980.

104. John G. Merriam, "Arms Shipments to the Afghan Resistance," in Farr and Merriam, *Afghan Resistance,* 91; Girardet, *Afghanistan: The Soviet War,* 187.

105. United States, Defense Intelligence Agency, "Iranian Support to the Afghan Resistance," briefing paper, July 11, 1985. Digital National Security Archive item number AF01634.

106. Hyman, "The Afghan Politics of Exile," 81.

107. Anthony Hyman, "Hands Across the Caspian," *The Middle East* (August 1986), 48.

108. United States, Defense Intelligence Agency, "Iranian Support to the Afghan Resistance," briefing paper, July 11, 1985. Digital National Security Archive item number AF01634.

109. McGirk, "Iran No Help to Afghans."

110. Iran reported in 1989 that about a third of the refugees were Pushtun, a fifth were Hazara (usually Shi'a), and a quarter were Tajik. Islamic Republic of Iran, Ministry of Interior, Bureau for Aliens and Foreign Immigrants Affairs, *Statistical Survey on Afghan Refugee Population in the Islamic Republic of Iran,* 1992, 19.

111. Roy, *Islam and Resistance in Afghanistan,* 213.

112. Ibid.

113. United States, Central Intelligence Agency, "Iran: Attacks on Afghan Refugees," cable, December 9, 1983. Digital National Security Archive item number AF01518.

114. USCR, "Refugees in Iran: Who Should Go? Who Should Stay?" June 1999. Found at http://www.refugees.org.

115. Annick Billard, "Islamic Republic of Iran: Unnoticed Country of Asylum," *Refugees* 23 (November 1985), 20; Anthony Hyman, "Afghan Refugees in Iran," draft of paper delivered at the international symposium on "The Crisis of Migration from Afghanistan: Domestic and Foreign Implications," (Oxford: Oxford University Refugee Studies Programme and Department of Ethnology and Prehistory, March 29–April 2, 1987); U.S. Department of State, "Afghan Refugee Situation—An Overview," par. 10.

116. "Report of the Technical Mission Undertaken to Iran and Western Afghanistan from 20th November to 16th December 1992," delivered to the International Consortium for Refugees in Iran.

117. Note that most statistical information about refugees' conditions is from the late 1980s and early 1990s, once there was an international presence. Iran was much more reticent about the refugees in the early 1980s, with the result that there is less information available about those years.

118. Azmoudeh Mohammad, "Health Problems of Afghan Refugees Reported" (Islamic Republic of Iran, Ministry of Health and Medical Education, July 1992).

119. "Report of the Technical Mission Undertaken to Iran and Western Afghanistan from 20th November to 16th December 1992," delivered to the International Consortium for Refugees in Iran.

120. UNHCR, "Refugees in Iran, An NGO Seminar," Tehran, July 1992, 4; and Islamic Republic of Iran, Ministry of the Interior, Bureau for Aliens and Foreign Immigrants Affairs, *Statistical Survey on Afghan Refugee Population in the Islamic Republic of Iran,* 1992, 14–15, 17. UNHCR estimates the lower percentage of males.

121. The proportion of working age men may be inflated since Iran often included 600,000 economic migrants in its count of 2.2 million refugees.

122. Edward Girardet devotes less than a page to the millions of refugees in Iran. Girardet, *Afghanistan: The Soviet War,* 209.

Chapter 4. From Refugees to Regional War in Central Africa

1. International Rescue Committee, "Mortality in the Democratic Republic of Congo: Results of a Nationwide Survey" (New York: IRC, April 2003).

2. The Great Lakes region encompasses Rwanda, Burundi, Tanzania, the Democratic Republic of Congo, Uganda, and Kenya.

3. Gérard Prunier, *The Rwanda Crisis: History of a Genocide* (New York: Columbia University Press, 1995), 41–54.

4. Catharine Newbury and David Newbury, "A Catholic Mass in Kigali: Contested Views of the Genocide and Ethnicity in Rwanda," *Canadian Journal of African Studies* 33:2–3 (1999), 297–99, 303.

5. Mahmood Mamdani, *When Victims Become Killers* (Princeton, NJ: Princeton University Press, 2001), 189.

6. African Rights, *Rwanda: Death, Despair, and Defiance* (London: African Rights, 1995 revised edition), 26.

7. The RPF was established in 1987, out of an earlier organization called Rwandese Alliance for National Unity that had been founded in 1980. The RPF originally operated as an organization to push for refugee repatriation but later changed its goal to toppling the Habyarimana regime. Gaudens P. Mpangala, "Ethnic Conflicts in the Region of the Great Lakes," unpublished manuscript (University of Dar es Salaam, Centre for the Study of Forced Migration archives, 2000), 143. See also Mamdani, *When Victims Become Killers*, ch. 6. Tanzanian scholar Bonaventure Rutinwa concurs that "the treatment of Rwandese refugees in Uganda around this period was one of the factors that gave impetus to the formation of the Rwandan Patriotic Front (RPF)." Rutinwa, "The End of Asylum? The Changing Nature of Refugee Policies in Africa," *New Issues in Refugee Research* working paper series (Geneva: UNHCR), May 1999.

8. Charles David Smith, "The Geopolitics of Rwandan Resettlement: Uganda and Tanzania," *Issue: A Journal of Opinion* 33:2 (1995), 55.

9. Mamdani, *When Victims Become Killers*, 175.

10. Newbury and Newbury, "A Catholic Mass," 305.

11. "Understanding the Great Lakes Crisis," report of an international conference, Nairobi, November 30–December 2, 1996. Printed in *Journal of Humanitarian Assistance*, sec. 4.2.0.

12. On the Rwandan genocide see, Prunier, *The Rwanda Crisis*; African Rights, *Rwanda*; Philip Gourevitch, *We wish to inform you that tomorrow we will be killed with our families* (New York: Farrar, Straus and Giroux, 1998); Mamdani, *When Victims Become Killers*; and Alan J. Kuperman, *The Limits of Humanitarian Intervention: Genocide in Rwanda* (Washington, DC: Brookings Institute, May 2001).

13. The actual number of refugees was a contentious issue throughout the crisis. While UNHCR talked of 1.9 million, General Paul Kagame, Rwandan vice president following the RPF victory, referred to about one million refugees. To be precise, in August 1994 UNHCR estimated 1.3 million in Zaire, 190,000 in Burundi, and 530,000 in Tanzania. The United States Committee for Refugees (USCR) estimated the total number at 20 percent less than official UN estimates. Dennis McNamara, Statement to House International Relations Committee, Subcommittee on International Operations and Human Rights, hearing on "Rwanda: Genocide and the Continuing Cycle of Violence," May 5, 1998; Jeff Drumtra, "Site Visit to Rwanda, Zaire, and Burundi, Oct. 20 to Nov. 17, 1994" (Washington DC: U.S. Committee for Refugees), Sec. 2A. On the number of militants, see Médecins Sans Frontières, "Deadlock in the Rwandan Refugee Crisis: Virtual Standstill on Repatriation," Amsterdam, July 1995, sec. 1.1.

14. Amnesty International, "Rwanda and Burundi, The Return Home: Rumours and Realities," February 20, 1996, 21.

15. Organization of African Unity (OAU), "International Panel of Eminent Personalities to Investigate the 1994 Genocide in Rwanda and Surrounding Events," July 7, 2000, sec. 19.28.

16. Inspection and Evaluation Service, UNHCR, "Lessons Learned from the Rwanda and Burundi Emergencies" (Geneva: UNHCR, April 1996), par. 23.

17. Save the Children, "Rwandan Refugees in Zaire," Bukavu, Zaire, Report for November 1, 1994–December 12, 1994, sec. 1.

18. "Exiled Rwandan Government Confirms Base," Paris AFP, FBIS Daily Report, April 26, 1995.

19. The RPF closed the Goma border on July 16, 1994.

20. Joel Boutroue, "Missed Opportunities: The Role of the International Community in the Return of the Rwandan Refugees from Eastern Zaire," *Rosemarie Rogers Working Paper Series* (Cambridge, MA: Center for International Studies, MIT), 1998, 4.

21. African Rights, *Rwanda*, 1093. Gérard Prunier confirms that Hutu leaders forced out the refugees. See Prunier, *The Rwanda Crisis*, quotation 304.

22. UNHCR official, interview by the author, Geneva, July 20, 1999.

23. UNHCR official, interview by the author, Geneva, July 15, 1998.

24. Eleanor Bedford, USCR, interview by the author, Washington, DC, November 2, 1999.

25. Human Rights Watch Arms Project, *Rwanda/Zaire: Rearming with Impunity* 7:4 (May 1995), 4n13.

26. Numerous sources concur that the cholera outbreak temporarily dislodged the power of the leaders. Between 100,000 and 200,000 people had voluntarily repatriated by mid-August, before the leaders had consolidated their power. By fall 1994, the militant leaders forced UNHCR to cancel organized returns after the convoys were attacked by mobs. Different sources report widely varying repatriation numbers. Bedford, interview with the author, November 2, 1999. See also McNamara, Statement to House International Relations Committee, May 5, 1998; Boutroue, "Missed Opportunities," 1998; Kate Halvorsen, "Protection and Humanitarian Assistance in the Refugee Camps in Zaire: The Problem of Security," in Howard Adelman and Astri Suhrke (eds.), *The Path of Genocide: The Rwanda Crisis from Uganda to Zaire* (New Brunswick, NJ: Transaction Press, 1999), 313–14.

27. African Rights, *Rwanda*, 1093.

28. Boutroue, "Missed Opportunities," 39.

29. Jeff Drumtra, "Site Visit to Rwanda, Zaire, and Burundi, Oct. 20 to Nov. 17, 1994" (Washington DC: U.S. Committee for Refugees), 23E.

30. Ray Wilkinson, "The Heart of Darkness," *Refugees, Crisis in the Great Lakes* (Geneva: UNHCR, No. 110, Winter 1997), 9.

31. World Bank, "Evaluation of Current Rwandan Refugee Camp Conditions and Structures in Goma and Bukavu-Zaire," report from World Bank Mission, March-April 1995, quotation par. 8.2. See also Amnesty International. "Rwanda and Burundi, The Return Home: Rumours and Realities," February 20, 1996, 32; and Médecins Sans Frontières, "Deadlock in the Rwandan Refugee Crisis: Virtual Standstill on Repatriation," Amsterdam, July 1995.

32. World Bank, "Evaluation of Current Rwandan Refugee Camp Conditions," par. 12.2.

33. The RDR later moved its headquarters to the Netherlands and also became active in Canada. Médecins Sans Frontières, "Deadlock," II.1.4; IRIN-Central and Eastern Africa, Update 1,089 for the Great Lakes (January 10, 2001).

34. Sheldon Yett, "Masisi, Down the Road from Goma; Ethnic Cleansing and Displacement in Eastern Zaire" (Washington DC: U.S. Committee for Refugees Issue Brief, June 1996), 14. See also William Cyrus Reed, "Refugees and Rebels: The Former Government of Rwanda and the ADFL Movement in Eastern Zaire" (Washington DC: U.S. Committee for Refugees Issue Brief, April 1997); Médecins Sans Frontières, "Deadlock," II.2.3; and OAU, "International Panel of Eminent Personalities," 20.6.

35. Human Rights Watch Arms Project, "Rwanda/Zaire: Rearming with Impunity," 3n7. Reed concurs with the estimate of 50,000 ex-FAR and militia in the spring of 1995. Reed, "Refugees and Rebels," 7. See also Gérard Prunier, "The Rwandan Patriotic Front," in Christopher Clapham (ed.), *African Guerrillas* (Oxford: James Currey, 1998), 132.

36. OAU, "International Panel of Eminent Personalities," sec. 19.22.

37. Human Rights Watch Arms Project, "Rwanda/Zaire: Rearming with Impunity" 7:4 (May 1995), 11–12; Médecins Sans Frontières, "Deadlock," II.2.1; Julian Samboma,

"Rwanda-Burundi: Hutu Extremists Rearming for Another Bloodbath?" article circulated on Forced Migration list, March 31, 1995.

38. Quoted in OAU, "International Panel of Eminent Personalities."

39. Quoted in Fiona Terry, *Condemned to Repeat? The Paradox of Humanitarian Action* (Ithaca, NY: Cornell University Press, 2002), 181.

40. Gérard Prunier, "Rwanda: Update to End of July 1995," Writenet Country Papers, Refworld, UNHCR, August 1995, sec. 3.4.

41. Refugees International, "Rwandan Repatriation: The Challenge for the Great Lakes Region," Report No. 1 (November 8, 1995).

42. *Summary Report from the International Workshop on the Refugee Crisis in the Great Lakes Region*, Arusha, Tanzania, August 16–19, 1995, 22.

43. The HRW report is based on interviews with ex-FAR and militia members, whose observations were corroborated by UNHCR and NGOs. Human Rights Watch Arms Project, "Rwanda/Zaire: Rearming with Impunity," 15.

44. For example, attackers killed twenty-eight people in Gisenyi prefecture on June 27, 1996. Thirteen civilians died in an attack in Kibuye prefecture on June 18, 1996 by an estimated forty assailants. Amnesty International, "Rwanda, Alarming Resurgence of the Killings," AFR 47/013/1996, August 12, 1996, sec. IV.

45. One UNHCR official claimed that the United Nations knew about some Rwandan attacks on Hutu in Zaire but chose to remain quiet. UNHCR official, interview by the author, Geneva, July 13, 1999.

46. Amnesty International, "Rwanda and Burundi"; Gérard Prunier, "Rwanda: Update to End of Nov. 1995," Writenet Country Papers, Refworld, UNHCR, December 1995, 1.2.

47. Gordon Smith and John Hay, "Canada and the Crisis in Eastern Zaire," In Chester A. Crocker et al. (eds.), *Herding Cats: Multiparty Mediation in a Complex World* (Washington DC: U.S. Institute of Peace, 1999), 99.

48. Eleanor Bedford, "Site Visit to Eastern Congo/Zaire: Analysis of Humanitarian and Political Issues, April 10 to May 10, 1997," (Washington DC: U.S. Committee for Refugees), sec. 4.7.

49. Reed, "Refugees and Rebels," 16.

50. Amnesty International, "Democratic Republic of Congo," Dec. 3, 1997.

51. The Hutu militants resurrected a version of their infamous hate radio called the Voix du Patriote, which spewed anti-Tutsi propaganda. OAU, "International Panel of Eminent Personalities."

52. In 1997, Hutu insurgents crossed the border from DRC to attack Congolese Tutsi sheltering in a Rwandan camp, Mudende, killing over 130 refugees. Other attacks followed, including another massacre at Mudende in December 1997. The survivors fled to the Nkamira transit center, which was also attacked, resulting in the death of 84 more Tutsi. Human Rights Watch, "Organizations Condemn Massacres of Refugees by Armed Forces," August 26, 1997; Gérard Prunier, "Rwanda: Update to End of February 1998," Writenet Country Papers, Refworld, UNHCR, March 1998.

53. OAU, "International Panel of Eminent Personalities," sec. 20.71.

54. The United Nations authorized 16,000 troops for Sierra Leone, a country less than 4 percent the size of Congo. OAU, "International Panel of Eminent Personalities," sec. 20.65. For more information on the conflict, see ReliefWeb at http://www.reliefweb.int.

55. Human Rights Watch Arms Project, "Rwanda/Zaire: Rearming with Impunity," 5.

56. Prunier, *The Rwanda Crisis*, 101.

57. African Rights, *Rwanda*, 1099.

58. UNHCR official, interview by the author, Geneva, July 14, 1998.

59. Hutu extremists also followed similar precautions regarding public opinion. In areas with high exposure to international agencies and the press, fighters did not wear uniforms or carry weapons. In the southern camps near Uvira, which were more obscure, men freely carried weapons and wore uniforms in the camps. Human Rights Watch Arms Project, "Rwanda/Zaire: Rearming with Impunity," 11, 15.

60. Richard Dowden, " 'No Amnesty' for Rwanda's Mass Killers," *Independent* (London), December 9, 1994.

61. Amnesty International, "Rwanda and Burundi, The Return Home: Rumours and Realities," February 20, 1996; Jim Hoagland, "Gen. Mobutu's Rwanda Game," *Washington Post*, August 27, 1995; Robert Block, "Mobutu 'Raising the Stakes in Search of Aid,' " *Independent* (London), August 24, 1995.

62. Bonaventure Rutinwa, "The Political Context of the Mandated Repatriations of Rwandese Refugees from Tanzania and Zaire in 1996," draft of paper presented at the Workshop on Physical Security and Protection of Refugee Populated Areas, Massachusetts Institute of Technology, Cambridge, MA, October 29–30, 1999, 6.

63. Kate Halvorsen, "Protection and Humanitarian Assistance in the Refugee Camps in Zaire: The Problem of Security," in Howard Adelman and Astri Suhrke (eds.), *The Path of Genocide: The Rwanda Crisis from Uganda to Zaire* (New Brunswick, NJ: Transaction Press, 1999), 311.

64. Peter Rosenblum, "Endgame in Zaire," *Current History* (May 1997). In 1993 the Nouveau Zaire started at NZ3 to the U.S. dollar; one year later, it had soared to NZ4000 to the dollar. Mel McNulty, "The Collapse of Zaire: Implosion, Revolution or External Sabotage," *Journal of Modern African Studies* 37:1 (1999), 67.

65. Abbas H. Gnamo, "The Rwandan Genocide and the Collapse of Mobutu's Kleptocracy," In Adelman and Suhrke (eds.), *The Path of Genocide*, 324–25.

66. Asteris C. Huliaras, "The 'Anglosaxon Conspiracy': French Perceptions of the Great Lakes Crisis," *Journal of Modern African Studies* 36:4 (Dec. 1998), quotation 599.

67. French troop presence reached 680 soldiers, who helped train the Rwandan army to combat the RPF. Human Rights Watch Arms Project, "Rwanda/Zaire: Rearming with Impunity," 6.

68. Reed, "Refugees and Rebels," 4.

69. Sources for this include interviews with airport staff, local businessmen, air cargo company crews, and Zairian officials. Human Rights Watch Arms Project, "Rwanda/Zaire," 7.

70. Reed, "Refugees and Rebels," 5. See also Prunier, *The Rwanda Crisis*, ch. 8; and Human Rights Watch Arms Project, "Rwanda/Zaire."

71. Chris McGreal, "Democracy in Africa: U.S. Hails New Breed of Strongmen," *Guardian*, December 22, 1997; Gnamo, "The Rwandan Genocide and the Collapse of Mobutu's Kleptocracy," 343.

72. Mahmood Mamdani, "Why Rwanda Trumpeted Its Zaire Role," *Mail and Guardian*, August 8, 1997.

73. Quoted in Terry, *Condemned to Repeat?* 185.

74. Peter Rosenblum, "Kabila's Congo," *Current History* 97:619 (May 1998), 198. See also Gnamo, "The Rwandan Genocide and the Collapse of Mobutu's Kleptocracy," 344; Amnesty International, "Democratic Republic of Congo, Deadly Alliances in Congolese Forests" (London: December 3, 1997), sec. 11.3.

75. Angola and Burundi also joined the alliance against Mobutu, but to a lesser degree than Rwanda and Uganda.

76. The web of alliances created strange bedfellows and constantly shifting loyalties. At one point, Uganda found itself attacked by an alliance of Hutu rebels, an Islamic sect based in Sudan, and disaffected tribesmen from the Bakonjo and Baamba groups. Gérard Prunier, "The Geopolitical Situation in the Great Lakes Area in Light of the Kivu Crisis," Writenet Country Papers, Refworld, UNHCR, February 1997, sec. 6. See also Gnamo, "The Rwandan Genocide," 337–38.

77. Gérard Prunier, "Rwanda: Update to End of July 1995," Writenet Country Papers, Refworld, UNHCR, August 1995, sec. 3.3.

78. Alexander Cooley and James Ron, "The NGO Scramble: Organizational Insecurity and the Political Economy of Transnational Action," *International Security* 27:1 (Summer 2002), 5–39; Terry, *Condemned to Repeat?* 25–31.

79. The U.S. government and the European Union donated 50 percent of the $1.4 billion. Eleanor Bedford, USCR, interview by the author, Washington DC, November 2, 1999; Médecins Sans Frontières, "Deadlock," sec. II.1.1; Jeff Drumtra, "Site Visit to Rwanda, Zaire, and Burundi, Oct. 20 to Nov. 17, 1994," (Washington DC: U.S. Committee for Refugees), 22E.

80. Terry reports that Caritas staff expressed sympathy toward the Hutu cause and repeated the Hutu claim of a "double genocide." Terry, *Condemned to Repeat?* 205. See also Human Rights Watch Arms Project, "Rwanda/Zaire: Rearming with Impunity," 16.

81. Joint Evaluation of Emergency Assistance to Rwanda, "Humanitarian Aid and Effects, Study 3," in *The International Response to Conflict and Genocide: Lessons from the Rwanda Experience* (OECD, March 1996).

82. John M. Janzen and Reinhild Kauenhoven Janzen, *Do I Still Have a Life? Voices from the Aftermath of War in Rwanda and Burundi* (Lawrence: University of Kansas Press, 2000), 50.

83. Terry, *Condemned to Repeat?* 191.

84. African Rights, "Witness to Genocide: John Yusufu Munyakazi: The Killer Behind the Refugee" (London: African Rights), June 1997, 21.

85. John Pomfret, "Aid Dilemma: Keeping It from the Oppressors; U.N., Charities Find Crises Make Them Tools of War," *Washington Post,* September 23, 1997; Amnesty International, "Democratic Republic of Congo," December 3, 1997, sec. 11.2.

86. Pomfret, "Aid Dilemma."

87. Janzen and Janzen, *Do I Still Have a Life?* 56.

88. Terry, *Condemned to Repeat?* 177.

89. Quoted in Rudolph Von Bernuth, "The Voluntary Agency Response and the Challenge of Coordination," *Journal of Refugee Studies* 9:3 (1996), 287.

90. UNHCR official, interview by the author, Geneva, July 13, 1999.

91. Jeff Drumtra, "Site Visit to Rwanda, Zaire, and Burundi, Oct. 20 to Nov. 17, 1994," (Washington DC: U.S. Committee for Refugees), 25E.

92. Amnesty International, "Democratic Republic of Congo: Deadly Alliances in Congolese Forests," December 3, 1997, AFR 62/33/97, sec. 11.2; Amnesty International, "Great Lakes Region: Still in Need of Protection," January 1997, AFR 02/07/97, sec. 2; Bedford, "Site Visit to Eastern Congo/Zaire," quotation 9.

93. Cooley and Ron, "The NGO Scramble," 25.

94. UNHCR official, interview by the author, Geneva, July 20, 1999.

95. Eleanor Bedford, USCR, interview by the author, Washington DC, November 2, 1999.

96. Médecins Sans Frontières, "Deadlock," sec. II.2.4. This position contrasts with earlier MSF reports which recommended smaller camps "so as to reduce the influence of the leaders on the distribution of humanitarian aid." MSF, "Breaking the Cycle," November 1994.

97. Halvorsen, "Protection and Humanitarian Assistance," 310.

98. Basically, the camps where placed wherever the refugees' leaders instructed the first batch of refugees to stop moving. Augustine Mahiga, a UNHCR official, admitted: "We practically had no choice in the location of the camps at the outset of the emergency. They were imposed on us by circumstances." UNHCR, "Information Bulletin, Burundi and Rwanda," June 1996, 6.

99. Dennis McNamara, "Everyone Is Found Wanting," *Refugees, Crisis in the Great Lakes* (Geneva: UNHCR, No. 110, Winter 1997), 22.

100. Amnesty International, "Rwanda: Alarming Resurgence of the Killings," AFR 47/013/1996, August 12, 1996, sec. II.

101. The rapid advance of the Rwandan army deep into Zaire also demonstrates that camps further from the border would not have been safe from attack.

102. Even the UNHCR statistical bureau provides demographic information on less than half of the refugees in Africa.

103. In sub-Saharan Africa, the United Nations estimates that 18 percent of the population is under five years old. Among the refugees, the high proportion of children probably declined following the cholera epidemic since young children are more vulnerable than adults. Center for Disease Control, "Morbidity and Mortality Surveillance in Rwandan Refugees—Burundi and Zaire, 1994," *MMWR Weekly* 45:5 (February 9, 1996), 104–7; Population Division, Department of Economic and Social Affairs of the United Nations Secretariat, *Sex and Age Distribution of the World Populations: The 1996 Revision* (New York, 1997), 37.

104. World Bank, "Evaluation of Current Rwandan Refugee Camp Conditions," par. 9.1.2.

105. For example, as of June 1994, UNHCR had only 11,000 blankets and 10,600 plastic sheets positioned in Zaire for the coming influx of over a million people. UNHCR, "Rwanda Emergency Crisis," memorandum, June 20, 1994.

106. This situation emerged because no NGO wanted responsibility for the unglamorous task of building latrines. Van Nieuwenhuyse, "Nutritional Assessment Mission in Goma and Bukavu (Zaire) and South West Rwanda," August 13–23, 1994.

107. The threshold for defining a situation as an emergency is one death per 10,000 per day. Dominique Legros et al., "The Evolution of Mortality Among Rwandan Refugees in Zaire between 1994 and 1997," in Holly E. Reed and Charles B. Keely (eds.), *Forced Migration and Mortality* (Washington DC: National Academy Press, 2001), 66.

108. Center for Disease Control, "Morbidity and Mortality Surveillance in Rwandan Refugees," 104–7; Legros, "The Evolution of Mortality," 57. The Population Reference Bureau gives slightly different numbers; it cites 0.25 deaths per 10,000 per day as the median death rate for developing countries. Quoted in Charles B. Keely et al., "Mortality Patterns in Complex Humanitarian Emergencies," in Reed and Keely (eds.), *Forced Migration and Mortality*, 7.

109. Jeff Drumtra, "Site Visit to Rwanda, Zaire, and Burundi, Oct. 20 to Nov. 17, 1994" (Washington DC: U.S. Committee for Refugees), 22E.

110. Sheldon Yett, "Masisi, Down the Road from Goma; Ethnic Cleansing and Displacement in Eastern Zaire" (Washington DC: U.S. Committee for Refugees Issue Brief, June 1996), 13.

111. For example, 20,000 refugees from Kibumba camp worked on the local plantations every day. Boutroue, "Missed Opportunities," quotation 51. Ann-Sophie Nedlund, UNHCR official, interview by the author, Geneva, July 15, 1999.

112. Amnesty International, "Rwanda and Burundi, The Return Home: Rumours and Realities," February 20, 1996, 4.

113. According to the Food and Agriculture Organization (FAO), the average consumption in Rwanda from 1995 to 1997 was 2050 calories. This is higher than consumption in the refugee camps, but the relative scarcity in Zaire did not lead to high levels of repatriation. During the same period, calorie consumption for Zaire/DRC as a whole was estimated at 1820 calories per day. Food and Agriculture Organization of the United Nations, *The State of Food Insecurity in the World* (Rome: FAO, 1999), 32.

114. Later chapters will explore the idea that opportunities for permanent settlement (e.g., local integration or resettlement abroad) might provide a material incentive to abandon violence. This option was not available at any significant level to the Rwandans.

115. Quoted in Dennis McNamara, Statement to House International Relations Committee, Subcommittee on International Operations and Human Rights, hearing on "Rwanda: Genocide and the Continuing Cycle of Violence," May 5, 1998, 9.

116. UNHCR official, interview by the author, Geneva, July 20, 1999.

117. A UNHCR official notes that refugees started making new machetes right away, since they were needed for farming. UNHCR officials, interviews by the author, Geneva, July 1999.

118. Smith, "The Geopolitics of Rwandan Resettlement," 56.

119. Prunier, *The Rwanda Crisis*, 265.

120. Quotation by John Muuyekure in Brian Murphy, "Refugee's Life Weaves Through Food Lines and Idle Times," *Associated Press*, May 26, 1994.

121. In response to the civil war in Rwanda, UNHCR had prepared a contingency plan for 50,000 people. Jacques Franquin, UNHCR, interview by the author, Geneva, July 15, 1998.

122. "Rwanda Rebels Shut Off Frantic Refugees' Retreat," *Houston Chronicle*, May 1, 1994.

123. During May 1994, leaders reported an increase of 100,000 people, but more neutral reports found an increase of only 10,000. Refugees were not formally registered until July 1994, bringing the population figures down to 230,000. Susanne Jaspars, *The Rwandan*

Refugee Crisis in Tanzania: Initial Successes and Failures in Food Assistance (London: Relief and Rehabilitation Network, 1994), 6–7.

124. Once the camp managers realized that this was counterproductive and stopped payment, the leaders became difficult and uncooperative. UNHCR official, interview by the author, Geneva, July 15, 1998.

125. UNHCR official, interview by the author, Geneva, July 15, 1998.

126. Keith B. Richburg, "Rwandan Refugees Riot, Threaten Aid Workers at Tanzanian Camp," *Washington Post,* June 17, 1994. Due to clashes between the political factions and an overall high level of crime, the Tanzanians later put about one hundred men in detention. Emile Segbor, UNHCR official, interview by the author, Geneva, July 15, 1998.

127. African Rights, *Rwanda,* 1090.

128. According to a UNHCR source present at the incident, the Tanzanian police negotiated the departure of Gatete from the camp but did not arrest him. When Gatete arrived in Dar Es Salaam, he was received by the French ambassador and sent to Paris to stay with the family of Habyarimana. UNHCR official, interview by the author, Geneva, July 15, 1998. Another source claims that Tanzania deported Gatete to Zaire in July 1994. Tony Waters, *Bureaucratizing the Good Samaritan, The Limitations to Humanitarian Relief Operations* (Boulder, CO: Westview Press, 2001), 123.

129. Jaspars, *The Rwandan Refugee Crisis in Tanzania,* 20.

130. After finding a group of men marching around in the camp, a UN official threatened to pull out of the camp. The militant groups then refrained from training openly in the camps. UNHCR official, interview by the author, Geneva, July 15, 1998.

131. Sam Kiley, "Hutu Refugees Train to Invade Rwanda," *Times* (London), April 10, 1995. MSF claimed that the ex-FAR was active in Tanzania. Médecins Sans Frontières, "Breaking the Cycle: MSF Calls for Action in the Rwandese Refugee Camps in Tanzania and Zaire," Special Report, November 10, 1994.

132. Smith, "The Geopolitics of Rwandan Resettlement," 56.

133. The suspicious UNHCR official offered to buy soccer uniforms and expressed interest in watching the games. The leaders then responded that the games took place at night—after UNHCR workers had retired to their guarded compound. UNHCR official, interview by the author, Geneva, July 22, 1999.

134. One observer reported that "the Tanzanian government distinguishes between military training and physical exercises by whether or not they use sticks or other dummies that resemble guns." Simon Turner, "Angry Young Men in Camps," *New Issues in Refugee Research,* working paper series (Geneva: UNHCR), June 1999, note 20.

135. UNHCR official, interview by the author, Geneva, July 20, 1999.

136. Johnson P. Brahim, "Refugee Crisis in the Great Lakes Region: How Tanzania Was Affected and Her Responses," Paper for the International Workshop on the Refugee Crisis in the Great Lakes Region, Arusha, Tanzania. August 16–19, 1995, 8.

137. Smith, "The Geopolitics of Rwandan Resettlement," 56.

138. Brahim, "Refugee Crisis in the Great Lakes Region," 8.

139. Paul Chintowa, "Rwanda-Politics: Tanzania Investigates Ethnic Killings," Inter Press Service, October 3, 1994.

140. Maureen Connelly, a UNHCR official at the Ngara camps, argued that the refugees were not hostages but rather brainwashed. According to Connelly, part of the willingness of the followers stemmed from the nature of Rwandan political culture, which emphasized organization and obedience to authority. Maureen Connelly, UNHCR official, interview by the author, July 20, 1999; and Médecins Sans Frontières, "Breaking the Cycle: MSF Calls for Action in the Rwandese Refugee Camps in Tanzania and Zaire," Special Report, November 10, 1994.

141. UNHCR official, interview by the author, Geneva, July 15, 1998.

142. Refugees International, "Rwandan Repatriation: The Challenge for the Great Lakes Region," Report No. 3 (December 6, 1995).

143. Waters, *Bureaucratizing the Good Samaritan,* 138.

144. Smith, "The Geopolitics of Rwandan Resettlement," 56.

145. "Refugees Swim Past Corpses to Safety," The Press Association Limited, May 6, 1994. See also Prunier, *The Rwanda Crisis,* 265–73.

146. UNHCR established a mass information program that used radio, press releases, reports from NGOs in Rwanda, and addresses by public officials. In its camp bulletin UNHCR warned the refugees to "please take note and obey [Tanzanian] laws, because if you do not, you will be punished according to the laws of Tanzania, arrested, imprisoned and sent back home." UNHCR also replied to a question in the bulletin that "it is no secret that refugees who want to go home are intimidated." Refugee Information Network, *News and Views: An Intercamp Bulletin for Ngara* 10 (May 1996), 1, 3.

147. Adrian Keeling and Carolyn Makinson, "Cross-Border Communication Between the Camps for Rwandan Refugees in Tanzania and Programs in Rwanda," Background Paper for the International Rescue Committee, September 30, 1995, 17.

148. Lutheran World Relief, "Tanzania, Aid Workers Face 'We Would Rather Die' Movement Among Rwandan Refugees," December 16, 1996. Found at www.reliefweb.int.

149. UNHCR official, interview by the author, Geneva, July 20, 1999.

150. Prunier, *The Rwanda Crisis*, 316.

151. Médecins Sans Frontières, "Deadlock in the Rwandan Refugee Crisis," sec. II, 4.

152. "Refugees Staying Put after Reported Persecution of Returnees," *Associated Press*, September 24, 1994.

153. UNHCR official, interview by the author, Geneva, July 22, 1999.

154. Amnesty International reported a spate of attacks from Tanzania into southeastern Rwanda in the fall of 1995. The victims described the assailants as former inhabitants of the village who had come back to kill Tutsi and demand resources for the Hutu extremists. Amnesty International, "Rwanda and Burundi, The Return Home," 22; Christopher Mwakasege, "The Impact of Refugees on Host Communities, The Case of Kasulu, Ngara, and Karagwe Districts in Tanzania," Study report presented at the International Workshop on the Refugee Crisis in the Great Lakes Region, Arusha, Tanzania. August 16–19, 1995, 14; Emile Segbor, UNHCR official, interview with the author, Geneva, July 15, 1998.

155. Paul Chintowa, "Rwanda-Refugees: Tanzania Confines Rwandans to Their Camps," Inter Press Service, October 11, 1994.

156. Paul Chintowa, "Rwanda-Politics: Kigali Claims Tanzania Supports Hutu Rebels," Inter Press Service, September 9, 1994.

157. In November 1995 UNHCR publicly stated that the Tanzanian army had been misbehaving. This increased tension between the government and the international organizations. UNHCR official, interview by the author, Geneva, July 15, 1998.

158. Part of the Tanzanian wariness may have stemmed from past experience with the spread of civil war involving refugees. The 1978–1979 war with Uganda began when Ugandan president Idi Amin sent fighters across the border to attack refugees there who supported the ousted leader, Milton Obote. With support from Tanzania, the refugees waged a guerrilla war from Kagera region in western Tanzania. Tanzanian forces eventually assisted in the invasion of Uganda and the toppling of Idi Amin. Anthony Clayton, *Frontiersmen, Warfare in Africa since 1950* (London: UCL Press, 1999), 104–8; Nicholas J. Wheeler, *Saving Strangers, Humanitarian Intervention in International Society* (Oxford: Oxford University Press, 2000), ch. 4; Christopher Mwakasege, "The Impact of Refugees on Host Communities, The Case of Kasulu, Ngara, and Karagwe Districts in Tanzania," Study report presented at the International Workshop on the Refugee Crisis in the Great Lakes Region, Arusha, Tanzania. August 16–19, 1995, 15.

159. Paul Chintowa, "Rwanda-Refugees: Threat of War Spilling into Tanzania," Inter Press Service, May 16, 1994.

160. "Radio Reports Influx of 'Large Numbers' of Armed Rwandan Refugees," BBC Summary of World Broadcasts, October 31, 1994. One official reported that the government was aware that fifty armed men, suspected to be *Interahamwe*, had crossed into Tanzania from Rwanda between August and October 1994. "Rwanda-Refugees: Tanzania Cracks Down on Rwandans," Inter Press Service, October 17, 1994. See also Paul Chintowa, "Rwanda-Refugees: Tanzania Confines Rwandans to Their Camps," Inter Press Service, October 11, 1994.

161. *Summary Report from the International Workshop on Refugee Crisis in the Great Lakes Region*, Arusha, Tanzania, August 16–19, 1995, 29.

162. Augustine Mahiga, "A Change of Direction for Tanzania," *Refugees, Crisis in the Great Lakes* (Geneva: UNHCR, No. 110, Winter 1997), 15.

163. Once there, most of the militants managed to escape. UNHCR official, interview by the author, Kigoma, Tanzania, February 2000.

164. Chris Maina Peter, "Rights and Duties of Refugees Under Municipal Law in Tanzania: Examining a Proposed New Legislation," *Journal of African Law* 41 (1997), 87. A new Refugees Act was enacted in 1998 that superseded the 1966 law.

165. UNHCR official, interview by the author, Geneva, July 22, 1999.

166. Sreeram Sundar Chaulia, "The Politics of Refugee Hosting in Tanzania: From Open Door to Unsustainability, Insecurity and Receding Receptivity," *Journal of Refugee Studies* 16:2 (2003).

167. Gérard Prunier, "Rwanda: Update to End of July 1995," Writenet Country Papers, Refworld, UNHCR, August 1995, sec. 3.2. See also William Cyrus Reed, "Refugees and Rebels: The Former Government of Rwanda and the ADFL Movement in Eastern Zaire," (Washington DC: U.S. Committee for Refugees Issue Brief, April 1997), 22n5. Mamdani also notes the contrast between Tanzania and Zaire. Mamdani, *When Victims Become Killers*, 254.

168. For example, former President Julius Nyerere harshly criticized the tepid Tanzanian government response to the genocide, whereas the ruling president, Ali Hassan Mwinyi, steered clear of such public condemnation. See "Nyerere Blasts Tanzania Over Rwanda Massacre," *Agence France Presse*, July 6, 1994. Also UNHCR officials, interviews by the author, Geneva, July 14 and 15, 1998.

169. As mentioned earlier, Tanzanian officials allowed the notorious genocidaire Gatete to leave the country rather than imprison or extradite him.

170. Augustine Mahiga, "A Change of Direction for Tanzania," 14–15.

171. James C. McKinley Jr., "Soldiers Force Refugees into Rwanda from Tanzania," *New York Times*, December 16, 1996; and Chris McGreal, "Refugees on the Move: Fear Forces Out Hutus," *Guardian* (London), December 13, 1996.

172. Agencies present in Tanzania included the International Federation of the Red Cross and Red Crescent Societies (IFRCRC), the Tanzanian Red Cross Society, CARE, Concern, IRC, Oxfam, Action Internationale Contre la Faim (AICF) and various national branches of MSF. Jaspers, "The Rwandan Refugee Crisis," 4.

173. Joint Evaluation of Emergency Assistance to Rwanda, "Humanitarian Aid and Effects, Study 3," 34.

174. Jaspers, "The Rwandan Refugee Crisis in Tanzania," 6–7, 25, quotation 29.

175. Cathy Lennox-Cook, "Kitali Camp, Ngara, Tanzania: A Year in the Life of a Rwandese and Burundese Refugee Camp, February 1995–February 1996," unpublished draft, February 11, 1996; UNHCR official, interview by the author, Geneva, July 22, 1999.

176. The provision of services is considered a model, but many NGOs denounce UNHCR's complicity in the forced repatriation of December 1996.

177. International Federation of Red Cross and Red Crescent Societies, "Rwandan Refugees in Burundi, Tanzania, Uganda, and Zaire," Situation Report No. 5, March 31, 1995, sec. 2.3.

178. UNHCR, "Rwanda Emergency Crisis," memorandum, June 20, 1994, 1.

179. Population growth among the refugees expanded at 4.5 percent annually, compared with 2.8 percent among Tanzanians and 3.1 percent for pre-genocide Rwanda. In April 1996 in Ngara camp, only 54 Rwandans returned home, whereas 2,000 babies were born. Mwakasege, "The Impact of Refugees on Host Communities," 1, 4; UNHCR, "Information Bulletin, Burundi and Rwanda," June 1996; Tony Waters, "The Coming Rwandan Demographic Crisis, or Why Current Repatriation Policies Will Not Solve Tanzania's (or Zaire's) Refugee Problems," *Journal of Humanitarian Assistance*. Found at http://www-jha.sps.cam.ac.uk/a/a021.htm, re-posted on July 4, 1997.

180. UNHCR's numbers for June 1996 are more reliable than earlier inflated statistics. UNHCR, "Information Bulletin, Burundi and Rwanda," June 1996. See also Waters, *Bureaucratizing the Good Samaritan*, 278.

181. Because of the low levels of violence, cross-camp comparisons are difficult within Tanzania. Since all the camps had lower levels of violence, one cannot reliably evaluate

the impact of the size of the camp. Also, information about the military activity within each camp is harder to obtain since the militants took care to hide their activities.

182. Refugees International, "Rwandan Repatriation: The Challenge for the Great Lakes Region," Report No. 3 (December 6, 1995).

183. There is information on Rwandan refugees in Burundi (142,000) and Uganda (6,800). Burundi's refugee population was 53 percent female and Uganda's was 49 percent female. UNHCR, "Demographic Characteristics of Selected Populations Assisted by UNHCR as of 31 December 1995," In *Populations of Concern to UNHCR, A Statistical Overview* (Geneva: UNHCR, 1996), table 10.

184. Waters, *Bureaucratizing the Good Samaritan*, 202, 260.

185. Between May and December 1994, the relief effort cost $1.4 billion. Waters, *Bureaucratizing the Good Samaritan*, 9.

186. International Federation of Red Cross and Red Crescent Societies, "Rwandan Refugees in Burundi, Tanzania, Uganda, and Zaire," Situation Report No. 5, March 31, 1995, 5.

187. As early as June 1994, UNHCR reported a low mortality rate of 0.51 per 10,000 people per day with no signs of epidemic. Later, in 1995, the Red Cross found mortality rates below normal, at 0.57 per 10,000 persons per day. UNHCR, "Rwanda Emergency Crisis," memorandum, June 20, 1994, 3; Jaspars, "The Rwandan Refugee Crisis," 11; International Federation of Red Cross and Red Crescent Societies, "Rwandan Refugees in Burundi, Tanzania, Uganda, and Zaire," Situation Report No. 5, March 31, 1995, sec. 4.

188. Beth Elise Whitaker, "Changing Opportunities: Refugees and Host Communities in Western Tanzania," *New Issues in Refugee Research* working paper series (Geneva: UNHCR), June 1999, 12.

189. Jaspars, "The Rwandan Refugee Crisis in Tanzania," 25.

190. Tony Waters, "Emergency Assistance and Development, or What Has a Cash Bath Done for Western Tanzania's Wahangaza?" unpublished paper, 11.

191. UNHCR official, interview by the author. Geneva, July 14, 1998.

192. Amnesty International. "Rwanda and Burundi, The Return Home," 4.

193. Waters, *Bureaucratizing the Good Samaritan*, 137, quotation note 3.

194. UNHCR, "Information Bulletin, Burundi and Rwanda," June 1995, 2.

195. Refugee quoted in Alphonso Van Marsh, "Refugees Describe Human Cost of Burundi's War," CNN, December 11, 1999. Found at http://www.cnn.com/1999/WORLD/africa/12/11/burundi.refugees/.

196. Jean-Francois Durieux, "Preserving the Civilian Character of Refugee Camps. Lessons from the Kigoma Refugee Programme in Tanzania," *Track Two* 9:3 (November 2000), 27.

197. The militancy of the refugees in Tanzania increased after the Rwandan invasion of Zaire in 1996. Rwanda expelled Burundian and Rwandan Hutu refugees from eastern Zaire, and many of the Burundian militants found their way to Tanzania.

198. Statement by a Burundian refugee in Tanzania. Quoted in "Tanzania: Burundi/Tanzania: IRIN Special Report on Returning Burundian Refugees," IRIN report, May 8, 2002.

199. There were also violent clashes among the various rebel groups in the camps. Differences of geography, family ties, and levels of extremism divided the parties. Within the Tanzanian refugee camps, supporters of FDD and PALIPEHUTU began to fight each other in Katale camp. During the fighting in January 1997, the army shot indiscriminately into the crowd. Gérard Prunier, "The Geopolitical Situation in the Great Lakes Area in Light of the Kivu Crisis," Writenet Country Papers, Refworld, UNHCR, February 1997, 58; and UN OCHA Integrated Regional Information Network for Central and Eastern Africa, "Burundi: IRIN Focus on Rebel Movements," October 13, 1999.

200. Aid workers noticed correlations between higher levels of malnutrition and increased rebel political activity in camps, due to greater taxation.

201. UNHCR Burundi office, "Memo on Activities in Ngara Camps," October 1999, information based on interviews with returnees. As the prospects for repatriation improved, more violent incidents of intimidation were reported. During January 2002,

rebels killed twenty-four people in attempts to discourage repatriation. IRIN, "Tanzania: Over 20 Burundi Refugees Said Killed Since Early January," February 1, 2002.

202. UNHCR official, interview by the author, Kigoma, Tanzania, February 13, 2000; Gérard Prunier, "Rwanda: Update to End of July 1995," Writenet Country Papers, Refworld, UNHCR, August 1995, sec. 3.1.

203. Emile Segbor, UNHCR official, interview by the author, Geneva, July 15, 1998.

204. Johnson Brahim, Tanzanian Ministry for Home Affairs official, interview by the author, Dar es Salaam, Tanzania, February 9, 2000. In September 1999, two hundred refugees were caught in illegal night meetings. UNHCR Kigoma office, "Tanzania Situation Report," September 1999.

205. IRIN, "Burundi: Interview with President Pierre Buyoya," April 18, 2002.

206. An independent Burundi news source quoted captured rebels who said they traded with Tanzanian soldiers to acquire ammunition. CNN, "Burundi Accuses Tanzania of Cross-Border Attack," October 27, 1997. Found at http://www.cnn.com/WORLD/9710/27/burundi/. See also IRIN-CEA Update 838 for the Great Lakes, "Tanzania: Commissioner Denies Supporting Burundi Rebels," January 13, 2000

207. IRIN-CEA Update 1,004 for the Great Lakes, "Burundi: Exchange of Gunfire on Border with Tanzania," September 5, 2000.

208. Gérard Prunier, "Burundi: Update to Early August 1995" and "Burundi: Update to Early February 1996," Writenet Country Papers, UNHCR Refworld. Found at http://www.unhcr.ch.

209. IRIN-CEA Update 1,014 for the Great Lakes, "Burundi: Tutsi Group Threatens to Attack Refugee Camps in Tanzania," September 19, 2000.

210. Bonaventure S.I. Rutinwa, "Refugee Protection and Interstate Security: Lessons from the Recent Tensions between Burundi and Tanzania" (Oxford: March 1999), 8.

211. International Crisis Group, "Burundian Refugees in Tanzania: The Key Factor to the Burundi Peace Process" (November 30, 1999), 6.

212. Durieux, "Preserving the Character," 27–28.

213. UNHCR official, interview by the author, Geneva, July 13, 1998.

214. Durieux, "Preserving the Character," 30.

215. UNHCR assistant protection officer, interview by the author, Kigoma, Tanzania, February 13, 2000.

216. Rutinwa, "Refugee Protection and Interstate Security: Lessons from the Recent Tensions between Burundi and Tanzania," 14.

217. Human Rights Watch, "In the Name of Security: Forced Round-Ups of Refugees in Tanzania" (July 1999).

218. UNHCR, "Progress Report on UNHCR's Response to the Great Lakes Emergency," Geneva, October 1997, 2.

219. Thuo Kimari, "ISLO Report, Kigoma and Kagera Regions," UNHCR Kigoma office, March 11–16, 1999.

220. UNHCR official, interview by the author, Geneva, July 16, 1999.

221. John Eriksson, "Synthesis Report of the Joint Evaluation of Emergency Assistance," March 13, 2000. Found at http://www.um.dk/danida/evalueringsrapporter/1997_rwanda/book5.asp#c3.

222. UNHCR, "Lessons Learned from the Rwanda and Burundi Emergencies," par. 35.

Chapter 5. Demilitarizing a Refugee Army

1. Charles Lane, "Picked Pocket," *New Republic*, December 19, 1994, 14.

2. In 1993 the number of refugees from the former Yugoslavia totaled 1.3 million, with an additional 1.6 million internally displaced. U.S. Committee for Refugees, *World Refugee Survey* (Washington DC: Immigration and Refugee Services of America, 1994), 130, 42.

3. For example, in 1993 Croatia hosted 800,000 refugees and displaced persons. Of those, 55,000 lived in collective centers, 89,000 were lodged in hotels, and the rest stayed

with host families. Department of Humanitarian Affairs, *United Nations Revised Consolidated Inter-Agency Appeal for Former Yugoslavia, April-December 1993*, Geneva, March 1993, 29.

4. Some observers claim that *all* male refugees were militarized due to forced conscription into one or another state army. However, these fighters were not recognized as refugees and did not receive humanitarian assistance. UNHCR officials, Geneva, July 1998, interviews by the author. NGO staff, Split, Croatia, June 1998, interviews by the author. On forced conscription in Croatia, see Human Rights Watch, *Civil and Political Rights in Croatia* (New York: Humans Rights Watch, 1995).

5. Igor Ivancic, UNHCR official, interview by the author, Split, Croatia, June 1998; Tanwir Shahzada, UNHCR official, interview by the author, Geneva, July 1998.

6. Anna Husarska, "Pocket Change," *New Republic*, July 19 and 26, 1993, 9.

7. The government accused his company, Agrokomerc, of issuing $1 billion in unbacked promissory notes, which created havoc in the banking industry. Misha Glenny, "The Godfather of Bihac," *New York Review of Books*, August 12, 1993.

8. Abdic received 1,010,618 votes to Izetbegovic's 847,386. Many interpretations of this supposed secret deal have been offered. Abdic has claimed he was forced to give up the presidency but at other times has stated that his desire was to forgo national politics for his business interests. UNHCR officials, interviews by the author, Geneva, July 1998; Laura Silber and Allan Little, *Yugoslavia: Death of a Nation* (New York: Penguin Books, 1995), 211.

9. Ivancic, UNHCR official, interview by the author, Split, Croatia, June 1998; and Gonzolo Vargaz Llosa, UNHCR official, interview by the author, Geneva, July 1998.

10. Ivancic interview.

11. Emma Daly, "Is Life Really Worth Living Under King Babo?" *Independent* (London), July 30, 1994.

12. UNHCR Office of the Special Envoy for Former Yugoslavia—External Relations Unit, *Information Notes on Former Yugoslavia*, February 1993, hereafter *Information Notes*. For more information on UNPROFOR, see Lawyers Committee for Human Rights, Refugee Project, *Protection by Presence? The Limits of United Nations Safekeeping Activities in Croatia* (New York, September 1993).

13. Judah explains that "so confident were those Serbs, however, of their good relations with their business partners in the 5th Corps that when it launched its attack only 20 per cent of Serbian troops who should have been at their positions along the Bihac front were actually there." Tim Judah, *The Serbs* (New Haven: Yale University Press, 1997), 243–45.

14. UNHCR officials, interviews by the author, Geneva, July 1998.

15. Husarska, "Pocket Change," 9–10.

16. Silber and Little, *Yugoslavia*, 359.

17. UNHCR officials, interviews by the author, Geneva, July 1998.

18. Roger Cohen, "Besieged Bosnian Pocket Fights Sense of Betrayal," *New York Times*, June 26, 1994.

19. The 1991 census counted 202,310 Muslims, 6,470 Croats, and 29,398 Serbs in prewar Bihac. All but 1,000 of the Serbs left when the war began, leaving about 199,000 Muslims and 5,000 Croats. *Information Notes*, June 1995.

20. In the September 1997 elections, Abdic's party won fifteen of the twenty-four seats in Velika Kladusa, a third of the seats in Cazin to the south, and zero seats in Bihac town still further south. Stephane Jacquemet, UNHCR official, interview by the author, Geneva, July 1998.

21. UNHCR official, based on interviews with 250 Abdic refugees. Interview by the author, Split, Croatia, June 1998.

22. *Information Notes*, Special Issue, November 29, 1993.

23. *Information Notes*, July 1994.

24. Daly, "Is Life Really Worth Living."

25. Davor Huic, "Bosnian Troops Take Rebel Stronghold," *Guardian* (London), August 22, 1994. Interview with Slobodan Jarcevic by T. Tomasevic, "Enemy Will Not Pass," FBIS Daily Report, Doc. No. FBIS-EEU-94-181, September 8, 1994.

26. "Bosnia Enclave Falls to Army Forces," *Star Tribune* (Minneapolis), August 22, 1994.

27. *Information Notes*, September 1994.

28. *Information Notes*, September 1994.

29. Adrian Brown, "Major Refugee Crisis Builds Up in Croatia," *Daily Telegraph*, August 29, 1994.

30. Quoted in Carol J. Williams, "Defying West, Bosnian Muslim Warlord Pushes Followers Toward Croatia," *Los Angeles Times*, August 28, 1994.

31. Refugee quoted in Tom Hundley, "Dispossessed Bosnian Muslims Remain Loyal to Their 'Papa,' " *Chicago Tribune*, December 5, 1994.

32. Sergio Viera de Mello, UN Director for Civil Affairs, quoted in "UN Tries to Convince Bosnian Moslem Refugees to Return to Bihac," *Deutsche Presse-Agentur*, August 29, 1994.

33. "Bosnian Refugees: Head of EC Monitor Mission Meets Abdic and Mikelic," *BBC Summary of World Broadcasts*, August 30, 1994; Ruzica Gavrilovic, "Refugees Ignore Pleas," FBIS Daily Report, Doc. No. FBIS-EEU-94–167, August 28, 1994; and Ruzica Gavrilovic, "UN Increases Efforts to Return Bihac Refugees," FBIS Daily Report, Doc. No. FBIS-EEU-95–167, August 27, 1994.

34. *Information Notes*, September 1994.

35. UNHCR official, interview by the author, Geneva, July 1998.

36. Landay, "Bosnian Army Takes Control."

37. Judah, *The Serbs*, 245–46.

38. UNHCR officials, interviews by the author, Geneva, July 1998.

39. Fran Visnar, "War in Cazin Krajina." Translated from Serbo-Croatian in FBIS Daily Report, Doc. No. FBIS-EEU-95–006, December 19, 1994. Quotation in *Information Notes*, Update to No. 11/94.

40. Judah, *The Serbs*, 246.

41. Six hundred and twenty-nine refugees decided not to return with Abdic and clustered on the Croatian side of Turanj. UNHCR convinced Croatia to accept those refugees. *Information Notes*, January 1995.

42. Misha Glenny, *The Fall of Yugoslavia* (New York: Penguin Books, 1996), 284.

43. "UN Recalls Aid Convoy," FBIS Daily Report, doc. no. FBIS-EEU-95–004, January 5, 1994.

44. "U.N. Food Aid to Serb, Muslim Groups is Cut," *Seattle Times*, March 9, 1995; "First Food Convoy in Month Reaches Bihac Pocket," FBIS Daily Report, Doc. No. FBIS-EEU-95–053, March 17, 1995. Quotation in *Information Notes*, February 1995; March 1995.

45. Charlotte Eager and Peter Beaumont, "Vengeance Drives Croats Forward," *Observer*, July 30, 1995. Silber and Little note that the Croatian military advantage "could only have been derived from their increasingly congenial relationship with the United States." Silber and Little, *Yugoslavia*, 357. American support for Croatia played a significant role in the Croat/Muslim alliance. Senior retired U.S. Army officers reorganized the Croatian military, indebting President Tudjman to follow American dictates. See Glenny, *Death of Yugoslavia*, 283; and David Shearer, *Private Armies and Military Intervention*, Adelphi paper 316 (New York: Oxford University Press for the International Institute for Strategic Studies, 1998), 56–63.

46. Rumor has it that "a lot was negotiated before the fight" between the Serbs and the Croatians, explaining the lack of Serbian intervention on behalf of the Krajina Serbs. UNHCR officials, interviews by the author, Geneva, July 1998. See also Glenny, *Fall of Yugoslavia*, 283–84.

47. UNHCR officials, interviews by the author, Geneva, July 1998.

48. "UN Reports Police Deport Abdic Supporters," FBIS Daily Report, Doc. No. FBIS-EEU-95–218, November 8, 1995.

49. UNHCR official, interview by the author, Geneva, July 1998.

50. UNHCR official, interview by the author, Geneva, July 1998.

51. Stephane Jacquemet, UNHCR official, interview by the author, Geneva, July 1998.

52. *Information Notes*, November 1995, January 1996; and Kurt Schork, "Bosnians 'Harassing Returnees,' " *Guardian* (London), January 26, 1996.

53. *Information Notes*, June/July 1996.

54. UNHCR official, interview by the author, Geneva, July 1998.

55. Quang Bui, UNHCR official, interview by the author, Geneva, July 1998.

56. Goran Andjelic, American Refugee Committee, interview by the author, Split, Croatia, June 1998.

57. Radio Bosnia-Herzegovina, "Former Bosnian Muslim Rebel Leader Urges Followers to 'Destabilize Situation,' " Sarajevo, March 3, 1998. From BBC Worldwide Monitoring.

58. Mario Marusic, " 'Babo' Returns Home?" May 17, 2000. Published as FBIS Daily Report, FBIS-EEU-2000–520.

59. "Croatian Court Sentences B-H War Criminal Abdic to 20 Years in Jail," Zagreb HINA, July 31, 2001. Published as FBIS Daily Report, FBIS-EEU-2002–0731; "DNZ Discusses Arrest of Party Leader Abdic in Connection with War Crimes," Sarajevo ONASA, June 10, 2001. Published as FBIS Daily Report, FBIS-EEU-2001–0610; "Nationalists Win Seats in Bosnian Presidency-Election Commission Results," BBC Monitoring International Reports, October 7, 2002; and "Strong Turnout in Jailed Bosnian War Criminal's Hometown," *Agence France Presse*, October 5, 2002.

60. Ivancic interview.

61. Cohen, "Besieged Bosnian Pocket." Estimates of numbers vary.

62. Delic interviewed by Zdravko Latal, "Reversal on the Bosnian Battlefield," FBIS Daily report, Doc. No. FBIS-EEU-94–129, July 1, 1994.

63. UNHCR official, interview by the author, Geneva, July 1998.

64. UNHCR official, interview by the author, Geneva, July 1998.

65. *Information Notes*, September 1995, October 1995, and November 1995.

66. The international actors involved in the Abdic refugee situations were UN organizations and NGOs, particularly UNHCR and the World Health Organization (WHO). The International Committee of the Red Cross (ICRC) was also present during both crises. UNHCR also cooperated with UN peacekeepers in the Krajina and with UN Military Liaison Officers.

67. On NGO incentives, see Alexander Cooley and James Ron, "The NGO Scramble: Organizational Insecurity and the Political Economy of Transnational Action," *International Security* 27:1 (Summer 2002), 5–39.

68. Steve Corliss, UNHCR official, interview by the author, Geneva, July 1998.

69. *Information Notes*, Update to No. 11/94.

70. Benny Otim, UNHCR official, interview by the author, Geneva, July 1998.

71. *Information Notes*, September 1994.

72. Roger Cohen, "For Rebel Bosnian Muslims, Life in Chicken Coops," *New York Times*, November 13, 1994.

73. Emma Daly, "Muslim Refugees Mass on Croatia's Border," *Independent* (London), August 31, 1994.

74. *Information Notes*, September 1994.

75. The entire letter is reprinted in the *Information Notes*, October 1994.

76. *Information Notes*, October 1994.

77. Steve Corliss, UNHCR official, interview by the author, Geneva, July 1998; and "U.N. Troops Wound Refugees Attacking Aid Workers," FBIS Daily Report, Doc. No. FBIS-EEU-94–191, October 2, 1994.

78. UNHCR official, interview by the author, Geneva, July 1998.

79. UNHCR official, interview by the author, Geneva, July 1998.

80. For statements of socioeconomic explanations see UNHCR ExCom, "The Security, and Civilian and Humanitarian Character of Refugee Camps and Settlements," Doc. No. EC/49/SC/INF.2, January 14, 1999, par. 11; UNHCR, *Handbook for Emergencies*, Geneva, 1999, chap. 6; Bonaventure Rutinwa, "Refugee Protection and Security in East Africa," RPN 22 (September 1996), 11–13; Organization of Africa Unity, *Convention Governing the Specific Aspects of Refugee Problems in Africa*, 1969, Article 2(6); Simon Turner, "Angry Young Men in Camps" (Geneva: UNHCR), *New Issues in Refugee Research* working paper series, June 1999; Simon Turner, "Vindicating Masculinity: The Fate of Promoting Gender Equality," *Forced Migration Review* (December 2000), 8–9; "Refugee Protection

and Security in the Great Lakes Region," OAU/UNHCR, *Regional Meeting on Refugee Issues in the Great Lakes,* Kampala, Uganda, May 8–9, 1998, 8.

81. In summer 1993, after strong protests by UNHCR and the international community, the Croatian government stopped arresting and repatriating Bosnian refugees. Human Rights Watch, "Civil and Political Rights in Croatia."

82. *Information Notes,* September 1994.

83. *Information Notes,* November 1994.

84. Jacquemet interview.

85. Daly, "Babo's Lost Tribe Is on the Road to Nowhere."

86. The United States eventually accepted about one thousand of the Velika Kladusa refugees.

Chapter 6. Collateral Damage

1. Fiona Terry, *Condemned to Repeat? The Paradox of Humanitarian Action* (Ithaca, NY: Cornell University Press, 2002), 219.

2. Using the context of the Ethiopian famine, Rony Brauman explains how NGO inaction or silence constitutes a political position. Brauman, "Refugee Camps, Population Transfers, and NGOs," in Jonathan Moore (ed.), *Hard Choices, Moral Dilemmas in Humanitarian Intervention* (Lanham, MD: Rowman and Littlefield, 1998), 177–94.

3. UNHCR, *Protecting Refugees, A Field Guide for NGOs* (Geneva: UNHCR, 1999), part I.

4. Quoted in Carola Weil, "The Protection-Neutrality Dilemma in Humanitarian Emergencies: Why the Need for Military Intervention?" *International Migration Review* 35:1 (Spring 2001), 101.

5. Médecins du Monde, "A Case by Case Analysis of Recent Crises Assessing 20 Years of Humanitarian Action," Paris, April 1999, sec. 2.b.

6. Inspection and Evaluation Service UNHCR, "Lessons Learned from the Rwanda and Burundi Emergencies" (Geneva: UNHCR, April 1996), par. 4.

7. OAU/UNHCR, "Regional Meeting on Refugee Issues in the Great Lakes," opening statement by Sadako Ogata, Kampala, Uganda, May 8–9, 1998, 2.

8. Jeff Drumtra, "Site Visit to Rwanda, Zaire, and Burundi, Oct. 20 to Nov. 17, 1994" (Washington DC: U.S. Committee for Refugees), sec. 27E.

9. Sergio Vieira de Mello, "The Humanitarian Situation in the Great Lakes Region, Speaking Notes for Address to the Excom Standing Committee" (New York: UNHCR, January 30, 1997), 3–4.

10. Project Description, "Screening of Rwandan Refugees in Tanzania," 1998, UNHCR document.

11. Joel Boutroue, "Missed Opportunities: The Role of the International Community in the Return of the Rwandan Refugees from Eastern Zaire," *Rosemarie Rogers Working Paper Series* (Cambridge, MA: Center for International Studies, MIT), 1998; UNHCR, "Information Bulletin, Burundi and Rwanda," June 1996.

12. One UNHCR official disagrees, arguing that the top leaders among the Rwandan Hutu refugees were well-known and that identifying and apprehending these leaders would not have been difficult. Boutroue, "Missed Opportunities," 43n159.

13. Ibid., 38–39.

14. United Nations, Security Council, "Report of the Secretary-General to the Security Council on the Protection of Civilians in Armed Conflict," S/2001/331, March 30, 2001.

15. "Security Council Blames Hutus for Part of Refugee Situation," *Associated Press,* October 14, 1994.

16. The soldiers subsequently renounced their combatant status and received refugee status from UNHCR. IRIN, "UN separates CAR soldiers from civilian refugees," October 8, 2001; IRIN, "UN begins separating civilian, military refugees," October 17, 2001; Lisa Yu, "Separating Ex-Combatants and Refugees in Zonga, DRC: Peacekeepers and UNHCR's 'Ladder of Options' " (Geneva: UNHCR, August 2002).

17. Drumtra, "Site Visit to Rwanda, Zaire, and Burundi," 1994, sec. 23E.

18. Inspection and Evaluation Service UNHCR, "Refugee Camp Security in the Great Lakes Region" (Geneva: UNHCR, April 1997), par. 6.

19. Eleanor Bedford, USCR, interview by the author, Washington, DC, November 2, 1999.

20. Resettlement abroad or integration into the host country may create a new problem—a politically active diaspora—but that phenomenon falls beyond the scope of this study.

21. Sadako Ogata, "Remarks," presented at the conference on "Humanitarian Response and the Prevention of Deadly Conflict," UNHCR and the Carnegie Commission on the Prevention of Deadly Conflict, Geneva, February 17, 1997.

22. Boutroue, "Missed Opportunities."

23. Memorandum of Understanding between the Tanzanian Ministry of Home Affairs and UNHCR, September 28, 1999.

24. UNHCR memo, Kigoma Office, 1999.

25. The police detained or fined 143 combatants in the first half of 2001. Jeff Crisp, "Lessons Learned from the Implementation of the Tanzania Security Package," UNHCR, Evaluation and Policy Analysis Unit, May 2001.

26. Quang Bui, "Ensuring the Civilian and Neutral Character of Refugee-Populated Areas: A Ladder of Options," Geneva: Center for Documentation and Research, UNHCR, July 1998.

27. The United States provided most of the funding for the Tanzanian security package.

28. Jeff Crisp, "Lessons Learned from the Implementation of the Tanzania Security Package," UNHCR, Evaluation and Policy Analysis Unit, May 2001.

29. Roy Herrmann, "Mid-Term Review of a Canadian Security Deployment to the UNHCR Programme in Guinea" (Geneva: UNHCR, Evaluation and Policy Unit, October 2003).

30. UNHCR, *Handbook for Emergencies, Second Edition,* 1999, ch. 24, par. 20.

31. On this point, see Carola Weil, "The Protection-Neutrality Dilemma in Humanitarian Emergencies: Why the Need for Military Intervention?" *International Migration Review* 35:1 (Spring 2001), 98.

32. ICRC statement quoted in Sean Greenaway and Andrew J. Harris, "Humanitarian Security: Challenges and Responses," Paper presented to the Forging Peace Conference, Harvard University, March 13–15, 1998. ICRC has accepted, however, the possibility of using armed protection to guarantee the safety of its personnel and the delivery of assistance. Médecins du Monde, "A Case by Case Analysis of Recent Crises Assessing 20 Years of Humanitarian Action," Paris, April 1999.

33. UNHCR, *Protecting Refugees: A Field Guide for NGOs* (Geneva: UNHCR, 1999), overview.

34. UNHCR, *Handbook for Emergencies, Second Edition,* 2001, ch. 7, par. 37.

35. Maureen Connelly, UNHCR official, interview by the author, Geneva, July 20, 1999.

36. Author's observation, refugee camps in Kigoma region, Tanzania, February, 2000.

37. Kathleen Newland, "Refugee Protection and Assistance," in *Managing Global Issues: Lessons Learned* (Washington DC: Carnegie Endowment for International Peace, 2001), 530.

38. Alex de Waal, "Dangerous Precedents? Famine Relief in Somalia, 1991–93," in Joanna Macrae and Anthony Zwi (eds.), *War and Hunger: Rethinking International Responses to Complex Emergencies* (London: Zed Books, 1994), 154.

39. Roberto Belloni, former OSCE official, personal communication to the author, November 21, 2002. See also Belloni, "Kosovo and Beyond: Is Humanitarian Intervention Transforming International Society?" *Human Rights and Human Welfare* 2:1 (Winter 2002), 42.

40. Terry, *Condemned to Repeat?* 224.

41. Françoise Bouchet-Saulnier, "The Principles and Practices of 'Rebellious Humanitarianism,'" Médecins Sans Frontières International Activity Report 2000. Found at http://www.msf.org/publications /activ_rep/2000/index.htm.

42. For a critique of the WFP position, see Mohammed Haneef Atmar, "Politicisation of Humanitarian Aid and Its Consequences for Afghans," *Disasters* 25:4 (2001), 321–30.

43. Myron Weiner, "The Clash of Norms: Dilemmas in Refugee Policies," *Journal of Refugee Studies* 11:4 (1998), 10, 17.

44. UNHCR, *Protecting Refugees: A Field Guide for NGOs*, Part II, Return.

45. See Mary B. Anderson, *Do No Harm: How Aid Can Support Peace—or War* (Boulder: Lynne Rienner Publishers, 1999) for the best statement of this idea.

46. Terry, *Condemned to Repeat?* 206.

47. Nicholas Leader and Joanna Macrae, "New Times, Old Chestnuts," in Nicholas Leader and Joanna Macrae (eds.), *Terms of Engagement: Conditions and Conditionality in Humanitarian Action* (London: Overseas Development Institute, Humanitarian Policy Group, Report No. 6, 2000), 12.

48. Arthur C. Helton presented a plan for a humanitarian coordinating body. See Helton, "Rescuing the Refugees," *Foreign Affairs*, March/April 2002.

49. Quoted in African Rights, *Rwanda: Death Despair and Defiance*, 1092.

50. ICRC, "ICRC Conditionality: Doctrine, Dilemma and Dialogue," in Leader and Macrae (eds.), *Terms of Engagement*, 23.

51. Amnesty International, "In Search of Safety: The Forcibly Displaced and Human Rights in Africa," Report AFR 01/05/97, June 20, 1997, sec. 1.

52. On the challenges facing UNHCR, see Gil Loescher, *The UNHCR and World Politics* (Oxford: Oxford University Press, 2001), ch. 10.

53. Impartiality is defined as using need as the only criterion for aid distribution.

54. Joel Boutrouc, UNHCR official, interview by the author, Geneva, July 2, 1998.

55. "Aid Agency to Abandon 'Killers' in Hutu Camps," *Herald* (Glasgow), August 29, 1995.

56. I thank Kurt Mills for this insight. Personal communication, March 27, 2002.

57. "Rwandans' Camps Reported Tense," *Gazette* (Montreal), October 4, 1994.

58. ICRC, "ICRC Conditionality: Doctrine, Dilemma and Dialogue," 25.

59. ICRC, *Strengthening Protection in War* (Geneva: ICRC, 2001), 48.

60. Austen Davies, "Thoughts on Conditions and Conditionalities," in Leader and Macrae (eds.), *Terms of Engagement*, 31.

61. Human Rights Watch, "Liberian Refugees in Guinea: Refoulement, Militarization of Camps, and Other Protection Concerns," (New York: November 2002), 22.

62. John Pomfret, "Aid Dilemma: Keeping It from the Oppressors; U.N., Charities Find Crises Make Them Tools of War," *Washington Post*, September 23, 1997.

63. Quoted in "Iraq: Operational Dilemmas for Humanitarians," *Talk Back, The Newsletter of the International Council of Voluntary Agencies (ICVA)* 5:1 (February 12, 2003).

Index

Abdic, Fikret, 16, 118–24, 131, 134. *See also* Bosnian Muslim refugees (Krajina, 1990s)

Actional Internationale Contre la Faim (AICF), 187n.172

Adelman, Howard, 169n.11

ADFL (Alliance des Forces Démocratiques pour la Libération du Congo-Zaire), 82–83, 86, 92

Afghanistan, 42, 44–47, 72, 159, 174n.17

Afghan refugees (Iran, 1980s), 16, 64–71; gender imbalance theory and, 69–70; international aid agencies and, 68–69; Iran-Iraq War and, 65; living conditions of, 70; militarization/political organization of, 65; persecution origins of, 45, 47–49, 64–66; receiving state responses and, 45, 49, 66–69, 71–72, 171n.34; resettlement and, 150–51; size/location/demographics of populations of, 36, 47, 64–65, 69–71; socioeconomic explanations and, 36, 69–71; third-party states and, 45, 69

Afghan refugees (Pakistan, 1980s), 16, 49–64; cross-border attacks and, 12, 44–45, 53–54; gender imbalance theory and, 61–62; international aid agencies and, 58–60; living conditions of, 61–63; local integration of, 63, 151; militarization/political organization of, 48–51, 53, 59–60, 150; persecution origins of, 45, 47–49; receiving state responses and, 54–56, 71, 171n.31; repatriation of, 51–52, 63–64, 150–51; resettlement and, 63, 150–51; size/location/demographics of populations of, 36, 47, 49–50, 61–62, 151; socioeconomic explanations of violence and, 36, 50, 60–64, 151; as state-in-exile, 48, 51, 150; third-party states' aid to, 12, 16, 32, 44, 52, 56–60, 71, 142

African National Congress (ANC), 11–12

African Rights, 141

Agrokomerc (firm), 120–22

AICF (Actional Internationale Contre la Faim), 187n.172

Akashi, Yasushi, 144

Akhundi, Abbas, 66–67

Albanian refugees (Macedonia, 1990s), 14

Albright, Madeleine, 88

Alliance des Forces Démocratiques pour la Libération du Congo-Zaire (ADFL), 82–83, 86, 92

Al Qaeda, 47, 72

American Refugee Committee, 90

Amin, Hafizullah, 46

Amin, Idi, 14, 186n.158

Amnesty International, 94

Anacleti, Odhiambo, 97

ANC (African National Congress), 11–12

Anderson, Mary, 7

Angola, 3, 8–9, 11–12, 87, 89, 159, 182n.75

Arab Nationalist Movement, 26

Arafat, Yasir, 26

Arusha Accords (1993), 74–75

Bagasora, Theoneste, 81, 88

Bangladesh, 13, 152

Bangladeshi refugees (India, 1971), 14

Barayagwiza, Jean Bosco, 1

Bizimungu, Augustin, 85

Boer, Andrea den, 37

border camps. *See* size/location of refugee populations

Bosnia, Autonomous Province of Western, 122–24

Bosnian Muslim refugees (Krajina, 1990s), 16–17, 35, 40, 118–40; gender imbalance theory and, 136–37, 139, information flows and, 125, 129, 134–35; international aid agencies and, 133–36, 140; legitimacy of leaders of, 133–34; living conditions of, 136–38, 140; local integration of, 119, 140, 149, 191n.41; receiving state responses and, 119, 129, 131–33; repatriation of, 22, 125, 127–28, 130, 134–35, 137–38; resettlement and, 40, 119, 127, 130, 138, 140, 149; size/location/demographics of populations of, 136–37, 139, 190nn.2–3; socioeconomic explanations of violence and, 119–20, 136–40; state-in-exile origin of, 124–28, 133; third-party states and, 132, 138–39, 142, 191n.45

Bosnian Muslim refugees (1990s), 22

Botswana, 3, 11–12

[197]

Index

Index

Sudan People's Liberation Army (SPLA), 31

Taliban, 47, 72
Tanzania: Burundian relations with, 152; capability/will of, 30, 94, 98, 103–6, 111, 116, 153; cross-border attacks and, 14; international aid agencies and, 106–8; legitimacy sought by, 114; political contexts in, 30, 105; Refugee (Control) Act of, 104; security partnerships and, 33, 104, 114–15, 152–53. *See also* Burundian refugees (Tanzania, 1970s); Burundian refugees (Tanzania, 1990s); Rwandan refugees (Tanzania, 1990s); Ugandan refugees (Tanzania, 1978–79)
Tapp, Charles, 6
Taraki, Nur Muhammad, 46
Terry, Fiona, 91–92, 141, 158, 160, 183n.80
Thailand, 3, 12, 29, 171n.31
third-party states: contributions to violence by, 5, 11, 14–15, 19, 32–33, 116; security partnerships and, 154. *See also specific countries*
Turkey, 163

Uganda, 12, 14, 31, 87, 89. *See also* Rwandan refugees (Uganda, 1990); Sudanese refugees
Ugandan refugees (Tanzania, 1978–79), 171n.31, 186n.158
Ulimwengu, Jenerali, 103–4
UNAMIR (United Nations Assistance Mission for Rwanda), 75
UNHCR (United Nations High Commissioner for Refugees), 32, 97, 164; Afghan crisis and, 57, 59–60, 62–63, 68; Bosnian Muslim crisis and, 120, 122, 124, 127 30, 133–36, 140; Burundian crisis and, 24, 112–15; employment/support of militant leadership by, 99, 106, 154–55; Kurdish crisis and, 163; Liberian crisis and, 164; militarization ignored by, 115, 133–35, 140; mission of, 143, 161–62; Nicaraguan/Salvadoran crisis and, 3; Palestinian conflict and, 27; "refugee" as defined by, 144, 167n.3; repatriation and, 111, 130, 134–35, 144, 159–60, 187n.176; Rwandan crisis and, 7, 78–79, 85, 90–92, 94, 96, 98–100, 102–7, 109, 117, 146–48, 152–53, 155, 164; security partnerships and, 33, 104, 114–15, 152–54; on socioeconomics of camps, 34, 36–39, 94, 137
União Nacional para a Independência Total de Angola (UNITA), 8–9, 87, 89

UNICEF, 39
Uniragiye, Jean-Baptiste, 97
United Nations: Bosnian Muslim crisis and, 127–28; Cambodian crisis and, 3; peacekeeping forces and, 33, 75, 82, 84, 121–22, 142, 147, 149, 153; relief organizations of, 5; Rwandan crisis and, 82–83, 95
United Nations Military Liaison Officer (UNMLO), 136
United Nations Office for the Coordination of Humanitarian Affairs (OCHA), 36–37
United Nations Protection Areas (UNPAs), 121, 125
United States: Afghan crisis and, 12, 16, 32, 44, 47, 54, 56–60, 71–72, 142; Bosnian Muslim crisis and, 132, 138–39, 191n.45; Burundian crisis and, 116; Cambodian crisis and, 3; Haitian crisis and, 15; international aid agencies and, 28, 32; militarization of World War II refugees by, 2–3; Nicaraguan/Salvadoran crisis and, 3; Rwandan crisis and, 32, 87–89, 116, 183n.79, 194n.27; security funding by, 194n.27
United States Committee for Refugees (USCR), 80, 83, 92, 96, 120, 146-47, 167n.3
UNPROFOR (United Nations Protection Force), 121–22, 127, 132
UNRWA (United Nations Relief and Works Agency for Palestinian Refugees), 4, 27–28
USCR. *See* United States Committee for Refugees

Vaux, Tony, 37
Velika Kladusa (Bosnia), 120–21, *126*, 131, 190n.20. *See also* Bosnian Muslim refugees (Krajina, 1990s)
Vietnam, 3
Vietnamese refugees (Hong Kong), 13

Wallis, Stewart, 81
war economies, financing of, 7–8, 24, 33, 40, 58–59, 90–91, 142, 159
war taxes, 7, 24, 91, 113, 115
Washington Framework Agreement (1994), *119*, 123
Weiner, Myron, 2–3, 19–20, 159
West Bank, 4, 12, 26–27
West Bank Liberation Front (Ugandan rebel group), 89
West Bengal (India), 14
Western Bosnia, Autonomous Province of, 122–24

CORNELL STUDIES IN SECURITY AFFAIRS

A series edited by

Robert J. Art
Robert Jervis
Stephen M. Walt